CHILD LABOUR
Issues, Challenges and Laws

CHILD LABOUR
Issues, Challenges and Laws

Edited by
S.C. Joshi

AKANSHA PUBLISHING HOUSE
NEW DELHI - 110 002 (INDIA)

AKANSHA PUBLISHING HOUSE
4649/21-B, Ansari Road,
Daryaganj, New Delhi - 110 002
Phones: 23263193, 9811582579
E-mail: ektabooks@yahoo.com

Child Labour: Issues, Challenges and Laws

First Published, 2006

ISBN 81-8370-030-6

Reprint 2011

PRINTED IN INDIA

Published by M.P. Misra for Akansha Publishing House, New Delhi - 110 002 and Printed at Tarun Offset Press, Delhi

Contents

Preface

It is commonly stated that children are the most valuable resources or assets of the society, their rights are largely ignored across the world. But unfortunately right from mother's womb and infancy stage a large number of children are subjected to various forms of discrimination, maltreatment, abuse and neglect, which affect their normal physical and mental development and as a result the nation loses a good amount of potential human resource. There is no accurate estimation about the magnitude and extent of the problems of children with regard to different issues addressed.

Child labour and trafficking in children are the simple examples of deep rooted-problem of a society which has failed to protect and care for its children, a community that is either ignorant of the exploitation or does not feel shame in trading its children for gain.

No doubt, there are a number of legislations in India to safeguard the rights of the children. Some of the legislations also have some shortcomings and some new legislations should be adopted to address specific problems which causes harm to children's career, and social and personality development. On prioritizing the problems faced by the huge number of children in the developing countries, the issue of child labour and neglect figure in the top areas. The support which is required for a large number of children in the developing countries, like India include adequate nutrition, immunization, other health care facilities, education and safe shelter. Hence, most governmental and non-government agencies give first priority to address the above issues. There is very little awareness, both in the general public and among welfare service providers, regarding the extent and severity of maltreatment and/or abuse of children in India.

The scenario with regard to problems of children has changed little despite continuous efforts made by the national and international agencies. Moreover, more and more serious steps should be taken in the developing countries to combat problems of children like child labour etc.

To highlight the problem of child labour which is still going on, even increasing in recent years, we have gathered information (old and new) from the studies made by various scholars and agencies. Under the rule of law, that too in a democratic society, perpetuation of 'Child labour' is a stigma on society. The need of the hour is to protect the rights of child to make them valuable asset for future. As sources of information are mainly secondary, the real credit for this work should go the researcher fraternity, and other national/international agencies concerned with the children. I am thankful to them all.

I am deeply beholden to Sri S.K. Muttoo, Secretary, Department of Social Welfare and Women Empowerment, Govt. of Uttaranchal for his patronage and guidance. I owe a deep sense of gratitude to Dr. H.C. Upreti, (Retd.) Associate Professor, Dept. of Sociology, University of Rajasthan, Jaipur. I am thankful to my colleagues at NIPCCD for their constant moral support and inspiration. I am grateful to my family members especially my wife and children for providing congenial work environment at home. Finally, Mr. M.P. Misra deserves all appreciation for bringing out the book superbly within short time.

—SCJ

Chapter 1

Child Labour: Concept & Issues

> "If a child is not disciplined and taught self-control early in the home, the grown up world will take care of him later on, perhaps cruelly and when it is too late. A child curbed, taught obedience, spanked when he is young, rarely requires punishment when he hits his teens.
>
> —*John Warren Hill*

Child Labour Defined

According to the Committee on Child Labour (1979: 8), "Child labour, however, can broadly be defined as that segment of the child population which participates in work either paid or unpaid" In their study of Working Children in Bombay, Singh *et al.* (1980: 23) have held the view: "Child labour means a working child who is between 6 and 15 years of age' is not attending school during the day, is working under an employer or is learning some trade as an apprentice.' In the study titled as Working Children in Urban Delhi conducted by the Indian Council of Child Welfare (1977: 125). "Every child below 14 years, who contributed to the family income or was gainfully employed including those marginally working was treated as a worker." V.V. Giri (1958: 360) has expressed the view: "The term "child labour" is commonly interpreted in two different ways: first, as an economic practice an second, as a social evil. In the first context it signifies employment of children in gainful occupations with a view to adding to the total income of the family. It is in the second sense that the term child labour is now more generally used. In assessing the nature and extent of social evil, it is necessary to take into account the character of the jobs on which children are engaged, the dangers to which they are exposed and the opportunities of development which they have been denied."

Hommerfolks, Chairman of the United Nations Child Labour Committee, has defined child labour as "any work by children that interferes with their full physical development, their opportunities for a desirable level of education or their needed recreation." (in Stein and Deavis, 1940: 112-113). Kulshretha (1978: 2) is of the view that "Child labour in a restricted sense means the employment of child in gainful occupations which are dangerous to their health and deny them the opportunities of development.... The term child labour not only applied to the children working in the industries but also to the children in all forms of non-industrial occupations which are injurious to their physical, mental, moral and social development." Whereas Sharma (1979: 9) states, "Child labour means the employment of children in gainful occupations (in industrial as well as non-industrial occupations) which are injurious to their physical, mental, moral and social development. Thus, the term includes wage-labour as well as self-employed children working independently as well as in family enterprises." Child labour therefore, can be defined here as any work undertaken by children below 18 years in agriculture and allied works injurious to their health and harmful to their proper development.

The precise age of what constitutes child labour has not been laid down anywhere because of variations in the age of child as given under different legislative enactments. Article 24 of the Constitution of India maintains: "No child below the age of 14 years shall be employed to work in any factory or mine or employed in any hazardous employment." Section 82 of the Indian Penal Code, 1860 reads: "Nothing is an offence which is done by a child under 7 years of age." Section 83 of the Indian Penal Code 1860, provides: "Nothing is an offence which is done by a child above 7 years and under 12 who has not attained sufficient maturity of understanding to judge the nature and consequence of his conduct on the occasion." Section 105 of the Indian Evidence

Act, 1872 lays down:" When a person is accused of any offence, the burden of proving the existence of circumstances bringing the case within any of the general or special exception including that of childhood of the Indian Penal Code (IPC) or any concerning law is upon him". Under the Indian Majority Act, 1874 the age of majority has been fixed at 18 years. Under the Vaccination Act, 1880, children have been defined as persons "who have not attained the age of 14 years in case of boys and 18 years in case of girls". "The Child Marriage Restraint Act, 1929 (Sharda Act) defines child as "a male below twenty one years and a female below eighteen years of age." Under the Motor Vehicles Act, 1939, child has been defined as a person under the age of 18 years. According to the U.P. children Act, 1951, "child" means a person under the age of 16 years. The Young Persons Harmful Publication Act, 1956 defines young person as "a person under the age of 20 years." Under the Suppression of Immoral Traffic in Women and Girls Act, 1956, "Girl" means a female who has not completed the age of 21 years." According to the Orphanages and Charitable Homes (Supervision and Control) Act, 1960, "Child" means a boy or girl who has not completed the age of eighteen years." As per provisions of the Children Act, 1960, "Child" means a boy who has attained the age of 16 years or a girl who has not attained the age of 18 years. Section 27 of the Code of Criminal Procedure, 1973 reads: "any offence not punishable with death or imprisonment for life, committed by any person who at the date when he appears or is brought before the count in under the age of Sixteen years, may be tried by the court of a Chief Judicial Magistrate, or by any court specially empowered under the Children Act, 1960 or any other law for the time being enforced providing for the treatment, training and rehabilitation of youthful offenders." According to Section 3 of the Employment of Children Act, 1938, "No child who has not completed his fifteenth year shall be employed or permitted to work in any occupation.... No child who has completed his fifteenth year but has not completed his seventeenth year shall be employed or permitted to work in any occupation unless the periods of work of such child for any day are so fixed as to allow an interval of rest for at least twelve consecutive hours which shall include at least such seven consecutive hours between 10 p.m. and 7 a.m. as may be prescribed...... No child who has not completed his fourteenth year shall be employed or permitted to work in any workshop wherein any of the processes set forth in the schedule is carried on. "Under Section 2(C) of the Factories Act, 1948, "Child means a person who has not completed his fifteenth year of age." Section 67 of the Act provides: "No child who has not completed his fourteenth year shall be required or allowed to work in any factory." Section 68 of the Act further lays down: "A child who has completed his fourteenth year or an adolescent shall not be required or allowed to work in any factory unless—(a) certificate of fitness granted with reference to him.... is in the custody of the manager of the factory, and (b) such child or adolescent carries while he is at work a token giving a reference to such certificate." "Adjacent", according to the Act, "means a person who has completed his fifteenth year of age but has not completed his eighteenth year." As per section 2 (c) of the Plantation Labour Act, 1951, "Child" means a person who has not completed his fifteenth year." Section 24 of the Act lays down: "No child who has not completed his twelfth year shall be required or allowed to work in any plantation." According to section 2 (e) of the Mines Act, "Child" means a person who has not completed his fifteenth year." Section 45 of the Act stipulates: "No child shall be employed in any mine, nor shall any child be allowed to be present in any part of a mine which is below ground or in any open cast working in which any mining operation is being carried on." In the Merchant Shipping Act, 1958, employment of children below 15 years as seamen has ordinarily been prohibited. Persons below eighteen years cannot be employed as trimmers and stokers. According to section 2 (c) of the Motor Transport Workers' Act, 1961, "child" means a person who has not completed his fifteenth year." Section 21 of the Act provides: "No adolescent shall be required or allowed to work as a motor transport worker in any motor transport undertaking unless—(a) a certificate of fitness granted with reference to him.... is in the custody of the employer, and (b) such adolescent carries with him while he is at work, a token giving a reference to such certificate." "Adolescent", according to section 2 (a) of the Act. "means a person who has completed his fifteenth year but has not completed his eighteenth year." According to section 2 (b) of the Bidi and Cigar Workers (Conditions of Employment) Act, 1966, "child" means a person who has not completed fourteenth years of age." Section 24 of the Act provides" "No child shall be required or allowed to work in any industrial premises." Under the Radiation Protection Rules, 1971 framed under the Atomic Energy Act, 1962, "A child has been defined as a person below eighteen years of age." According to Section 2 (2) of the U.P. Dookan Aur Vanijya Adhishthan Adhiniyam, 1962, "Child" means a person who has not completed his fourteenth years." Section 1 of the Act clearly says. "No child shall be required or allowed to work in any shop or commercial establishment except as an apprentice in such employment as may be notified by the State Government in the Gazette." In Shops and Commercial Establishment Acts passed by other States and Union Territories, child has been defined as a person between 12 and 14 years. It is because of this variation in age of a child in different laws that child labour will have to be defined in the context of a vocation in which a child is employed (Madan, 1975: 92). Since children employed in agriculture are not covered under any statutory provision, the age of child labour in agriculture has to be defined keeping in view the nature of agricultural work. In this regard an observation made by Mendelievich (1979: 4) seems to be pertinent: "Agriculture is one of the most hazardous sectors for the physical safety and health of workers for several reasons: the prevalence of dangerous modern machinery; prolonged exposure to heat, sunlight, dust, wind and insects; the almost constant physical effort that agricultural work demands; contact with various chemical products such as fertilisers and pesticides whose long-term effects on man may be completely unknown and for the majority of which, in cases of poisoning, no specific antidotes exist. Children are particularly at risk from endemic and parasitic diseases, diseases of the respiratory tract, dermatosis and fatal accidents." The Convention concerning the Minimum Age of Employment, 1973 lays down that as regards work which is likely to adversely affect health, or morals of young persons, minimum age for admission to any type of employment or work of this kind shall not be less than 18 years. This is why the minimum age in the context of child labour in agriculture with which the present study has been concerned, has been fixed at 18 years.

Information gathered regarding age at which the child workers started working and analysed in relation to their nature of employment on the assumption that the age of starting work may be different in case of children working on their own land, on land owned by others and on own as well as others' land, reveals that the largest single group of child workers (25.00%) had started work between 7-9 years followed by those who had started work between 9-11 years. (19.00%), below 5 years (13.60%), 5-7 years (12.40%), 11-13 years and 13-15 years (9.00%) each and 15-17 years (3.00%). It is noteworthy that as many as 9.00% of the child workers did not remember their age of starting work. The average age of starting work has been 8.57 years. Singh *et al.* (1980: 75) have found in their study: "Thus one out of every four working children, joined the workforce before completing 9 years of age and a little less than of half before completing 12 years of age and again a little more than one fourth as soon as they entered their thirteenth year of life". Gangrade (in Mendelievich, 1979: 82) has concluded that "children only 6 years old have been found working, although the usual age of entry into employment seems to be 8 to 9 years. Boys of 10 to 12 have been found working on regular term contracts of several years duration."

Khandekar and Naik (1972: 369) have found that "a fairly large number of children below what is considered to be the working age, are called upon to supplement the economic activity of their elders."

An analysis in terms of nature of employment reveals that in the case of the child workers working on their own land, the largest single group (27.14%) has started work between 7-9 years of age, followed by those who had begun working between 9-11 years (20.48%), below 5 years (16.19%), 5-7 years (14.05), 11-13 years (9.05%), 13-15 years (5.00%) and 15-17 year (0.48%). As many as 7.61% of the child workers did not remember the age of starting work. The average age of starting work on own land has been 7.93 years. In case of the child workers working on land owned by others, the largest single group (42.86%) had started working between 13-15 years of age, followed by those who had started doing so between 7-9 and 11-13 years (14.29% each) and 5-7, 9-11 and 15-17 years (7.14)% each). There have been 7.14 per cent children working on land owned by others who did not remember the age of starting work. The average age of starting work on land owned by others has been 12 years. As for children working on their own land as also on land owned by others, the largest single group (27.27%) had started work between 13-15 years of age followed by those who had started doing so between 15-17 years (18.18%), 7-9 years (13.64%) 9-11 years (12.12%), 11-13 years (7.58) and 5-7 years (3.03%). As many as 18.18% children working on their own land as well as on land owned by others did not remember the age of starting work. The mean age of starting work on own land as also on land owned by other has been 12.33 years. It is noteworthy that none of the child workers working exclusively on land owned by others or on own land as well as on land owned by others had started working below 5 years of age because in wage employment, efforts are made by inconsiderate employers to take maximum work within minimum time which children are not in a position to physically bear.

Employers and Child Labour

Children are forced to take up work out of necessity to fulfil the basic unmet needs of their own as also of their family members. Information gathered regarding persons for whom the child workers might have been forced to work and analysed in relation to their age on the assumption that child workers in different age-groups might have been working for the fulfilment of the needs of different categories of persons, reveals that an overwhelming majority of the child workers (68.70%) have been working for satisfaction of their own as well as family members' needs followed by those who have been working for the sake of their family members only (10.20%) and those who have engaged in work for their own sake (9.00%). As many as 12.20% have not given any response in this regard.

In the age-group of 8-12 years, majority of the child workers (61.07%) have been working with a view to satisfying their own as well as family members' needs followed by those who have been involved in work for the sake of their family members (8.05%) and their own sake (4.70%) only. 19.46% of the child workers in this age-group have not given any response.

In the age-group of 13-18 years, an overwhelming majority of the child workers (71.79%) have been participating in work in order to fulfil their own as well as family members' needs followed by those who have been engaged in work for the sake of their family members (11.11%) and for their own sake (7.98).

As many as 9.12% of the child workers in this age-group also did not give any response. Thus the child workers, irrespective of their age composition, have, by and large, been working to satisfy their own as well as family followed by those who have been engaged in work for the sake of their family members' needs.

Motivators to Child Labour

Children may get motivation to work from different sources. They may themselves decide to work when they see that even basic needs of their own as also of their family members are not properly et despite the best possible efforts made by their parents. They may be motivated by their parents to take up work out of sheer compulsion of family circumstances. Other members of their family, and even those outside their family, may suggest children to share the burden of their parents unable to afford the family expenses. Data gathered regarding persons who have motivated the child whokers to take up work reveal that in a majority of cases (54.8%) motivation to work has been provided by child workers themselves and their parents followed by those where such motivation has come from self (21.80%), parents (14.20%), self and brothers (3.60%), self and guardians (0.80%), brothers (0.40%) and guardians (0.20%). It has not been possible for 4.20% of the child workers who motivated them to take up the work.

Causes of Child Labour

A number of reasons with different types of combinations have been held responsible for work by Children. Labour Bureau (In NIPCCD, 177:179), the first to undertake a detailed survey of child labour in India, had come to the conclusion: "The major reason for the prevalence of child labour in a developing country like India is not far to seek. In these countries, the poverty of the parents compels them to send their children to work at an early age.... the existence of child labour in differential degrees in almost all sectors of economy-organised or unorganised—can mainly be attributed to economic causes." George (in NIPCCD, 1977: 166-167) has cited these reasons for seeking employment: "To supplement family income (72.50%); death of father (23.00%) do not like to depend on others (19.00%); parents asked to search for job (17.00%); for out-of-pocket expenses (10.00%); no one to look after (7.00%); no other earning member (5.00%); to earn for education (5.00%); to learn the job (4.00%); parents asked to assist in occupation (3.00%), interested in the job (3.00%); just to escape attending school (0.50%)." Punekar (in NIPCCD, 1977: 129) has maintained: "In the rural area, employment of children (i.e., persons below the age of 15) as wage-paid labour is mainly to supplement the meagre income of chronically poverty-stricken households" Govil (in NIPCCD, 1977: 82) has pointed out that "poverty is the root cause for child labour" Kulshrestha (1978: 12-19) has mentioned poverty, absence of scheme of family allowance, large family, cheaper rates of child labour, absence of compulsory education, illiteracy and ignorance, slow process of protective labour legislation and inadequate inspecting machinery as the causes of child labour. Jain and Chand (1979: 322) have observed: "Children work not because their parents are wicked or those that employ them are wicked but because their income is essential for the survival of the family or themselves, if they have left their home for lack of means of survival." Mendelievich, while detailing the reasons, (1979: 8-9) has made a mention of (1) need to reduce to the greatest possible extent the poverty, (2) parents' wish to keep their children occupied and off the streets, (3) poor performance at school, (4) situation at home characterised by tension and uncertainty absence of one of the or both the parents etc. and (5) instability and insecurity caused by migration from rural to urban areas. Citing a study undertaken in Bangkok, Mendelievich has made a pointed reference of these reasons: poverty (23.40%) need to assist parents in household economic activity (32.90%), parents want them to work (26.30%), need to earn their own living (7.90%), better than doing nothing (6.90%) and other reasons (2.60%). K.D. Gangrade (in Mendelivich, 1979: 81) has maintained: "The poverty of many families forces the parents to put their children to work instead of sending them to school." Singh *et al.* (1980: 9-12) have thrown light on tradition and poverty as the main causes of child labour. Ministry of Labour, Government of India (1979: 10-13 and 70) has maintained tradition, poverty, lack of adequate awareness among parents for educating children, illiteracy, large size of family, inadequate schooling facility, loss of parents or breadwinner of the family, unemployment and lack of land as the causes of child labour. Sharma (1979: 67) has come to the conclusion that "child labour originates due to the prevalence of poverty in the society.... non-realisation on the part of parents of the important role of education, and their preference for work to education might have contributed to social evil". Kusum (Government of India; 1978: 16) has expressed the view that "it their children to seek employment. Inadequate income of the adult bread-earner of the family, unemployment absence of any family allowance or subsistence allowance on one side, and the large family on the other, death of the adult bread-earner, drinking habits and other social evils in adults and absence of school and provision of compulsory education, illiteracy and ignorance of parents etc. are the main reasons of the child labour." Pichholiya (1980: 99) has held the view that "children's participation in labour force for wages is mainly due to the need to supplement household income." Nadeem Mohshin (1980: 27) has held that "the supply of child labour is governed mainly by two factors: (1) non-availability of adult labour in the family, (2) inadequate income of the family... in India where a large section of population suffers from acute poverty; child labour, by and large, is a product of unemployment, under employment of the adult wage earners." The Labour Bureau Simla (1981: 53), on the basis of survey of child labour in Indian industries, has observed; "Extreme poverty, lack of opportunity for gainful employment and intermitancy of income and low standards of living are the main reasons for the wide prevalence of child labour."

It is thus sufficiently clear that poverty is the main reason for children's employment in India. Facts relating to poverty in India reveal that 48.13% of the population in 1977-78 has been living below poverty line of Rs. 65.00 per capita per month on 1977-78 prices corresponding to daily calorie requirement of 2400 per person in rural areas and Rs. 75.00 per capita per month on 1977-78 prices corresponding to minimum daily calorie requirement of 2100 in urban areas (Indian Worker, 1980: 2). Assuming that the poverty line is drawn at consumption level of Rs. 65.00 per capita per month for rural areas and Rs. 75.00 per capita per month for urban areas, children below the poverty line would the about 18 million, embracing 55% of the rural children and 45% of the urban ones (Majumdar: 1981). There are certain circumstances which compel the children to take up work at an early age. Data collected regarding such circumstances and analysed in relation to age of the child workers on the assumption that such circumstances may be different in case of children of different age-composition, reveal that majority of the child workers (64.67%) have been compelled to take up work by poor economic condition followed by apathy in studies (22.60%), preference fro work (21.15%), need for extra working hands (12.98%), weakness in studies (11.45), no other employment opportunity (10.34) and parents' desire (9.38). Further analysis in terms of age indicates that in both the age-groups of 8-12 (62.96%) and 13-18 (62.26%), majority of the child workers have reported poor economic condition as the factor which has compelled them to take up work. Analysis of data relating to such circumstances in relation to sex reveals that in case of the male child workers, poor economic condition (67.22%) followed by apathy towards studies (21.74%), preference for work (16.72%), weakness in studies and need for extra working hands (13.04%) each), no other employment opportunity (7.36%) and parents' desire (3.01%) have been the reasons behind taking up work whereas in case of female child workers, poor economic condition (58.12%), preference for work and parents desire (32.48% each), apathy towards studies (24.79%), no other employment opportunity (17.95%), need for extra working hands (12.82%) and weakness in studies (7.69%) have been the compelling factors.

This shows that poor economic condition has been the main factor compelling the child workers to take up work, irrespective of their sex differences.

Further analysis in relation to state of education unravels that in case of the child workers without any education, poor economic condition (70.40%) followed by preference for work (32.80%), need for extra working hands (8.80%), no other employment opportunity (7.20%) and parents' desire (5.60%) have been the compelling circumstances. As for the child workers who have discontinued their education, poor economic condition (67.02%) followed by apathy towards studies (38.46%), preference for work (27.47%), need for extra working hands (19.78%), weakness in studies (13.29%), no other employment opportunity (12.08%) and parents' desire (9.89%) have been the reasons. In so far as the child workers who have been able to continue their education are concerned, poor economic condition (60.00%) followed by apathy towards studies (22.50%), weakness in studies (18.00%), need for extra working hands (12.50%), parents' desire and no other employment opportunity (11.50% each) and preference for work (11.00%) have been the forcing factors.

In a nutshell, it has been the poor economic condition of child workers that has compelled them to take-up work irrespective of their age, sex and state of education.

Reasons of Employers' Preference for Children in Work

There are a number of reasons due to which children are preferred by employers. Reasons stated in the Report of the Committee on Child Labour (Government of India, 1980: 11-12) are:

(1) less developed ego and status consciousness;

(2) lesser affliction by feeling of guild and shame;
(3) no hesitation to do non-status, even demeaning, jobs;
(4) activeness, agility and quickness and lesser feeling of tiredness;
(5) greater discipline and control;
(6) less expensive to maintain;
(7) superior adaptive abilities;
(8) lack of organisation;
(9) moral consideration of the employers to help and to provide succour to the destitute or forsaken children; and
(10) acquisition of fineness through initiation in the early age.

Singh et al. (1980: 12-13) have made a mention of (1) hesitation among adults to perform certain jobs; (2) cheapness of child giving larger surplus value to the employed (3) superior adaptability of children; (4) absence of many negative qualities among children; (5) lack of organisation; (6) religiosity of the employer to provide succour to destitute and forsaken children; and (7) acquisition of fineness as reasons behind employers' preference for children in work. The National Commission on Labour (1969: 386) has also pointed out that "quite often it is the feeling of sympathy rather than the desire to exploit which weighs with employers in employing child workers.... We have been told by some employers that unless the fingers were thus trained at very early age, their adaptation later would be difficult." Information gathered regarding reasons of preference for employment of children by employers and analysed in relation to age of the child workers on the assumption that reasons given by the child workers in different age-groups may be varied, unreavels that the largest single group of child workers (36.25%) has given shortage of working hands and high economic status of employers followed by more land (20.00%), and high economic status of employers (16.25), more land and high economic status of employers (13.75%), shortage of working hands (8.75%) and intensive cultivation (5.00%). An analysis in terms of age reveals that in case of the child workers in the age-group of 8-12 years, shortage of working hands and high economic status of employer (56.25%) followed by more land and high economic status of employer (18.57% each) and shortage of working hand (6.25%) have been spelt out as reasons for preference. As for the child workers in the age-group of 13-18 years, shortage of working hands and high economic status of employer (31.25%) followed by more land and high economic status (21.31% each) more land and high economic status of employer (12.5%), shortage of working hands (9.38%) and intensive cultivation (6.25%) have been put foward as reasons for preference.

In a nutshell, shortage of working hands coupled with high economic status, of the employer has been given by the child workers irrespective of age composition, as the main reason behind employer's, preference for children in work.

There may be a number of reasons responsible for a person's liking for any kind of work. Information gathered from the child workers regarding reasons for their liking for agricultural work and analysed in relation to their age on the assumption that reasons may differ according to age-composition, clearly indicates that apathy towards studies (28.63%) followed by a combination of apathy towards studies and desire to stay at home (27.35), no other employment opportunity (11.56%), desire to stay at home (19.68%), no other employment opportunity and desire to stay at home (8.55%), apathy towards studies and poor economic status of family (5.56%), relatively more economic benefit (4,79%), and poor economic status of family (2.99%), have been given as reasons for liking agricultural work. Age-wise analysis shows that in both the age-groups of 8-12and 13-18 years, the largest single group has given apathy towards studies followed by a combination of apathy towards studies and desire to stay at home as the reasons.

Impact of Child Labour

"Child labour deprives children of educational opportunities, minimises their chances for vocational training, hampers their intellectual development and by forcing them into the army of unskilled labours, condemns them to low wages all their lives." (T.N. Chaturvedi, 1977: 369)

It is beyond doubt that children are forced by circumstances to do labour in the tender age when they should have been at schools. The mere fact that it is not the work but labour that children are coerced to do has manifold repercussions for them, for their family and for the society as a whole. In the context of child workers themselves, harmful effects of child labour can be seen in the form of their improper physical development, varied kinds of illness and physical deformities, damage to central nervous system, impoverishment of the entire mental world, lack of capacity to adjust with other persons in society, inability to express views, indulgence in various social vices etc. Khandekar and Naik (1972: 369) have observed: "Since the early years are meant to equip oneself with knowledge, techniques and skills for one's different adult roles in the society, having to take up a job at a young age to earn a living, is bound to affect the very process of growing up."

Induction of children in work from the early stage deprives them of opportunities for acquiring various abilities and skills through education and training which are necessary for getting important positions in the contemporary competitive society; and thus they become unable to contribute their mite to their families which they would otherwise have done, had they been sent to educational and training institutions in their formative period. Participation of children in work outside the family dissociates them from their family members and creates a physical distance between them and thereby reduces the degree of intimacy, love and affection towards the family among them. The incidence of earning money from childhood generates a feeling of independence among children due to which they like to behave freely and promiscuously and do not like to be subjected to control and discipline by other family members and are seen, in many cases, adopting many a bad habit and separating from their families immediately after their marriage, and in some cases, even before marriage. Thus the family not only suffers the economic loss in the long run but also becomes subjected to loose social bonds and ties within the family, and at times, even family disorganistion.

Finally the society is the great sufferer because of incidence of child labour. Work by children means not only decrease in opportunities for adult employment but also reduction in the wages of adult workers. It is estimated (T.N. Chaturvedi, 1979: 9-27) that if workers under 18 years of age in India could be taken out of the labour force and provided educational and vocational training, some 15-20 million unemployed adults would be able to find jobs on standard wages. In the long run, child labour means prevalence of unskilled and incompetent labour force in society. Thus the society not only suffers the economic loss but also has to bear the blame of having child labour in a welfare state despite whose commitment to ensure a minimum desirable standard of living, children are forced, out of necessity, to take up employment in their tender age.

Chapter 2

The Root Causes of Child Labour

"The ones who will suffer most for the mistakes we make in raising our children will be our grandchildren."

—*Imogene Fey*

Being a socio-economic problem, child labour is generally conceded that illiteracy, ignorance, low wages, unemployment, poor standard of living, abject poverty, deep social prejudices and appalling backwardness of the countryside are all, severally and collectively, the root causes of child labour.

Officially, it has been stated that, "child labour is no longer a medium of economic exploitation but is necessitated by economic necessity of the parents and in many cases that of the child himself." While Prof. Gangrade believes that child labour is a product of such factors as customs, traditional attitude, lack of school or reluctance of parents to send their children to school urbanisation, industrialisation migration and so on.

MAJOR CAUSES

1. Poverty

Mostly, of the population of India lives below the poverty line. The gross national product income had decreased by 5 per cent, and per capita real income by 7 per cent during 1979-80. According to the annual report of the Ministry of Programme Implementation for 1988-89, the poverty percentage got reduced from 48 per cent in 1977-78 to 37 in 1984-85. Out of 316 million people who fall below the poverty line, 118 millionare children. Out of these children, 99 million are in rural areas and 19 million are concentrated in urban areas.

The parents of the poverty-ridden population are faced with the bewildering question as to whether they should send their children to educational institutions to learn and equip themselves with adequate knowledge in order to prepare themselves for adulthood, or to send them to the labour market augment the income of their starving families.

Widespread poverty is one of the major causes of child labour. In India, which is a developing country, poverty forces the parents to send their children to seek employment because augmentation of their income is essential for the survival of the family including the children themselves. Illness and other contingencies demand extra money in hand and the employment of children is resorted to as a quick and easily accessible way to get it. The Institute of Public Opinion conducted a survey in 1969, which showed that 41.2 per cent of the Indian population was below the poverty line. Half of these belong to the scheduled castes and tribes. In villages a vast majority of agricultural labour belongs to these communities.

The Mumbai study on working children found that low economic status of the family was the single largest factor for non-schooling of the children and their coming into the labour market. A study on child labour in Khurja potteries revealed that most of the parents of working children had less than five bighas of land. These families owned one or two milch animals which the parents tended and the children worked in the potteries of Khurja.

As such, due to extreme poverty, the parents are not only incapable of investing in their children's development, they are even reluctant to support them and want them to become a source of income to the family as early as possible.

The Report of Committee on Child Labour opines that chronic poverty is the factor responsible for the prevalence and prepetuation of child labour. It reports:

> "Nearly half of India's population subsists below poverty line. In the countryside, the distribution of land is most iniquitous. The lower 50 per cent households own only 4 per cent of the land. As many of 27.2 per cent of the rural households are agricultural tenants and 30.4 per cent agricultural labourers. Nearly one-third of the metropolitan population lives in slums and improvised tenomant. In Madras 90.8 pre cent of the families of working children have an income below Rs. 500/- per month. In Bombay 78 per cent and in Delhi, 88 per cent of such families have a monthly income of Rs. 500/- and below. In these families, the child, since his very appearance in this world, is endowed with an economic mission. The child is compelled to shed sweat of brow to keep the wolf away from the door. In some families, when disease or other forms of disability upset the delicate balance of the family budget, there may not be any alternative but to send the child to work. These families cannot sacrifice the smaller gains of the present for the larger gains of the future, as they do not have any surplus to sustain them. The income accruing from child labour may be a pittance but it plays a crucial role in saving the family from a shipwreck. Economic compulsions weighed heavily on the consciousness of poor parents that they would not mind colluding with the child's employer in violating the law and putting the child under risks of inhuman exploitations. Poverty and child labour thus always beget each other and tend to reinforce themselves in families and communities."

Undoubtedly, the above statement is generally valid and poverty compels the parents to send their children to the labour market. But, it is not true for each and every society as a rule because there are some communities or societies in which, irrespective of their composition, the number of child labour is insignificant despite high levels of poverty. For example, it defies explanation that in Bihar and Uttar Pradesh which, going by the per capita income, could be termed as poor states, child labour constitutes only 4.8 per cent and 6 per cent of the total labour force respectively, whereas Andhra Pradesh and Karnataka, which are better off in terms of per capita income nave a higher percentage of child labour, constituting about 9 per cent and 8 per cent of the total labour force respectively. Another example is that of Africa. It has been noted that in regions, or amongst "Tribes," where the concept of market relationship has not yet gained any considerable ground employment of children in gainful occupation within the family or outside it is not significant at all despite the general level of existing poverty.

2. Unemployment

The unemployed has worse living conditions than that of the poor. Low wage make a an poorer but unemployment makes him absolutely poor. It turns the weak into a cripple. Poverty dempens his spirit but unemployment kills it mercilessly. So, can one muster sufficient courage to suggest the poverty-stricken unemployed not to send his child to work? Partly employed people sail in the same boat. And, unfortunately, the curse of unemployment is an universal one. It exists in the most affluent countries, like United State of America, also, does exist child labour and its accompanying problems. In their book, 'Child Workers in America," Lumpkin and Douglas have very rightly pointed out that two-fifth of the children seek work due to the unemployment of the adult member of the family. Nearly two-third of children were at work because the adult member of the family had no employment or had some part time job, and one-third of children wanted to work due to the serious cuts in the pay of the adult.

In the opinion of Padmini Sengupta:

> "Labour is employed on the average for 189 days in agricultural pursuits. There are other rural employments which exist but the overall position would appear to be 100 days in the year of total unemployment. During the period of unemployment many women migrate to cities

with families, and beg with babies in their arms. Thy are, therefore, employing the children from infancy for begging which is an important employment, especially now, and children of the baby group are exploited while older children are pests in every part of the city including railway stations where begging is prohibited by law but where it thrives as officials turn a deaf ear to the wails of boys and girls."

Sivakasi and neighbouring areas of the newly created Kamraj district get scanty rains. As a result, little agricultural operations are being carried out over there. This has forced the people to look for non agricultural jobs. The Sivakasi stretch has a number of match and fire-work factories where most of the operations are annual. To man these factories children are preferred because they are very hard working and cheap. This has resulted into widespread unemployment among adults.

In Khurja potteries, the incidence of child labour is high due to the unemployment of adult members of the families. Ms. Burra feels that, "Bulandshahr district, although agriculturally prosperous, has little work on its mechanised arms for the bulk of rural poor who face unemployment on a massive scale. The only work available is in the potteries of Khurja.

3. Low Wages of the Adult

The wage structure of the adult workman has a direct bearing on the occurrence of child labour. The employer has a vested interest both ways. It is all the more so in the case of statutorily fixed minimum wage. The less an employer pays to his adult workman, the more is the exploitation and the more he stands to gain on the wage bill. The more exploited a workman is the more will be his compulsions to send his children to work, who will be paid all the more less. So, in order to ensure adequate and regular supply of cheap child labour even in violation of the protective laws, the vested interest of the employer will be to keep the wage structure of his adult workers at its lowest.

As per Report of International Labour Organisation the problem of child labour is not problem by itself. In reality, the problem is that of maintenance of the child which is directly connected with the question of ensuring a living wage to the adult wage earner so that he may be able to maintain his family at an adequate standard.

The above facts were also observed in a number of seminars, workshops and conferences on the problem of child labour, and it was felt that if the adult workmen could get a real living wage, they are likely to desist from sending their children to work.

4. Absence of Schemes for Family Allowance

Another direct cause of child labour, which is as causative as poverty, is the unfavourable condition at home. There may be tension and uncertainty, provoked or increased by poverty; the father may have left home; the mother may be alone; the father or mother or both may have fallen ill or become physically unfit to work, or may have died. In such families, these contingencies upest the delicate balance of the family budget, leaving the family with no alternative but to sent the children to work. These starving family would prefer a bare bread in hand today rather than go without it in the hope of buttered bread in indistinct future.

The study on child labour in Aligarh lock industries shows that 8 per cent of children have taken up employment because they have neither mother nor father to support them, while 13 per cent of child labour have only mother alive. On the other hand, 10.75 per cent of children had joined this industry because they had no mother at home and the father thought that it would be better to send them to work.

However, the argument that the most of the children go

to work because of the compelling circumstances in the event of loss of the bread winner is also fallacious to some degree because it is usually the head of the family himself who forces his children to go to the labour market. The absence of statutory provisions and schemes for family allowance also adds up to the problem of child labour. In India, there are no schemes for such allowances that many help the needy families maintain an adequate standard of living, so that they may not have to send their children to the work place.

5. Migration to Urban Areas

Migration to cities due to industrialisation and urbanisation, is one of the factors responsible for the problem of child labour. The Delhi study shows that there is a substantial number of migrants among child workers, particularly in the field of domestic services. They also work in tea-stalls and 'dhabas.' A large number of domestic servants belonged to Almora and Garhwal district of north-eastern Uttar Pradesh, while most of those working in tea-stalls and 'dhabas,' and also those hawking evening newspapers, had migrated from Azamgarh, Basti, Gorakhpur and Gonda district of Uttar Pradesh and, to some extent, from Bihar. The rag-pickers were partly local and partly from West Bengal. The shoe-shine boys mostly hailed from Agra, Jhansi and Shahjahanpur districts of Uttar Pradesh. It is not just a coincidence that the migrant child workers invariably belonged to the relatively poor and backward regions of the country, and not the economically developed areas, such as, West Bengal, Haryana and Western Uttar Pradesh.

The Mumbai study showed that 58.2 per cent of the child labour was the exclusive result of the internationalisation of the urban slum culture, as their families had migrated to cities before their birth. In all, there were 90 per cent of them who belonged to migrated families. The reasons for the migration of 87 per cent families were economic and presence of friends and relatives in the city who could help them.

Urbanisation had even allured the children to run away from their rural homes to the cities to find employment.

5. Child Labour, A Cheap Commodity

Generally, the employers prefer to take in children when the given job can be accomplished by them better than the adults or at par with them, and even otherwise. To them the labour power of the children is a cheap commodity. By employing them they save on the wage bills. Besides, children are apt to be docile and more obedient, and can be easily bullied into submission. They readily do all sorts of odd jobs without a whimper. The more needy a child happens to be, the less he will be paid by the employer.

Child labour is not only very cheap, it is also trouble-free since children cannot organise agitations by themselves and, being minors, the membership of trade unions is not open to them. Neither can they demand any overtime, nor the medical and other benefits. The activeness, suppleness and agility of the child's delicate body is an additional asset to the employer, making him more desirable for employment, for he can be made to rush in and out on errand, run up and down the stairs, bend or lie down, fetch and take back things, or hand over the tools to the adult workers. He readily dos all this and much more without whimpering, protest, sense of shame or hurted ego. No adult can be expected to do all this.

It is apt here to quote the Committee on Child Labour:

> Children have less developed ego and status consciousness. They are also less affected by feelings of guild and shame. Children can be put on non-status, even demeaning jobs, without much difficulty. Children are more active, agile and quick and feel less tired in certain tasks. They can climb up and down staircase of multistoreyed buildings several times during the day carrying tea and snacks for employees of offices located in these buildings. They are also better candidates for

> tasks of helper in a grocer's shop or an auto-garage. Employers find children more amenable to discipline and control. They can be coaxed, admonished, pulled up and punished for default without jeopardising relations."

Most often, when seasonal work demands additional hands, children are more in demand, for example, during harvesting seasons when adult workers are not readily available to cope up with the work in hand.

In India, children of very young age are engaged for domestic work because they are very cheap. The middle class families, falling within low income groups, especially prefer boys and girls of the age group 8 to 14 to work in their homes as domestic servants for food and some pocket money. These employers, though educated in formal sense, appear to have the least concern for these children and their conscience hardly pricks.

6. Large Families

Large families, with comparatively low income, cannot afford to nourish high ideals and notions about family ties. Resultingly, such types of families fail to provide a protected childhood to their children. If the family is small and well planned, there will hardly be any need of sending their children to work in order to earn whatsoever they may. The children of small and planned families can be carefully looked after and educated. But, unfortunately, the improverished and illiterate parents have a thought that when God has given the body, he will feed it also. They also consider three or four children better than having just one or two. For them, more children means more income. They argue that whereas every human body has just one mouth to eat, it has got two hands to feed it.

7. Lack of Compulsory Education Facilities

The Child labour and non-schooling of children have a

vital linkage among the poorer sections of the population. The provision of compulsory education upto a prescribed age would compel the children to attend school, leaving hardly any scope for their employment by the self-styled benevolent masters.

Due to inadequacy in schooling facilities and lack of opportunities for education, in Aligarh lock industries 41 per cent of the child labour were illiterate, 31 per cent had left the school before passing the fifth standard and only 28 per cent had studied upto middle standard. Further, many of the parents, especially that of the rural and slum areas, cannot afford the prescribed minima of uniforms, books and stationery etc., even though education is free upto primary level. Apart from the consideration of expenses, the allurement of the child's income also plays a major role in their decision against schooling of their children. They are also not sure that schooling will really brighten up their children's future prospects. They dread uncertainty, and prefer to follow the saying that one bird in hand is better two in bush. The plight of the educated unemployed youth India lends support to their views.

In relation to child labour, the importance of need for compulsory education gets confirmed by the report of the National Commission on Labour, 1969.

> "The gradual reduction in the employment of child labour since independence is due partly to the expansion of educational facilities by the state and also to relatively better enforcement of statutory provisions relating to child labour."

The major hurdle in the way of making education compulsory for all children up to a prescribed age has been rightly indicated by the above report in the following:

> "An artisans cannot afford to educate his wards though education is free. For him an uneducated child is an

asset; desire to be educated becomes a double liability because of (a) loss of earnings, if the child does not work, and (b) expenditure on education, howsoever small."

No doubt, the role of education cannot be underestimated for proper development of children. Each and every parent wants his child to become a reputed 'A' class person but the unfortunate children have neither the means for education nor they have time to spare for it. They just cannot afford to wait for a bright future tomorrow, rather than having the bread crumbs right now.

8. Illiterate and Ignorant Parents

Most of the illiterate people belong to the lower socio-economic strata of the population in India. These people are only concerned with the present and have rather much at hand to worry about. So, naturally, they deliberately try to escape from the stress and strains of worrying about the future. They are pleased with what they gain by the earnings of their children. Complacently, they do not care to avail of the educational opportunities for their children, including vocational training, even if the same may be available, though such opportunities are rare for the employed children. They are also unmindful of ill effects on the health of their working children.

The Madras Study had come to the conclusion that children who were in employment, were from low literacy groups of the society. About 44 per cent of the parents of child labour were alliterate and another 33 per cent of them were of low literacy groups having studied upto standard V only. Therefore, a large number of parents and guardians were not aware of the importance of education. Their sole concern was the monetary aspect of their children's employment, and not the development of their intelligence in the least.

Thus, the child labour is prevalent extensively in the

lower socio-economic groups because of the lack of appreciation on the part of the parents of the role of education in improving life and the living conditions.

9. Traditional Attitudes

Many sociological factors also contribute to the evil of child labour. In the rural setup, the tradition of family occupation often motivates the child to become a bread winner. For example a goldsmith's son takes to gold-smithery, or a carpenter's child prefers his ancentral vocation. It is worth noting that 15.75 per cent of the child labour had joined the Aligarh lock industries because of their family traditions.

Besides the above mentioned factors responsible for child labour, there are several other causes too. Firstly, the provisions of the protective labour legislations are lopsided and do not cover agriculture and small scale industries. Further, the enforcing machineries, which are provided by the state governments, are inadequate almost every where and fail to check up on child labour. The Factories Act itself is defective in many respects, mainly so because it does not apply to craftsmen on the untenable ground that they do not use power.

To conclude, the child labour emerge due to multiple causes—some economic, some social, some psychological and otherwise. This can be curbed only after striking at the root causes.

REFERENCES

Acharji, N., *Child Labour in India,* (Unpublished).

Addam, Jane (1983), *Child Labour and Pauperism,* p. 17.

Burra, Neera (1988), "Where Children are Cast in Misery's Mould," *The Hindustan Times,* Feb. 14.

Burra, Neera (1988), *Where Children are Caste in Misery's Mould,* The Hindustan Times.

Gangrade, K.D. (1978-79), *Child Labour in India,* Department of Social Work, Delhi University, Delhi, (Unpublished).

Gangrade, K.D. (1978-79), *Child Labour in India*, Department of Social Work, Delhi University, Delhi, (Unpublished).

George, K.N. (1977), "Child Labour in the City of Madras," in National Seminar on Employment of Children in India, organised by National Institute of Public Cooperation and Child Development, New Delhi.

George, K.N. (1977), Child Labour in the City of Madras," in National Seminar on Employment of Children in India, organised by the National Institute of Public Co-operation and Child Development, New Delhi, August, (Unpublished).

Government of India (1954), *Child Labour in India.*

Institute of Public Opinion (1973), *Monthly Commentary on Indian Economic Condition.*

Khandekar, M. (1970), "A Report on the situation of Children and Youth in Greater Bombay," Tata Institute of Social Sciences, Bombay.

Lumpkin, K.D. and Douglas (1938), D.W., *Child Workers in America.*

Madan, G. (1975), *Review of Legal Provisions Relating to Facilities for, and Working Conditions of Employed Children—The Impact on Their Health, Education and Development,"* (Unpublished).

Report of the International Labour Organisation quoted in the book *"Needs of Children"* pub. by UNICEF, p. 144.

Sengupta, Padmini, *Child Labour as a Social Problem* (Unpublished).

Study of Child Labour in Bombay (1978), National Institute of Public Co-operation and Child Development, New Delhi, (Unpublished).

Study of Child Labour in Bombay (1978), National Institute of Public Co-operation and Child Development, New Delhi, (Unpublished).

The Hindustan Times (1989), April 27.

Yojana (1981), Vol. XXV/S, March 16-31.

Chapter 3

Child Labour in India

> "The first duty toward children is to make them happy. If you have not made them happy, you have wronged them; no other good they may get can make up for that."
>
> —*Charles Buxton*

The phenomenon of child labour has existed in one form or another in all historical times. The problem of child labour has been prevalent in India since long and it constitutes an ugly feature of the social life of our country. Historycal accounts prove that 'Child Labour' was in vogue in Indian society from time immemorial. Children gave helping hands to their parents in the household chores and also in family occupations. Various Sanskrit books have described how children in Indian families shared the work-load of their parents and of their gurus during their Brahmacharya Ashrama (study-life). The famous story of Krishna and Sudama clearly establishes that children (students) were used by their gurus for carrying out certain household chores. In the modern period with the advent of new industrial culture, this practice has assumed an alarming proportion only to attract the attention of social workers, philanthropists and social activists to its various negative aspects. It was never a problem till children were used as helping hands. The need for more production at cheaper costs and the motive to earn more and more resulted in using the helping hands as working hands. Many social organisations and leaders took serious notice of this practice and made hue and cry. Consequently, it attracted attention of the Parliamentarians and social scientist who made several attempts to understand this problem from different angles. This chapter will make a modest attempt to review all such efforts and link these findings with the present study on child labour in the Carpet Industry. The studies available on the subject can be categorised broadly into four areas.

As regards Child Labour in Ancient India, it can be said that it existed in the forms of child slaves. The children of less than 8 years were purchased as slaves like articles of trade for doing low and dishonourable works. Children of slave took birth as slaves, live and died as slaves unless the master liked to release them from slavery.

Kautilya pointed out that the trade of children as slaves was not prohibited in Mlechchas, because they were backward and uncivilised. On the other hand, Arya child was prohibited to become a slave. Thus, though there is little evidence of the employment of children for wages, but if child slavery could be regarded as that, the existence of child labour in ancient India cannot be denied.

Later on Kautilya realised that children were not physically fit to do ignoble work. Therefore, the first reform, in the field of slavery, that Kautilya sought to bring about was to impose a ban upon the sale and purchase of children as slaves. Any person pledging or selling his own minor children or children of his relatives as slaves was heavily fined.

I

CHILD LABOUR—THE PRODUCT OF ECONOMIC FACTORS

The economic practice of child labour in India, dates back to the Industrial Revolution in the country. Since then the demand of Industry for cheap labour grow so rapidly and the poverty of the masses become so acute that the tendency to exploit child labour among the employers increased in an unprecedented manner.

In introduction of 'Permanent Settlement' by Lord Cornwallis in March 1793 resulted in the collection of land revenue which for exceeded the volume collected in the past. The small holdings and landlordism were factors which were directly responsible for increasing indebtedness of the rural population. The British Land Policy made deadly assult on the Indian handicrafts. The handicrafts of ancient India, had provided jobs to the surplus population and controlled pressure on land. Industries like Saltpetre, glass-making, paper making, handlooms etc., were the worst hit by the British Policy on Industry and tariff. The industries started declining, the cities started shrinking and this led to the increasing pressure on the land. It was this policy which put the vicious circle of poverty operating in India, as it resulted in the pressure of population on the soil, mass indebtedness in rural Indian and created conditions unfavourable to the health of the rural economy. This was the story of small holdings and indebtedness, the two great evils of the agrarian economy in the modern times, resulting in the problems of child labour which continued unabated. With the advent of the industrialisation and urbanisation, children become subject to economic and social exploitation by employers whose main consideration was maximisation of profits. This was pointed out by the Royal Commission on Labour (1929—31) which described at length the extremely unsatisfactory employment and working conditions of child workers.

Traditional Indian Economy

The plunder of the wealth and resources of this vast territory and the life and labour of its people and finally absolute domination for the last two centuries by the Britishers, reduced Indian people to a miserably impoverished mass. The British East India Company acted as the vehicle for draining India's wealth into Britain. The sweat and blood of the Indian people, reduced to money, became one of the principal sources of the primitive accumulation of capital in Britain. Wages, working hours, employment of child labour, housing and in all other spheres the extent of exploitation was appallingly excessive. But the nature of that exploitation on the Indian Labour during its germinating period and for a long time therefore, for reasons of its being under a rupacious colonial rule, was more terrifying.

Women and Children at Work

Fifteen to sixteen hours of working at a stretch was a most common practice during the early phase. Even the women and children as little as between five and six years of age were also inhumanly tied to the grinding wheels of the factory. The exploitation of Indian working class was expressed chiefly in the fact both British and Indian Capitalists secured absolute surplus value. Working hours of maximum length, from dawn to dusk and often longer was the most striking indication of the brutal manner in which labour was exploited.

Indian Factory Labour Commission of 1908

The employer did not show any sense of proportion or any human consideration in exploiting female and child labour children even of such tender age as between 5 and 7 were worked most cruely everywhere. Investigations conducted by the Indian Factory Labour Commission of 1908 revealed that half of the time, 30 to 40 per cent of these employed in the factories were tender aged children. The Commission while narrating the mode of work of a jute mill in Bengal stated that the workers lived three to four miles away from the mill. But when the siren struck at 3 O'clock in the night, the child labourers below 7 years of age attended the factory travelling on foot that distance of three to four miles in the darkness of night. Regarding female labourers also the commission pointed out that their health break down under the strain of working whole of the night. Many of these women labourers attended the factory with suckling babies in arms. When the workers physically broke down under the strain of his labour unbearable for any human being, one set was replaced by another of new recruits just like replacing a broken cog of a wheel by a fresh one.

Dewan Chamanlal noted down a heart-rendering story about the brutal exploitation on child labour as reproduced below:

It is very apt to quote Dewan Chamanlal in this connection Slavery is the key note of Industrial life of India. We do not have to look to countries like Libenia or Abyssinia to find forms of child slavery. We have it here in the heart of India. Not long ago a well-known public man, in the days when he was working as a school-master, disclosed that in the house adjoining his own, a large number of children used to be drafted in everyday and that sometimes at night he used to hear their pitiable cries, which gave him no rest. He thought that the adjoining house was a school and that it was his duty as a school-master to report to the authorities regarding the crucities that were being inflicted upon innocent children. When enquiries were made, it was discovered that the adjoining house was a Lace Factory in which little children of tender age were made to work unheard of hours and it was when they were tired and when their heads bent in sleep over their work that the kind-hearted factory owner would cane with his wheep and make them up thinking that their cries and their tears were an aid to their industrial education. The name of this public man was the right Hon'ble Srinivas Sastri.

Chronic poverty is responsible for the prevalence and perpetuation of child labour. Nearly half of India's population subsists below poverty line. In the countryside, the distribution of land is most iniquitous. The lower 50 per cent households own only 4 per cent of the land. Thus, the problem of child labour is the by-product of exploitation by a few socially and economically powerful persons trading on the misery and suffering of large number of poverty-striken labourers. Economic exploitation of child labourers is the result of the concentration of national wealth in a fewer hands who enjoy all the privileges of affluent living, condemning the under-privileged to distress and despair.

Poverty and Indebtedness

The social customs and obligations like births, marriages, death in the families and drinking habits play an important role in compelling the poor to resort to borrowing. The money lenders use to take advantage of the deteriorating economic conditions of the poor. They advance small loans from time to time in lieu of binding them to work as agricultural labourers till the final payment of loans. Indebtedness becomes an economic inevitability and child labour and exploitation a way of life to many of them. thus, one of the potent causes of child labour in India is the poverty of landless agricultural labourers. Poverty forced them to incur loans for consumption and their inability to repay the loans lead to their children to work in industrial and non-industrial occupations.

Due to poverty, low-birth or degraded nature of occupation the fate of many child labourers were sealed by forces of socio-economic nature. The Scheduled Tribes, the Scheduled Castes and other backward classes are the main victims of the child labour problem.

Thus, socio-economic, demographic factors like size of the family, poverty, indebtedness and illiteracy compelled the children from the poor families to participate in the labour force. With limited or total absence of skill and training, a traditional society with conservative and fatallistic outlook provides congenial ground for employment of children.

Child Labour: Some Studies

The studies of Ashok Mitra, Kulshreshtha, Pandhe, Jain and Chand have attempted to identify the reasons for the large scale incidence of child labour. The large-size of the families, poverty, illiteracy of the parents, their ignorance about the importance of education as well as about the impact of labour on the health of the child, infirmities of state protection programmes, and poor implementation of universal primary education programmes are considered to be the important causes of child labour in India. Besides, the economic benefits accuring from child employment are also high as it generates an income which is higher than what they actually consume in the family.

These factors contribute the reasons for prevalence of child labour in India. In brief, the problem of child labour is undoubtedly very complex as historical, sociological political and economic considerations come into play.

Preference for Child Labour

Employer generally prefer children to adults because of various reasons. Children are less egoistically developed, less status conscious and they are affected by the feelings of guilt and shame. They are more agile, active and feel less tired and can put up with even more demanding works. They are more amenable for discipline, are cheaper to buy and by employing children the employers avoid many a labour problem. They are better candidates for tasks of helper in a grocer's shop or an auto-garage. They can be coaxed, admonished, pulled up and punished for defaults without jeopardising relations. Thus, children are employed because they are available at cheaper wages and they are exploited because they are poor. All this explains why children are liked more for jobs.

Children in India: A Demographic Profile

As per 1971 census, there were 230.3 million children in India accounting for 42.02 per cent of the total population. The distribution of child population varies from 34.76 per cent in Haryana to 46.86 per cent in Assam. The factor behind these variations are quite numerous. It is observed that 41.86 per cent of the male population and 42.19 per cent of the female population belong to the child age-group (i.e., less than 14 years). Of the total child population, 14.94 per cent belongs to the Scheduled Caste while 6.94 per cent belongs to be Scheduled Tribes. The ratio of the Scheduled Caste/ Scheduled Tribe child population to the total population is depending upon the general distribution of Scheduled Caste/ Scheduled Tribe population in a particular administrative division. Of the total population 17.55 per cent in estimated to be migrant population. The percentage varies from as high as 35.11 in West Bengal to as low as 9.63 in Bihar. The analysis of migration data revealed that migration rates have been higher amongst the rural children than the urban children. The child population has increased by 27.9 per cent between 1961 and 1971. The change has been as high as 67.1 per cent in Delhi and as low as 4.87 in Pondicherry.

Child Work Force

Out of 230.3 million children in India, 10.7 million were enumerated as workers by the census in 1971 of these nearly three-fourths were males. The child workers constitute 5.95 per cent of the total work force of the country. There are 7.9 million male child workers and 2.8 million female child workers in the country. Earlier study has revealed that child work force is low is areas where literacy level is high, and where urban and industrial development is high. In rural and backward regions, or in areas where Scheduled Caste/ Scheduled Tribe concentration is high, child workers also tend to be high.

The male child workers proportion varies from 0.56 per cent in Alleppy district of Kerala to 14.1 per cent in Kalahandi district of Orissa. The proportion of female child workers varies from 1.05 per cent in Ganganagar district to 25.9 per cent in Dungarpur district (Rajasthan) during 1971. The participation rate of children in the work force is 2.42 per cent in the urban areas while it is three times of it in the rural areas. Owing to the large rural population in the country, a high proportion of children (92.78 per cent) are engaged as workers in the rural areas. Nearly 87.23 per cent of the child workers are engaged in primary sector, that is, agriculture and allied activities. Secondary and tertiary sectors employ 6.67 per cent and 6.13 per cent respectively.

It is observed that where literacy is low, child workers is high. In Kerala, where literacy rate is the number of high (69.75 per cent), the proportion of child work force is low (1.79 per cent) and in Rajasthan where literacy is low (22.57 per cent) the proportion of child workers is high (7.29 per cent). The development of the region generally leads to the reduction of the size of the child work force.

Child Labour: Statewise Distribution

Extent of child labour and its magnitude has been discussed in the first chapter. It is, however, necessary to discuss in brief, the dimensions of child labour in Indian States.

According to 1981 census Jammu and Kashmir had the highest number of Child labourer that is 10.3 per cent. The figures for the other states are as follows. Madhya Pradesh 7.9 per cent. Sikkim 6.8 per cent, Himachal Pradesh 5.8 per cent, Rajasthan 5.6 per cent, Bihar 3.7 per cent, Manipur 3.6 per cent, Tripura 3.0 per cent, West Bengal 2.8 per cent. Meghalaya 7.9 per cent, Karnataka 7.6 per cent, Maharashtra 6.4 per cent. Nagaland 5.6 per cent, Gujarat 4.7 per cent, Haryana 3.6 per cent, Punjab 3.6 per cent. Uttar Pradesh 3.0 per cent, Kerala 1.0 per cent. The figure for whole of India was 5.1 per cent. For some states the 1981 figures are not available and hence the findings of 1971 census, Andhra Pradesh 9.2 per cent. Assam 3.4 per cent, Orissa 5.3 per cent. Tamil Nadu 4.5 per cent. According to one report the trend during the last decade (1971—81) has been such that the work participation by boys of 0-14 years has decreased by 3.5 per cent while that for girls has increased by 3.2 per cent.

Types of Child Labour

The number and types of occupations in which children are being employed in endless and includes almost every aspect of human work and life. Generally, children are employed in the agricultural sector helping in agricultural operations like sowing, weeding, harvesting and threshing. Their activities also include looking after animals, collecting firewoods, carrying water, spreading manure and fertilisers in the farm land. In urban areas, they are engaged in more diversified activities such as loading-unloading hawking, looking after parked vehicles, shoe-shining. Besides, they are also employed as helpers in tea shops and auto-repair shops or are engaged as domestic servants, house and road construction works, brick-kiln, stone breaking, carpet-weaving, beedi making, match making etc. Quite a large number of child labour is in existence in unorganised sector including small scale and cottage industries viz., handlooms weaving, leather tannery, glass bangles, mat-making, tailoring pottery, fireworks.

Child Labour in Indian Industries

The Labour Investigation Committee (1946) remarked that "one black spot of labour conditions in India is illegal employment of children in certain industries." Some case studies on the plight of child labour by social workers and researchers have contributed a lot for the raising consciousness about the problem. The more horrible features of exploitation of child labour are found in the match-box industry and printing presses of Sivakasi (Tamil Nadu) lead mines and state pencil factories of Mandsaur (Madhya Pradesh), glass factories of Ferozabad (Uttar Pradesh), the carpet industry in Mirzapur-Bhadohi (Uttar Pradesh).

Match-Box Industry in Sivakasi (Tamil Nadu)

In recent years, several write ups in newspapers and periodicals have focussed light on the deplorable position of child labour employed in the match and fireworks industry in Sivakasi. The Gurupadaswamy Committee (1979) had estimated about 50,000 child labourers employed in Sivakasi area. In these match factories, child workers in the age group of 5 to 15 work about 12 hours in a day and receive wages in the range of Rs. 1 to 8. Because, the wages are determined on the basis of piece rates, the child workers work feverishly in time available to them to show the maximum output. This results in a complete neglect of their own requirements and many of the children were found rather frail and anaeomic in their looks. There was no medical assistance available to them, and children even in sick conditions had no option except to sit in the factory and work on box making, frame filling, labelling and band role pasting. In spite of their best efforts for the day, their return was very meagre one.

Carpet Industry in Mirzapur-Bhadohi (U.P.)

One of the largest employers of children is the carpet-weaving industry. In Kashmir, this sector employs more than one million children. The carpet industry utilises child labour in Bhadohi Mirzapur, Allahabad and Varanasi. The carpet industry has only increased oppression and reinforced the feudalistic structure of social relations. Dr. B.N. Juyal has observed, "Indulging in physical violence and other abuses on child labour becomes a matter of routine and ordinary occurrences which may not disturb anybody.

Roughly, 1.5 lakh children work in the carpet industry and they do the major part of the work. The Industry could not survive without the children. A carpet is not woven; it is knotted and each individual knot has to be made by hand. Eighty per cent of the knotting work is done by children under the age of sixteen. They work long hours without protest, are easily coerced and will also do a lot of unpaid work for the owner willingly. The difference in the earnings of a weaver boy and the final seller tells the whole story. A square yard of carpet which a boy may weave in a day can sell for anything between Rs. 100-400 in the export market. For that, the boy who actually made it, is paid the princely sum of Rs. 5-10. And from it is loom owner will deduct the expense of food, medicines and clothes.

Handloom Weaving at Kanchipuram

In the state of Tamil Nadu, in Kanchipuram a large

number of children in the age group of 7 to 14 are working on looms. It was pointed out that, because of their nimble fingers, they were particularly deft in weaving designs and borders. Most of them had never been to school. They were getting a wave between Rs. 60 and 100 per month. Some of the very young children were being paid as low as Rs. 15 per month. In some cases, it was also observed that children had been pledged into work by the guardians on a long term basis.

Inhuman Exploitation

The Child Labourers rescued in the Famous Bilwaria incident bore visible marks of physical torture, such as branching with hot iron, bruises and lathi blows. They were severely beaten with iron rods if they were slow at work, made mistakes in weaving, asked for adequate food, or even if they went to case themselves without the master's permission. At night, they were all locked up in a small room. This happened to them daily. But once they were caught in the act of escaping, their feet were fied together and they were slung upside down from the branch of a tree and then, to "Properly" drive the lesson home, they were branded with hot irons. (Juyal)

It has been found that about 50 per cent of child labourers are anaemic and/or suffering from the worst infestation. The evil consequences of remaining cramped in damp pit looms, resulting in boils, the swelling of the lower limbs and aching joints, etc. have been frequently observed.

Glass Bangle Industry in Ferozabad

The glass industry is another important child employer. Children are employed in Jurai (joining of ends), Chhatai (Sorting), Katai (engraving of different patterns with the help of abrasive wheels), Pakai (heating) and then in counting and packing. The decoration of bangles with hill. (liquid gold) is done by girls and women. The factories run for about 8 months in the year and work only at night. In Ferozabad alone, there are about 250 such factories which employ about 60,000 children out of a total labour force of 1 lakh. Many of these children have to stand about 4 feet away from furnaces and ovens with temperatures as high as 800-1200 F. The cases of asthma and bronchitis are many. Workers suffer from various eye diseases. Ferozabad ranks first as far as tuberculosis is concerned among child workers.

Bidi-Rolling Industry in Madhya Pradesh

The bidi-rolling industry is located at various places but in Madhya Pradesh alone it employs about 2 lakh children. In such industries, child workers roll bidies and assist the adult workers by cleaning and cutting the leaf and closing the ends. Employers pay the children much less than the adults on the pretext that the products do not come upto the required standard of quality. There was sufficient indication to suspect a high incidence of tuberculosis among the bidi workers and this, was due to starting work at a tender age, very long hours of work.

Zari Making Industry in Lucknow

Children are also employed in the zari-making and embroidery industry. About 7000 child workers in the age group 8-15 were employed in Lucknow with an average monthly Rs. 50 payment towards waves. They sit and work in over-crowded rooms with poor lighting and ventilation. Many of them suffer from eye diseases.

Pottery Industry in Khurja

In Khurja (Uttar Pradesh) out of the 20,000 pottery workers, about 50,000 are children below the age of 14. Here, children carry lamps of clay for cutting and moulding. They clay is fitted in the moulds and then taken out into the open for drying. They then return with empty moulds. All this work is done at a very fast pace as the employer aims at a rapid output with the maximum profit. The total weight to be carried per trip is about 8 kgs. Thus in his 8 hours of work a child has to reach a distance of virtually 5 kms with this load, thus making about 1000 trips. Despite such harsh and hard work, the child workers are labelled as mere helpers and therefore, paid a negligible amount of money.

Stone-polishing Industry in Jaipur

The precious stone-polishing industry of Jaipur employs 10,000 children, all of whom work in slums or miserable hovels. The work is done through middle-men who procure children for a pittance. Similarly, in the diamond-polishing industry of Surat, the child workers develops eye defects very soon. They are ruthlessly retrenched with the first early signs of eye fatigue. Many are jobless in their teens.

Child Labour in Kolkata

It is Kolkata and its surroundings that can safely claim having the biggest contingent of teen-age workers 90 per cent of the children in Calcutta hail from different rural districts, 30 per cent of these children come from Midnapur alone, with Howrah occupying the second position. There is also a sizeable migration from Bihar, Orissa and Uttar Pradesh. Agricultural Labour families, owning a bit of land or absolutely landless, are migrating to the cities in large numbers. According to physicians' estimate, 100 per cent of the City's child workers suffer from Vitamin deficiencies, 52 per cent from worm infections, 32 per cent from skin diseases, 22 per cent from eye complaints, 23 per cent from asthma and respiratory infections and quite a good number from T.B. and lung cancer.

Mumbai: Child Labour in the Unorganised Sectors

Thousands of children work like robots in the various hotels and restaurants in Bombay despite the civic fathers' pretence that child labour does not exist in their dream city. With an estimated 50,000 of the 3 lakh people employed in the City's nearly 12,000 food shops of various nature, Bombay has the largest number of working children among the Indian Cities, next only to Calcutta. A team of the All India Guild of Law Graduates and the Bombay Labour Union, that jointly conducted a survey in the recent past, found a majority of the kids belonging to the migrant families hailing from the Souther States, for whom 12 to 13 hours labour against a monthly pittance of Rs. 100 to Rs. 150 is the order of the day. A study made by Kumar Ketkar in 1977 reveals that children and women work beyond 12 hours, in filthy working conditions, all safety measures being ignored, not to speak of bonus or exgratia payments. Thus, child labour is essentially a problem of poor and destitute families, where parents cannot afford the education of their children. It is not uncommon to find especially in the urban areas, that families below the poverty line depend on the earnings of their children. Moreover, in the majority of cases, there is no liability on the part of the employer to give any service benefits such as provident fund, gratuity, leave, promotion and annual increments.

Child Labour in Delhi

There are over 2.5 lakh of child workers on the Capital's streets who have to work for long hours just for two square meals a day. From Bihar, Uttar Pradesh, Rajasthan and Madhya Pradesh about 15-20 of them arrive in the Capital each day in search of jobs. A majority of these children sleep on the pavements near the New Delhi and Old Delhi railway stations, the Inter-State Bus Terminus, Jama Masjid, Connaught Place and the Walled City areas. Sexual harassment is the major problem among girls. A large number of children are sent from the Uttar Pradesh villages by their parents during weekends to work in Delhi. Those who join dhabas and shops are found to be exploited most, as they have to work for 14 to 16 hours daily and due to the accommodation and food provided by the owners, such children are not in a position to bargain for better wages.

Child Pledging in Tamilnadu

There are innumerable cases where unfortunate children are being exploited both by their parents and the agents for their own selfish needs. These innocent little ones an being treated like cattle, pledged and mortgaged at the will of their masters. In their case, the masters are the parents and, later, the agents. In the society of around one lakh people subsiding on the Bidi Industry located mainly in the district of Vellore and its suburbs. The deep-rooted traditons and customs among bidi workers together with the strong and cut culture of this community has made child pledging an accepted practice. The ironical fact is that they perceive the agents as their saviours who provide work to their children and the subsequent meal to the family. But in reality children are abused, pledged, redeemed and repledged to different agents for a higher amount from the agents.

In the bidi industry of Vellore, child pledging has become an organised trade where the term 'Pledging' refers to the bondage of children by their parents to an employer or his agent against a loan on an agreement, written or oral, that the child would work till the repayment of the debt. The term 'Child' means the son or daughter of a migrant who has not completed 15 years of age involved in bidi rolling. Due to continuous drought, economic compulsions or death of the main head earner, the landless labourers were forced to take up employment elsewhere, preferably in the Bidi industry since the whole family could be employed by it. The migrant families became squatters on the road side or any other 'Promoke' land in these villages. Except their children, they had nothing at hand to rely upon. As a last resort, to feed themselves they preferred to pledge their children for survival.

A study reveals about the ill-treatment and the stories of exploitation meted out to these children, the pledged children work 12 hours a day and are paid a daily sum of

Rs. 1 to Rs. 4, depending upon the amount pledged, if the contractual obligations are not violated by the child. It was reported that the parents have to provide another family member to replace the pledged boy. The children have no recreation, no freedom and no basic human rights. They are like caged birds. Their only world is their work spot and their home which is place only to sleep. At an early stage in their lives, they have frustrations resulting in a high rate of alcoholism and smoking. They study further reveals that excessive hours of work and over exertion results in back pain, hip pain and nervous problems among the pledged children.

Child Bonded Labourers

There are reports about child bonded labour in Andhra Pradesh especially in the Medak district. All the villages in Sidipet, Medak and Gogipet Taluqs that have been surveyed had child labourers chained by leand lords and money lenders. A substantial number of child bonded labourers in every village without exception has been manifested. In some villages of the Medak district, land lords were found thriving upon child labourers, known as Jute Gadus. It has been noticed that once a jute gadu (child bonded labourer) complained to the police inspector about the cruelties committed against him by his master. He was beaten up and thrown out of the police station. It is obvious that such illegal actions made the child labourers silent and they did not dare to approach any government agency or raise their voice against their masters.

Deplorably, annual wage for a child bonded labour on the verge of starvation and aged between 7-15, ranges between Rs. 25 and Rs. 250. In some parts of Madhya Pradesh and Bihar, the situation is even more pitiable. In these areas, the annual wage ranges between Rs. 70 and Rs. 175 for the same age group.

Several studies indicate that the plight of working children has some relationship with Industrial capitalism. The gradual shift to cash crops and the growing number of landless labourers also adds to the exploitation of child labour.

Many of the children are exploited by being trapped in pilferage, the blackmarketing of cinema tickets, the selling of alcohol, gambling and the life. In riots, bus and vehicle burning, harassment of women in buses and lonely places, and in bank robberies, criminal elements make use of this frustrated youth power, while political parties use them for their dirty works departments'. Mafia elements in the Bengal Coal Fields, Matka elements in the Bombay slums and smugglers on the Punjab Circuit are only some constituents of a manpower group spawned from the harsh realities of neglected childhood. For the child who could not tolerate abundonment, who grew up with no habit of responsibility or concern for others, drifting into the easiest path available to him, stress and fear have inevitably created the anti-social personality.

The children inteviewed in the carpet industry in the Mirzapur-Badoli area, or in the matchworks in Sivakasi and countless other industrial centres that exploit child labour, demonstrate how they have cheerfully accepted abysonal working conditions, long hours of work and health hazards. They have nowhere to sleep, no education or opportunity to train for employment as adults. Many such children are bonded and slave on year after year as the family's continuing poverty cannot release them.

A large number of children are working in the unorganised and self-employed sectors in towns as servants and in machine-tools and repair shops. A significant proportion of child labourers are found in the handloom industry of Kashmir, in the private mines of Meghalaya, in the Sugar factory of Lucknow, in the fish industries of Kerala, in the tea gardens and industries of Assam and in innumerable unorganised industries.

II

PREVALENCE OF CHILD LABOUR

The study on the working children in urban Delhi (1977) tried to examine the extent, causes and consequences of child labour in urban Delhi. The study estimated 21,000 child workers in Delhi in 1973. Out of 1,992 household surveyed, only 60 families had working children numbering 18. Most of the local children were employed in the workshops. Children working in tea stalls, dhabas and as domestic servants came from the eastern and north-eastern parts of Uttar Pradesh and Bihar. The average size of their household was 5.5 and the average monthly income including the earning of working children was Rs. 321.5 per month. Another study by the Committee on Child Labour (1979) appointed by the Ministry of Labour, Govt. of India examined various dimensions of child labour in different occupations. The study revealed that the incidence of child labour was highest in Andhra Pradesh where it accounted for about 9.0 per cent of the total labour force, 9.2 per cent of the total child population and 3.7 per cent of the total population of state in 1971. The Child labour was more prevalent in rural areas than in urban areas. A higher percentage of children (5.31 per cent) in rural area were workers whereas this ratio in urban areas was only 1.82 per cent. The participation of children in the labour force in the age-group of 10-14 years was very high (28.9 per cent) for males as compared to females (20 per cent).

The census figures (1971) also reveal that out of 10.74 million working children, 36.03 per cent are cultivators, 42.70 per cent agricultured labours and 8.24 per cent are engaged in live-stock, forestry, fishing, etc., 0.22 per cent in mining, and quarrying and 6.08 per cent in manufacturing process, 0.54 per cent in construction, 1.95 per cent in trade and commerce, 0.39 per cent in transport and 3.7 per cent in other services. Another study of child workers conducted in rural Haryana (1979) was based on a sample of 200 child labour families in four villages. It was found that 89 per cent parents of child labour were illiterate, about 49 per cent working children had never gone to school, 40 per cent had discontinued schooling and only 11 per cent child workers were regular in carrying on the burden of schooling and earning of both. In Rewari Tehsil, under study, 70.7 per cent were boys and the rest were girls; 19.4 per cent were between 6 and 8 years of age and 47.6 per cent were of 11-14 years of age; 30.5 per cent of them belonged to Rajput casts and Yadav each and the largest group of child workers consisted of Chamar (Scheduled Caste). The family size of the majority of these workers was 6 to 8. The greater load was on the shoulders of children belonging to nuclear families (70 per cent) than to those (30 per cent) of the joint families. The maximum number (66.0 per cent) of children came from the most prevalent family size of 6 to 8 member whereas the small size of families of 3 to 5 members contributed 34 per cent only. Due to limited coverage, it did not present the working conditions, perception of child labour by their parents, relationship between children and employers and the Child Labour Laws in different working settings.

Another study on Problems and Social Services Needs of Child Labour in Agriculture in Uttar Pradesh (Singh, 1982) revealed that the average age of the child workers was 13.6 years while the majority of child workers (70.2 per cent) belonged to the age-group of 13-18 years. The majority of the child workers were from non-tribal Hindus and Scheduled Castes. The maximum number of child workers who discontinued the studies were in the age group of 8-12 years.

The study on the working condition of children employed in unorganised sector (CSIR 1984) which was based on a sample of 900 male and female child workers below the age of 16 years, indicated that the majority of children employed in match units in Sivakasi were girls (67 per cent). Only 8 per cent were children below 8 years of age and a majority of the child workers (71 per cent) were in the age-group of 13-16 years. Another study on the working children in Bombay (Singh M., 1980) in the age-group of 6-15 years found that most of the working children belonged to low income groups in urban centres who generally reside in slums and depressed areas. This study was conducted on 203 boys (67.7 per cent) and 97 girls (32.3 per cent): three per cent of them belonged to the age-group of 6-9 years, 25.7 per cent to the age-group of 9-12 years and 71.3 per cent to the age-group of 12-15 years. Out of these 300 working children 211 (70.3 per cent) worked under the employer and 89 (29.7 per cent) were self-employed, 287 lived with their parents and 13 with guardians and relatives. The majority of the families of the working children (63.8 per cent) had 5 to 8 members, the average being 5.8 per family. There were more male members than female members in these families. Out of 703 children in the age-group of 6-15 years, as many as 319 (45.4 per cent) were found working. Out of these 703, 403 (57.39 per cent) were boys and 300 (42.7 per cent) girls. Out of 319 working children, 200 (62.7 per cent) were boys and 119 (37.3 per cent) girls. The working children from Hindu families were more than those from Muslim families. The percentage of the working children increased with age, 9 per cent were in the age-group of 6-9 years; 39 per cent in 9-12 years; 78 per cent were in 12-15 Years. Most of the children joined the labour force by the time they were 10 years. Male children shouldered the family's economic responsibility to a large extent than the female. Irrespective of sex, the eldest child in the family invariably had to work, the percentage being 96 per cent boys and 90 per cent girls.

Coming to Himachal Pradesh, a study on the problem of the working children in the state had revealed that about 1/3rd of the children of the age-group of 10-14 years in rural and 1/8th of those in urban areas were at work in India. Children working in agriculture and in households on an average worked for 280 days in a year. In villages, children were used as bonded labour and as contract labour in urban areas. Of the working children, 36.79 per cent belonged to Schedule Castes and Scheduled Tribes, and 20.75 per cent to lower castes. Thus, incidence of child labour is much higher in economically backward communities. As regards their literacy, 71.52 per cent were illiterate. A majority (80.35 per cent) of them belonged to agriculture and 16.75 per cent to households. Most of them owned houses but a majority lived in Katcha houses. Regarding income, 5.44 per cent were getting less than Rs. 900, 24.78 per cent between Rs. 901-1800 and 34.71 per cent between Rs. 1801-3600 as their annual income. Another report (Gangrade, 1983) reveals that the states like Uttar Pradesh, Jammu and Kashmir and Tamil Nadu have flourishing centres of carpet weaving. Varanasi, Bhodhi, Mirjapur are also big centres of carpet weaving. It is in Mirjapur where 50,000 workers are engaged in carpet weaving of which nearly 20 per cent are children. Employment of children in activities suited to them keeps the cost of production low. They also work as apprentices. In household carpet weaving enterprises children are considered indispensable as helpers and as trainees who continue the craft.

Factors Responsible for Child Labour

The survey of children at work (Mendelvich, 1979) tried to highlight the problem of child labour in India and its causes. In fact, the problem of child labour in India may be seen as the result of traditional attitudes, urbanisation, industrialisation, migration, lack of schools or the reluctance of parents to send their children to schools, etc. In the ultimate analysis, main causes are extreme poverty and agriculture being the main occupation of the majority of population requiring more hands.

Child labour is essentially a problem of the poor and destitute families, where parents can not afford to provide education to their children. A study of the working children in Mumbai (Singh M. 1980) found that 20.6 per cent of the interviewed employers were employing children because they were quick and efficient, 12.6 per cent preferred them because they were more amenable to discipline, some found them better suited for some types of jobs, 30.5 per cent said that their plight had greater sentimental appeal, 9.3 per cent were in favour of them as they were cheap and 1.9 per cent favoured because of their honesty. Out of 287 respondents (parents), the majority (170 i.e. 69.2 per cent) mentioned economic compulsions as the main factor. As many as 74 (25.8 per cent) mentioned that the child was idle and doing nothing. Therefore, he was put to work to save him from the demoralising effects of idleness. There were 69 (24 per cent) respondents who said that the child had left the school and there was no alternative but to put him at work at keep him busy. Sixty two of them (21.6 per cent) attributed the early entry to work on the part of their children to death, disease or loss of job of the earning member of the family. A few did not mention any special reason or circumstances and said that child labour was their family tradition. Seventeen of the respondents (6.0 per cent) said that their children were keeping bad company and slipping into delinquency so they had to put them on some job so that they might inculcate a sense of discipline. Twelve of the respondents mentioned that the child himself was keen to earn; so they did not stop him from working.

Taking the case of Haryana State, another study on the working children in Hisar (Sharma 1982) revealed that a majority of the child workers joined the labour force due to acute poverty of their family, death and chronic illness of the earning members and there was no source to supplement their family income. Children came from different States. About 4/5 of the children came from the families whose average monthly income was less than Rs. 300 and the size of the family was 8 on an average. The social circumstances which also motivated the child workers to seek jobs were company of friends, rude behaviour of fathers and lack of affection in the family, etc.

One more study on the working conditions of Children employed in unorganised sector, in Sivakasi (CSR, 1984) found that children were the main bread winners in most of the families there. A large number of families depended on the income from match units either as main source or as supplementary source of family income. About 36 per cent of the families had more than two children employed in match units. Most of the children were under compulsion to work due to poverty. A majority (95 per cent) of them took up jobs in match units because of the poor financial conditions of their families. Another 6 per cent of them were interested to continue their studies but were forced by their parents to work to support their families or to supplement the family income. Similarly, another study on Child labour in Himachal Pradesh found that it was the economic necessity which compelled the families to send their children to work. Increasing incidence of debts created more pressure for sending all possible hands to work for wages.

Employers preferred child labour, because it was easy to manage them and also they had to pay less wages to them. About 14.67 per cent employers expressed their opinion that children should be employed but 82.67 per cent replied in the negative. It was also found that in certain handicrafts like Zaribrocade, carpets which need training at the early ages children are preferred to adults.

Working Conditions

A study conducted (Singh M., 1980) in Mumbai presents the working conditions of both self-employed and employed children. Self-employed child workers were found to be working for 10 hours a day who earned around Rs. 82 per month on an average. The Lack of fixed place of shelter, inadequacy of equipment and harassment by officials were the main problems in carrying out the job smoothly. According to me parents, work developed a sense of responsibility in their children made them sober, considerate and well-behaved. The findings about the employed children revealed that none was asked to produce a certificate of medical fitness by the employer nor the employer got him/her medically examined. A majority of the children (68.2 per cent) were getting a monthly salary of Rs. 100 and below. The Children engaged in construction work, arts and crafts and production received the highest payments whereas those in households and restaurants were paid the lowest emoluments in terms of hard cash. Out of 205 children who were earning, as many as 133 (64.9 per cent) received pocket money, 64.9 per cent, i.e., 133 children worked on regular basis and the rest on daily wages. The minimum number of hours a child worked was 4 hours and the maximum was 14 hours, the average being 8.7 hours. Out of the total sample, 5.10 per cent working children had no fixed rest interval. Similarly, 35 per cent of the children did not get an off-day during the week.

According to employers, protection against sun and rain was available to 79.9 per cent of the working children, separate rest places to 20.6 per cent, proper lighting to 88.7 per cent, medical facilities to 41.2 per cent, drinking' water and bath facilities to 79.4 per cent, protection against job hazards to 52.9 per cent, proper ventilation to 83.8 per cent, recreational facilities to 17.2 per cent and toilet facilities to 57.4 per cent. As many as 54 per cent children did not express any difficulties in the performance of their jobs. Another 88.60 per cent of the children were satisfied with the treatment accorded to them their employers and only 11.4 per cent were not satisfied.

So far as the employers satisfaction is concerned, 68.1 per cent of the employers were satisfied with the work behaviour of the children and 6.4 per cent were not satisfied. According to the parents, none of the employed children ever met with any accident at the work place. It was further that 47.3 per cent were satisfied with their salaries, 66.6 per cent were satisfied with the length of their working hours, 13.7 per cent with the physical conditions of their work, 5.9 per cent with the facilities and benefits available, 10.2, per cent with the security to their jobs, 3.9 per cent with the treatment of their employers and 2.4 per cent with the treatment of their colleagues. Another 36 per cent of the children had to do household chores also in addition to the regular job. The study under discussion covered most of the aspects of child labour which were not found in other studies. However, due to limitations of its coverage, it could not present the acute problems, of the children working in the carpet weaving industry.

Statistics show that the total employed children in two units of the carpet industry in Srinagar, wages varied from Rs. 2 to Rs. 10 per day for weavers. The wages were Rs. 2 to Rs. 4 per day when full skill of the trade was obtained. In both the units, children were required to work for the same hours as fixed for adult workers. There 'were no special provisions for education, recreation, social security and other welfare amenities for children.

Another study was conducted to find out various dimension of child labour and occupations where children are employed. The study revealed that chronic poverty was a stronger factor than tradition in respect of child labour. The income accruing from child labour might be a pittance but it played a crucial role in saving the family from a shipwreck. Accordingly to this report, children, too in many cases had the fear of being discarded by their parents, if they failed to earn and prove that they were useful to the family. In case of parental incapacitation, children become the sole bread winners. The child workers are not organised on the lines of trade unions which can fight for their causes. Child labour is also justified on the ground that it trains the child's fingers for the required skill. This study, though conducted on an all-India basis, does not throw light on all the aspects of the problem. Moreover, there is hardly any meaningful preferences to the child labour in weaving industry.

A study (Gopunjkar 1980) on the working children in the tribal areas of Maharashtra, conducted with a view to preparing a detailed note on different types of work children did, revealed that children participated in all the occupations/ jobs available to them and activities of home/family occupations and kept themselves engaged through-out the year. The child starts working from about 5 to 6 years of age. The income from the work of the child is of two types in cash and in kind. Wages in cash are governed to some extent, by the Minimum Wages (Amendment) Act of 1979. But in many cares labourers are paid less than what is due to them. The wages in kind are given at rates in accordance with the local practice.

Except for a few activities like Saldari, children enjoy real free life and do not feel the constraints of work. They are not overburdened and feel free in the working atmosphere. However, proper education and health facilities are not available in the country. Diseases resulting from malnourishment and unhygienic conditions and practices are very common.

Another study on child labour in Himachal Pradesh based on a sample of 438 children, 419 parents and 337 employers highlighted that most of the children worked for less than a year but those engaged in tea plantations (Kangra) were more stable. Similarly, agricultural jobs appeared to be more stable than non-agricultural jobs. As reported, 41.10 per cent children were having temporary jobs whereas 30.14 per cent had sessional jobs and 42.85 per cent of child workers lived within one kilometer from their places of work. Others had travel 1 to 5 Kilometre. They procured their jobs on the basis of personal contracts and a few through newspapers, etc. Less than half (37.59 per cent) conceded that the working children were getting better treatment at home in the form of better food, clothes, etc. A majority of the children were working for long hours, e.g., 5.26 per cent for more than 15 hours and 18.31 per cent for 10-15 hours. In Kangra 76 per cent of the children worked for 7-8 hours. About 9.07 per cent reported about the poor safety conditions; but most of them felt no problems. One complained that their work affected their lungs.

A survey report revealed the working conditions of children working in industries were unhygienic and deplorable. The work places in most cases were overcrowded, dark and dingy. The workers were poor and hard-pressed and had to work for long hours to earn their livelihood, especially in view of the prevailing low wage rates.

Dr. S. Singh's study in 1982 on problems of social service needs of child labour in agriculture in U.P. showed that an average monthly income of the child worker had been Rs. 68, Rs. 86 which came to about Rs. 2 per day. A majority of child workers were engaged in carrying water, house watching, buying domestic things, cattle grazing, working in night on irrigation and crop watching, etc. Mean monthly income of the child workers was Rs. 60.86 and in the majority of cases, payment of wages was made directly by the employers and received directly by the child workers. Child workers were suffering from minor ailments only caused by seasonal variations though they were exposed to various serious diseases. A majority of the child workers stated that employers did not exploit them for undue work. The health of the majority of the child workers was poor and their guardians were illiterate without any technical knowledge. The entire monthly earning was between Rs. 200 to Rs. 400 only.

Another study by Sharma (1982) on the working children to examine the extent of exploitation and socio-economic background of child labour found that 56 per cent respondents had to work for 15 to 18 hours per day for earning their livelihood and 44 per cent for 10-15 hours per day. The average daily working hours was 16 hours. As for the payment of wages, 81 per cent of the respondents were receiving upto Rs. 50 per month whereas 16 per cent were paid Rs. 50 to Rs. 100 per month while only 3 per cent respondents received more than Rs. 100. The respondent contributed the maximum of their earnings to support their families.

Another study (CSR 1984) conducted on working conditions of children employed in unorganised sector in Sivakasi reported that about 53 per cent of the child workers had been working for more than two years. They worked for more than 10 hours per day in ill-ventilated places without basic amenities and rest which affected their health and retarded their physical and mental growth and development at this age. The employers were found to be very strict with the employed child workers. Thus, 11 per cent of the children stated that they were treated harshly by their employers, 88 per cent stated that they were scolded when mistakes were committed and the rest were beaten on such occasions. Primarily, this study was based on a sample of 900 child workers only. Therefore, the required information could not be verified by the parents and the employers of the child workers.

Combating Child Labour

So far as the implementation of various laws for the working conditions and welfare of child labour is concerned, a study, revealed that employers had colossal ignorance about the existing laws. Only 20 were in favour of legislation regulating employment of children. Out of 159 employers owing establishments, only 9 mentioned that officials visited their establishments for inspection purpose. Similarly, another study had found that to remove the legal binding, the employers did not enter the name of the working—children in the register maintained by them. Children disappeared as soon as the inspector arrived in the factory. The record did not reflect child employment.

Coming to plantation, a survey report revealed that the working hour of the child workers were very lengthy in the most of the factories. It was observed in 44 cases that the daily working hours varied between 6-8 hours as against 4½ hours prescribed under the Factory Act, 1948. Practically, there was no much difference between working hours of the child workers and the adult workers in 30 units. Thus, the weekly hours of work for children were more than 41 in 17 plantation units. There is no uniformity of age for employment of children as prescribed under the employment of Children Act, 1938, the Plantation Labour Act, 1951, Mines Act, 1952, etc. Wages paid to children varied from state to state and also industry to industry. Analysis of results showed that the daily wages of the working children in different industries was upto Rs. 5 only. There is no statutory provision for providing educational facilities under labour laws except in the Plantation Labour Act, 1951. Welfare, recreational and other facilities were also not available to the child workers. Another study (Sharma, 1982) conducted in Hisar in Haryana revealed that the problem of child labour was on the increase inspite of legal enactments to prevent the practice. Hence, in the organised sector the problem of child labour practice is on the decrease whereas in the unorganised sector it is on the increase.

A study conducted in Sivakasi in 1984 found a big contrast in the statement given by the employers. For instance, according to match units 35 per cent to 50 per cent more than the minimum wages fixed by the Govt. was paid to the child workers while an analysis showed less than what was stated. According to another statement of the employers of the match units, almost all the child workers were provided with facilities as available under the Insurance Act, Providend Fund Act, etc., but in actual practice, these were not made available. The toilet facilities were almost non-existent in their places of work as well as in their homes. There were no recreational facilities except movies.

Apart from a number of studies conducted in both urban and rural areas in different occupations, a few Enquiry Committees, Commissions were set up by the State and the Central Govts. Economic books dealing with labour problems which are based only on secondary data and a few articles in different journals have been published. Surveys were also conducted to assess the working conditions and effects on child labour. But the reports were often casual, sketchy, impressionistic and limited in scope which did not give a comprehensive and integrated picture of the problems.

To conclude, this chapter is intended to highlight the deplorable condition of working children during last three decades of 20th century. Now in the 21st century this problem is taking more pernicious turn with growing unemployment compounded by growing population. The situation in Bihar, Orissa, Uttar Pradesh, Rajasthan and Madhya Pradesh is more grim.

NOTES

Baig, Tara Ali (1988), 'The Child: The Trauma of a Change' *Social Welfare*, pp. 7 and 39.

Bhagoliwala, T.N. (1982), *'Economics of Labour and Industrial Relations'*, Chapter-31, Sahitya Bhavan, Agra, p. 196.

Gangrade, K.D. & Gathia, J.A. (ed.) (1983), *'Women and Child Workers in Unorganised Sector'*. Concept Publishing Company, New Delhi, p. 60.

Gathia, J.A. (1983), 'Child Workers in the Informal Sector' in *Women and Child Workers in Unorganised Sector*. Concept Publishing Company, New Delhi, p. 77.

Juyal, B.N. (Dr), Kumari Sudarshan Chandola, L.M (1985), 'Child Labour: The twice exploited' Gandhian Institute of Studies, Varanas.

Ketkar, Kumar (1977) 'Bombay Workers up in Arms', *Economic Times*, 26 May, 1977.

Khan, A.M. (1988), 'Child Labour, Causes and Remedy', *Yojana*, December 16-31, p. 18.

Kulshreshtha, J.C. (1978), *Child Labour in India*, Ashish Publishing House, New Delhi, p. 49.

Lorenzo, A.M., *Agricultural Conditions in Northern India*, New Book Company Ltd., Bombay, p. 58.

Mukhopadhyaya, Ashim (1989), 'Children Without Childhood', *Frontier*, June 24, p. 23.

Nigam, Sevanti, 'Child Labour and Education' (1982), *Voluntary Action*, Vol. 24, No. 7, pp. 286-287.

Panwar, Brijendra Singh (1988), 'Pledged for Rs. 100, *Free Press Journal*, September, p. 11.

Punekar, S.D. (1975), 'Child Labour in Unorganised Industries'. Rural Vocation paper presented at the National Seminar on the Exployment of Children in India, New Delhi, November 25-28.

Report of the Committee on Child Labour (Gurupadaswamy Committee) (1979), Ministry of Labour, Government of India, December, p. 10.

Report of the Indian Factory Labour Commission (1908), Vol. I, pp. 6, 7, 11.

Roy Choudhary, S.C. (1978), *'Social Cultural and Economic History of India'* (Modern Times), Surjeet Publications, Delhi, p. 50.

Seal, K.C. (1980), *Profile of the Child in India*, Ministry of Social Welfare, Government of India, New Delhi, p. 181.

Sen, Sukomal (1977), *Working Class of India, History of Emergence and Movement* (1830-1970), K.P. Bagchi and Company, p. 18.

Sinha, Swapan Kumar (1985), 'A Profile of Child Labour in Calcutta' *Social Welfare*, Vol. XXXII, November-December, p. 24.

Tripathy, S.N. (Dr), *Bonded Labour in India*, Discovery Publishing House, New Delhi, p. 32.

Chapter 4

Child Labour Protection: Global Scenario

'...Child is the father of man."

—*W. Wordsworth*

'Children need special protection because of their tender age and physique, mental immaturity and incapacity to look after themselves. The future of global civilisation will depend upon on how the children grow and develop. According to great poet Milton 'child shows the man, as morning shows the day.'

Even before the establishment of the International Labour Organisation (I.L.O.), the attention was drawn by various social reformers such as Robert Owen (1771-1858) of England that the problem of child labour should be taken up at global level. The beginning of the children rights movements can be traced back to the mid-nineteenth century with the publication of an article in June 1852 by Slagvolk 'the Right of children', followed by 'Kate Kliggin', 'Childrens-Rights' in 1982.

I.L.O. and Labour Conventions on the Child Labour

With the establishment of the I.L.O., there has been greater impeties to prescribe international legal norms for child protection. In view of their exploitation and the indifference and insincerity shown by the national government, it is now being increasingly realised that the problem of child labour should not be thrown at the mercy and discretion of the nations. It has become an important aspect of human rights. There are more than 100 million children engaged in employment after hearing and hazardens. India contributes more than a quarter of the world's working children and one-third of Asia', child labour. The problem is of such a magnitude and multi-dimensional. That it require international cooperation.

Effects were made by the I.L.O. for the protection of child labour at the global level as is evident from the following conventions.

Minimum Employment Age (Industry) Convention 1919 (No. 5)

It provided that children under the age of 14 years should not be employed or work in any public or private undertaking. Even though India gave effect to this convention by making provisions in the Factories Act 1922 and the Mines Act 1923, but the convention was ratified only in 1955.

Night Work by Young Person (Industry)

Convention, 1919 (No. 6) which prohibited employment of young persons of 18 years of the age and any public or private undertaking during night. Though India had adopted this convention in 1921, but its application for India was limited only to 'factories' and the age limit was kept at 14 years. Thus the exploitation of children in other undertaking e.g. construction remained unabated.

The Minimum Age (Trimmess and Strokers) Convention, 1921

It provided that young persons under the age of 18 years shall not be employed on vessels as trimmers and strokers. Though India adapted their convention in 1922, the age-limit for India was kept at 16 years.

Minimum Age for Employment 1937

(No. 59 and 60) to implement these convention, the employment of Children Act, 1938 was passed to prohibit children under 15 years of age occupations connected with transport of goods, passengers, mails and railways. This was ammended in 1978 having wide coverage.

Minimum Age far Admission to Employment 1973 (138)

The convention has revised the earlier ILO conventions prescribing minimum age for admission to employment. The convention aims at the effective abolition of child labour and to raise progressively the minimum age of admission to employment. The minimum age shall not be less than the age of completion of compulsory schooling and in any case shall not be less than 15 years (Art, 2(3)). For those member state whose economy and educational facilities are insufficiently developed may specify a minimum age of 14 years. For those employments which are likely to jeopardise the health, safety or morals of young persons, the minimum age has been prescribed at 18 years. This provision does not apply to employment to children on light work, in that case national laws may permit the employment of work of persons 13 to 15 years of age provided it is not likely to be harmful to their health or development (Article 7). India has to ratify this convention. However there has been concensus of the South Asian Countries including India to ratify this convention and to included in its National Policy.

Indian Enactments

Besides implementing ILO 4 conventions on the child-labour, certain other enactment were also passed in India for the protection of child labour—such as Children (Pledge of Labour) Act, 1933, prohibiting pledging of children, the Plantation Labour Act, 1951, prohibiting the employment of children under 12 years in plantations. Our national leaders did not have the matter of child labour in the hands of politicians and made provisions Basic Document of self. Article 24 of our Constitution provides that no child below the age of 14 years shall be employed to work in any factory or mine or engage in any hazardens employment. Article 39 states that 'tender age of children are not aroused and the citizens are not forced by economic necessity to inter avocations unstated to their age and strength. The national policy for children adopted in 1974 also provided as one of the objections that no child under the age of 14 years shall be permitted to the hazardens and heavy work. It is unfortunate, that it took 36 years to our legislation since the commencement of the constitution to plan the Child Labour (Prohibition and Rejection) Act, 1986 banning the employment of children labour 14 years of age in specific occupation and process. The Act covers only 10% of the that working children. Those working under the unorganised sections are not protected. The Act does not cover child labour even in hazardens process where they are carried out in any Workshop by the occupier with the help of his family or any where established by or receiving assistance or recognition from the Government. Is it not the violation of Art. 24 of the Constitution which respectively prohibited the employment of children in any hazardens employment:

In spite of the ILO convention and the constitutional mandate and the Child Labour Act, 1986, 6.7% of the work force consists of children labour of 14 years. Most of them are bonded labour. As late as in 1985, the Union Labour Ministry conceded the existence of child labour as a 'harsh reality.' What is worse that this 'harsh reality' is not only acknowledged by the state but is also justified by saying that 'the poor parents get income of their children. It is matter of social in justice that only the children of the poor be allowed to work. The child labour continues the bulk in prohibitive and non-prohibitive industry and areas of employment. Perhaps, free and compulsory education upto age of 14 years (Artical 45) could not be would have come in way of the employment of children.

Efforts Made at the Universal Basis

Besides I.L.O. conventions, the concern to protect the child at the international level for the special care and attention is manifest by Geneva Convention of the Rights of the Child, 1924 the Universal Declaration of Human Rights, 1948 and the two conventions relation to Human Right—i.e. the International Covenants on Level and Political Right (Articles 23 and 24) and the International Convention on Economic, Social and Cultural Rights (Art. 10).

U.N. Declaration on the Right of the Child, 1949

The first universal document was the Declaration on the Right of the child adopted by the General Assembly of the U.N. on November 20, 1959. It categorically recognised that the child by reason of his physical and mental immaturity needs special safeguards and care, including appropriate legal protection. The declaration contained only general principle and carried no legally binding obligations-Principle 9 stated that 'The child shall not be admitted to employment before an appropriate minimum age.

U.N. Convention on the Right of the Child, 1989

Although there were more than 80 treaties and desertion particularly since the days of the League of Nations, but they lacked comprehensive vision of children needs in today world. The. 1970 witnessed an upsurge of interest in the Rights of the child. In 1978, Poland made a proposal for a convention on the Right of the child and the 1979 International Year of the child followed. During this year, the U.N. Human Right Commission set up working group to draft a convention, which after ten long years was presented to and passed by the General Assembly in 1989, The UN. convention on the Rights of the child was unanimously adopted on November 30,1989. It come into force on September 2, 1990 when it was ratified by 30 stats—10 more than the minimum required under Article 49. The poll of ratification was much faster than any other human right convention. The convention become binding just weeks before world Summit for children was giving to be held on September 30, 1990.

The convention modified and consolidates the existing standards. The convention may be called the first binding statement on children's rights emerging form the full partnership within developing and developed countries.

Article 32 of Constitution of relevant for over purposes. It states:

32(1) states parties recognise the right of the child to be protected form economic exploitation and from performing any work that is likely to be hazardens or to interfere with child education, or to be harmful to the childs health or physical, mental, spiritual, moral or social development.

(2) State parties shall take legislative, administrative, social and educational measures to ensure the implementation of the present Article. To this end and having regard to the relevant provisions of other international instruments, States parties shall in particular:

(a) provide for a minimum age for admission to employment.

(b) provide for appropriate regulation of the house and condition of employment.

(c) provide for appropriate penalties or other sanctions to ensure the effected enforcement of the present Article.

World Declaration on the Survival, Protection and Development of Children

Later, the world summit for children was held at the United Nations on 30 September, 1990 and adopted world declaration on the survival, protection and development of children. Over 150 nations, including India, participated in it. They made a commitment to implement the convention of the Rights of the child. The nations committed themselves to work for special protection of the working child and for the abolition of illegal child labour, (10 point programme—Point

No. 7). It was divided that there should be universal efforts to promote the welfare of children through U.N. and other international and regional organisations. It was also stated that there should be greater involvement of non-governmental organisations (NGOs). It was also decided to adopt and implement the plan for Action.

Plan for Action

The plan for action for implementing the world declaration in the 1990 was also adopted. This plan for action is intended as a guide for national government, international organisation, non-governmental organisations (NGOs) in formulating their own programmes of action ensuring the implementation of the declaration of the world summit for children. It was observed that it was true that the needs and problems of children may very from country to country, but there are certain common aspiration throughout the world for the well being of the children. Their survival, protection and development was the pre-regulate for the development of humanity as a whole.

It was asserted that the convention of the rights of child sets universal international legal standards for the protection and well being of the children. The plan for action urged that every possible efforts should be made in all countries to disseminate the convention and wherever it has been ratified to promote its implementation and monitoring (Article 8).

It was, further, asserted in the plan for action that more than 100 million children are engaged in employment, after heavy or hazardens and in continuation of international conventions which provide for their protection form economic exploitation and form performing work that interfere with their education and is harmful to their health and full development. With this in merit the states should work to end such child labour practices and how the condition and circumstances of children in legitimate employment can be protected to provide adequate opportunity for their healthy upbringing and development Art. 23.

Both action as the national level and international level was considered necessary to enable developing and the best developed countries (LDCs) to participate effectively in the world wide effect for child survival, protection and development. All development agencies are to contribute to the achievement of goals enunciated in the declaration and the plan of action—the United Nation was requested to institute appropriate mechanism for monitoring the implementation of the plan for action through its agencies especially UNICEF.

Conference on Human Rights, Vienna, June 1993

In June 1993, conference on Human Rights was held in Vienna. The world conference urged that the efforts be made to achieve universal ratification of the U.N. convention on the Right of the Child by 1995 and universal signing of the world summit Declaration and plan for action as well as their effective implementation. The world conference urged all governments to take effective measures against harmful child labour.

The convention has since been ratified by 35 countries. It has also been re-affirmed by the SAARC conference on children 1991 and 1992, where it has been resolved to eliminate child labour progressively and in accelerated manner. In its national child Policy, now India has stated that 'No child under 14 years shall be permitted to be encouraged in hazardous occupations or heavy work.

Unfortunately, the U.N. convention 1989 also adopts a 'regulatory' model instead of the 'prohibitory' model. The child labour is perceived as an inevitable evil and attempts to provide adequate safeguards and a regulatory framework for it continuance. The ideal of absolute prohibition of child labour appears to be an every town on account of economic reality, social attitudes and family constraints. It may be remembered that ideal for free and compulsory education is defendant on the ideal of total prohibition of child labour. It is necessary that there should be progressive movement towards a ban on child labour within a specified time. All than child labour is likely to be the principal obstruction in the realisation of the goal of free and compulsory child education. There is no doubt about the inter-linkage of child labour and universabily of primary education children law to be withdrawn from the child market, last these child word will be confiscated. They have to be rehabilitated and given some economic incentives and the families below poverty line. The NGOs and other interested groups can make a major contribution in this direction.

It is also suggested that the government should be import of products which are manufactured by implication of child labour. In fact plea was made for all government to enact suitable legislations banning import of goods made fully or partially by children dare the Vienna Conference, June, 1993. Indeed USA (Harkin Bill) and Germany are going to ban import of carpets from India, when children are employed. This may be extended to other goods and commodities as well.

It has been observed that India has been also in adopting International Labour standards. India acceded to the convention on the Right of Child only on December 11, 1992. The delay was justified by our Foreign Secretary that before according to any International convention, the government has to examine whether there is any conflict between the International convention and the provisions of domestic law. It has then to be approved by the Parliament. ILO Programme for the Elimination of Child Labour (IPEL). It aims at encouraging and promoting action oriented programme by NGOs and other institutes.

There is no exaggeration in admitting that ratification of International Labour standards has been effective more as 'status symbol' and for upholding the country's image abroad rathar for their sincere implementation and compliance in practice. Swami Agnivesh has called it 'some window dressing'. It may be remembered that Article 51 of our Constitution provides that India must honour its international obligation. Our Supreme Court has also held that International convention, if retified by the Government of India would be binding on India. There is a lack of political will to enforce the binding International treaties and conventions.

REFERENCES

Abhishek Manu Singhvi 'the Right of the Child—Reality and Promise.'

Justice Bhagwati in L.K. Pandey v Union of India 1982 (2) SCC 249.

Meena Gupta (1992), 'Special problems of enforcement of child labour and Regulations' Workshop on child labour in U.P..

Mohinder Singh, Child Labour and Law Constraints and Policy—Workshop, on Child Labour in U.P. organised by Deptt. of Labour and UNICEF.

N. Vaidyanathan (1975), 'I.L.O. convention and India', p. 39.

Plan for Action for Implementing the World Summit for children held at the United Nation (1990), New York.

R.C Singh (1990), 'Economic Rights of the Child'.

Richard II Young (1993), 'Labour Exploitation and the Rights of the Child', UNICEF publication.

Sheela Barse v Union of India (1983) SCC 1775, and Legal Aid Committee v U. of India (1989) SCC 331.

Upendra Ban (1993), 'Unconstitutional Polities and Child Labour' Mainstream.

Chapter 5

Looking at Child Labour

"Children left to grow up like weeds are not likely to produce the fruits of genius."

There is no exaggeration in admitting that the origin of the problem of child labour lies in the process of industrial revolution. Industrialisation process leads to migration of labour, including child labour, from rural to urban areas to employers of factories, mines etc. who exploit child labour to minimise their costs and maximise profits.

The Constitution of India is committed to the protection and promotion of the interests of the child. This has established the superiority of the welfare considerations over the economic ones. It was not surprising, therefore, that a series of committees and commissions have been appointed by the Government of India either specifically on the question of child labour or on labour conditions in general, which give us insights into the problem and give suggestions to alleviate this problem. The Royal Commission on Labour in 1929, the Labour Investigation Committee in 1944, The National Commission on Labour in 1966, Gurupadswamy Committee on Child Labour in 1979 and Sanat Mehta Committee in 1986 are the major committees which deserve special attention.

While the social concern is genuine and widespread, the wide cleavage between intentions and reality calls for a deep understanding of the interrelated processes of economic development, social and political development and population. Children's activities are after all determined and often a consequence of these realities. This paper attempts to understand children's activities, so that their determinants and implications are placed in a proper perspective for conceptualisation of the issues involved in the child work. Such an understanding would also lead to a better appreciation of legislations on the subject, which may help in formulating an integrated approach for child welfare. Rogers and Standing have developed a very thorough typology of child work across the countries which may prove useful in this context.

Rogers and Standing divide children's activities into different categories: (1) Domestic non-monetary work is usually within the family. It is self-employment and is generally 'time intensive'. (Examples, cleaning, cooking, washing, child care etc.). (2) Non-monetary and non-domestic work which is usually found in the poor agrarian/rural economies. This is self-employment, which is a part of family activity and includes activities like tending of livestock, protecting crops from birds and animals, hunting, gathering and weeding. This work is also time intensive and is often intermixed with domestic work. (3) Children also work in the non-agrarian environment, such as artisan production, small scale production and in the informal sector activities in trade, manufacturing and services, (such as, running errands, looking after goods for short periods and marketing of domestic produce). Although there is a low level equilibrium in many such activities, it represents an efficient allocation of the available family time and to that extent the activities of the children and the activities of the adults become complementary. (4) The fourth type is the work where children work as bonded labourers and are pledged by their parents in lieu of debt.

Although bonded labour is abolished by law the prevalence of the practice is noted in a number of studies. While the above types represent unpaid work mainly within the family and is self-employment, as Rogers and Standing point out child labourers are also employed on wages. A child wage labourer is sometimes a part of the family labour force wherein the entire family works on wages and children become a part of the group. These practices are noted in agricultural field labour, brick making, carpet making, domestic service, digging operations etc. The other part of the child wage labour is where children are independently employed as wage earners either on fields or in factories in the service sector.

All of these activities of children either directly deprive the child from opportunities for full physical and mental development of or indirectly cause low level equilibrium in terms of a life-times chance. In fact, sometimes children's work is such where they work under such conditions that it would lead to physical handicaps and even cause death. Even when alive, they end up as a family and social burden. It is these consequences which are at the back of one's mind when one looks at the social concern for the children which is voiced all over the globe.

Child Workers in India: An Estimation

Inadequate data are available in India regarding the extent of child labour. One major source, namely, the Census of Population does not permit a study over time due to the changes in definitions etc. National Sample Survey (NSS) data are usually regarded more reliable. In addition, the extent of child labour was indicated in the first and the second agricultural labour enquiry reports and in periodic surveys of the labour bureau.

As is evident from the data the number of child labourers has gone up from 16.33 million in 1972-73 to 17.36 million in 1983, although as the percentage of the child labour to the total labour force, it shows a decrease. NSS figures too are disputed as underestimates. Unofficial figures of child labour are in the range of 44 to 100 million. Roughly 91 per cent of the child labour in accordance with the Census of Population are in the rural areas as per the 1981 Census. About 86 per cent of child labour is in agriculture and allied activities (43 per cent agricultural labourers, 36 per cent cultivators and 8 per cent livestock) and broadly 44 per cent self employed in non-domestic and non-monetary activities mainly in rural areas. Outside agriculture, manufacturing, processing and repairs accounted for 6 per cent, other services 4 per cent, and trade and commerce 2 per cent. There is a reduction in the percentage of child workers in 'cultivators', partly attributable to definitional change, and partly to the generally accepted phenomenon of growing marginalisation and inability of marginal holdings to sustain more labour. An increasing proportion of children opting for wage labour in agriculture is, therefore, in conformity with the same process which is observed for small and marginal landholdings.

TABLE 1: ESTIMATED NUMBER OF CHILD WORKERS IN INDIA

Agricultural labour enquiry reports	*Percentage of child labour (Below 15 yrs. of age)*
1. First (1950-51)	4.8
2. Second (1956057)	7.7
3. Population Census, 1961 (14.50m)	8
4. Population Census, 1971 (10.74m)	6
5. Population Census, 1981 (11.17m)	

National Sample Survey Rounds: (Million)

Round	Year	Rural	Urban	Total
27th	1972-73	15.04	1.29	16.33
32nd	1977-78	14.68	1.57	16.25
38th	1983	15.57	1.79	17.36

Children Employed in Factories

The percentage of child workers to the total average daily employed workers in factories submitting returns under the Factories Act has been 0.14 per cent in 1972, 0.10 per cent in 1973, 0.07) per cent in 1976 and 0.1 per cent in 1977 (Appendix -3). It is worth noting that there were only 4,178 child workers in the factory sector in India in 1977. Though there is likely to be some underestimation in this, it is generally accepted, that the incidence of child labour in factories has decreased over the years and the number has now become insignificant. Within the factory sector however, food and food products, textile products, and hosiery and chemicals, employ more child labour. In general, child labour is seen most concentrated in organised manufacturing activities and in plantations.

TABLE 2: PERCENTAGE DISTRIBUTION OF CHILD WORKERS ACCORDING TO THEIR MAIN OCCUPATIONS (1971)

Activity	Percentage
1. Cultivators	36.10
2. Agricultural labourers	42.70
3. Livestock, forestry, fishing, hunting and orchards etc.	08.10
4. Mining and quarrying	00.20
5. Manufacturing, processing, servicing and repairs.	06.10
6. Construction	00.60
7. Trade and commerce	02.00
8. Transport, storage, communications	00.40
9. Other services	03.80
Total	*100.00*

COMMITTEES AND COMMISSIONS ON CHILD LABOUR IN INDIA

We may briefly look at some of the observations and the findings of various Committees and commissions which have investigated the conditions of labour in general and of child labour in India from time to time in particular. The following are the main among these in chronological order.

1. The Royal Commission on Labour (1929)

The Royal Commission on Labour (1929), which was set up in 1929, observed that there was considerable incidence of child labour in *bidi* making and plantations as well as in carpet weaving in Mirzapur district (United Province) and in tanneries in Amritsar district (Punjab). The Commission referred at length to the child labour on plantations where children, accompanied by parents, lived on tea gardens. Chances of education of these children were almost nil and hence the Commission recommended that the owners of the tea plantations should contribute towards the establishment of facilities for ensuring their minimum education. The employers, however were interested in the steady supply of labour and employed children of four to six years and nine to eleven years. The Commission recommended legal prohibition for children to work below the age of 10, and to have any entry of the names of all working children in the wage book. The commission observed that in many cities a large number of young boys were employed in *bidi* making, who worked for long hours and under strict discipline. As regards the children working in ports and on loading of coal on ships, the 1922 Act made it obligatory for the local governments to frame rules under the Indian Ports Act 1908 which prohibited employment of children under the age of 12 years in handling goods at piers, jetties, docks, warehouses and ships. The commission wanted that this minimum age for employment should be raised to 14 years. The Commission's efforts to prohibit and regulate the work of children below the minimum age was faced with contrasting issues such as dislocation and hardship of parents of these children. The Commission recommended that children should not be allowed to work overtime or take work home and prohibited the pledging of children, observing the economic realities of the time and of child labour. It observed that "child's right to childhood and even to such education as may be available should make no appeal comparable to its earning capacity."

In nutshell, the Commission adopted a conciliatory approach and recommended cooperation between the government, the local authorities and the employers to develop child welfare centres and clinics for children.

2. Labour Investigation Committee (1944)

The Labour Investigation Committee, popularly known as Rege Committee, observed that child labour declined from the peak of 74,620 (5.3 per cent of total employment) in 1923 to 9,403 (0.5 per cent in 1939, but showed a slight increase during war time. As the data were thought to be unreliable, the committee concluded that "the employment of children (between 12 and 15 years as well as below 12 years) has gone down considerably since the beginning of the century." The child labour aspect was predominant in *bidi* making, carpet weaving, glass and other small scale industries. The report specially referred its prevalence in the match industry in South India, in cement industry in Rajasthan, in the spinning industry in Cochin, and in carpet weaving in Kashmir. The Committee recommended that it is not enough to prohibit the employment of children, but it is also essential to adopt simultaneously positive measures to wean them away from industrial employment.

3. National Commission on Labour (1966)

The National Commission on Labour observed that the employment of children is indeed more of an economic problem than anything else. However, denial of opportunity to children for their proper physical development and education was considered a serious issue keeping in view the larger interest of the society. The Commission recommended fixing of the minimum age for children, fixing working hours of child labour and making arrangements for work with education for them.

4. Gurupadswamy Committee (1979)

The Gurupadswamy Committee on Child Labour was set up in 1979 which was further evidence of the nation's resolve to initiate concrete policy measures for the protection of working children. The report, which was both analytical and comprehensive, dealt at length with the questions, such as, the dimensions of child labour, status of legislation and its implementation, and welfare and training schemes for child labour. The report also carried out some enquiries for ascertaining the points of views of workers, employers and the government on aspects such as what is child labour, what compels children to work, what are the occupations in which children are employed, why child labour is preferred etc.

The main observations and the recommendations of the committee are: (1) A multiple policy approach is necessary in dealing with the problems of working children. (2) Child labour is not a homogeneous group and therefore should be divided among the categories of wage earners, family workers, apprentices in traditional crafts and children who are both working and going to school. (3) The minimum age for entry into employment should be 15 years. (4) The existing law relating to prohibition and regulation of employment of children should be consolidated into a simple comprehensive one. (5) There should be a minimum educational qualifications say the eighth standard, for entry into any regulated employment. (6) The government should initiate dialogue with the trade unions for developing institutional framework for collective bargaining in respect of the needs of the working children. (7) The Planning Commission should work out the feasibility of removing children below 15 years from the labour market in order to find out employment for the unemployed and able-bodied persons. (8) The educational policy should have an appropriate curriculum and suitable schedules of vacations and holidays to suit the rural environment. Non-formal educational facilities should be arranged in the areas, where there are more working children. (9) Creches/child-care centres should be established at the school premises or at community centres in rural areas so as to encourage girls who have to take care of young siblings in the family to attend school. (10) Periodical medical check-up should be arranged for child labour and rules should be made to ensure a hygienic working environment. (11) The

Apprenticeship Act should be enforced effective. (12) Systematic efforts should be made to identify hazardous jobs for children and their occupational diseases and treatment.

5. Sanat Mehta Committee

The Sanat Mehta Committee reiterated the concerns which have been voiced both in the report of National Commission of Labour and in the Gurupadswamy Committee. The Committee emphasised the need for a uniform age for children for entry into employment and wanted to combine work with education.

6. The Child Labour Act (1986)

The latest act called the Child Labour (Prohibition and Regulation) Act of 1986, prohibits engagement of children in certain employments and regulates the condition of work of children in certain other employments. When viewed in the context of the earlier reports on the problems of child labour, the present act represents the concerted effort of the nation to realistically meet the aspirations expressed from time to time. The act has identified some hazardous industries and 11 hazardous industrial processes in which employment of children under 14 is prohibited. The act also provides for the inclusion of more processes in the banned category with the appointment of a committee. In the rest of the sectors, the approach is regulation of the employment of child labour through various measures.

Educating Child Labour

Ironically, all children who are not at work are not necessarily in schools. Even if they are enrolled in schools, the drouput is a major problem particularly among the children of the weaker sections. Out of 100 children enrolled in class I, about 25 to 30 reach standard V and those who complete the middle level education are even less. The reasons for this seem to be academic failure, lack of availability of middle school, parents' low incomes and so on. Restructuring of content of education, different schedules for vacations, timing for schools etc. have been suggested by Gurupadswamy Committee for longer retention of more and more children in schools.

When the poor see widespread unemployment around them, they prefer early entry into 'informal sector' work. However, this does not allow them to complete middle school education, which may not be an entry into the job market, but may be a base for the further learning process.

How do we expect an agricultural labour household to dispense with child's work which is supplementing the family income? What can be done when the family cannot afford to send the child to school even when free schooling is available? It can be said that an assurance of the legal minimum wages to adults may motivate them to send their children to school. Fixing up minimum wages for child labour is, however, likely to be counter-productive. It will be desirable if the concerned industries bear a financial burden for hostel for working children which can also provide subsidised food, recreation and education-cum-training.

The economic activity and schooling are sometimes combined. For example, in the manufacture of incense—sticks, which is a home-based industry, majority of the child workers attend schools and also work at home for three to four hours a day. This flexible production system is seen in the manufacture of ready made garments, *bidi* etc. It is however, often the parents who force long hours of work on their own children.

It is argued that the abolition of child labour would increase the employment for adults and relieve the unemployment problem. The child workers, particularly the wage paid in the total labour force is hardly 3 per cent. The removal of child workers therefore, cannot ease the unemployment problems although in a few specified activities, more adults could find jobs. It is however not sure that these adults come from the families of children who are removed from work.

To conclude, prohibition of child labour in selected works and the provision expanding this list, as it is laid down in the latest act in India, is a realistic approach at this stage of socio-economic development. The strategy to progressively retain more and more children in schools for longer period would need action on: (1) poverty alleviation programmes, (2) creation of more avenues for production employment, (3) educating parents through functional literacy programmes about the role of education, (4) establishment of working children's hostels to take care of foods, and (5) education-cum-training and recreation programmes for children in major cities of India.

REFERENCES

Enid, Schildkrout (1981), "The employment of Children in Kano (Nigeria)" in *Child Work, Poverty and Underdevelopment*, International Labor Office, Geneva.

Mead, Cain & A.B.M. Khorshed (1981), "Labour Market Structure and Reproductive Behaviour in Rural South "Asia" in *Child Work, Poverty and Underdevelopment*, International Labour Office, Geneva.

Patel, B.B. (1980), *Slums in Ahmedabad: A study of Migration, Employment and Housing* (Mimeo), Sardar Patel Institute of Economic and Social Research, Ahmedabad, India.

Patel, B.B. (1986), *Work, Working Conditions and Earnings: Agarbathi Workers in Ahmedabad*, Gandhi Labour Institute, Ahmedabad, India.

Report of the Committee on Child Labour (1979), Ministry of Labour, Government of India.

Report of the Labour Investigation Committee (1958), Government of India, Delhi.

Report of the Labour Investigation Committee (1969), Government of India, Ministry of Labour and Employment and Rehabilitation.

Report of the Royal Commission on Labour in India (1931), Government of India, Central Publication Branch.

Rodger, Gerry and Guy Standing (1981), *Child Work, Poverty and Underdevelopment*, International Labour Office, Geneva.

S. Marla (1977), "Bonded Labour in Medak District (Andhra Pradesh)" In *National Labour Institute Bulletin* (New Delhi), Vol. 3 No. 10.

Sanat Mehta Committee Report on Child Labour (1984), Ministry of Labour, Government of India.

Chapter 6

Child Labour in Developing Countries

The Declaration of the Rights of the Child proclaimed by the United Nations General Assembly on 20th November 1959 can be considered important for initiating the discussion on 'Child Labour'. The following principles enunciated by the United Nations through this Declaration relate to child labour.

Principle 2

The child shall enjoy special protection, and shall be given opportunities and facilities to enable him to develop physically, mentally, morally, spiritually and socially in a healthy and normal manner and in conditions of freedom and dignity.

Principle 4

The child shall enjoy the benefits of social security. He shall be entitled to grow and develop in health.... The child shall have the right to adequate nutrition, housing, recreation and medical services.

Principle 9

The child shall be protected against all forms of neglect, cruelty and exploitation. He shall not be the subject of traffic, in any form .... The child shall not be admitted to employment before an appropriate minimum age; he shall in no case be caused or permitted to engage in any occupation or employment which would prejudice his health or education, or interfere with his physical, mental or moral development.

International Labour Organisation (ILO) also has declared its commitment to protection of the child in the preamble to its constitution. Abolition of child labour has been one of its basic aims since its establishment. At the same time, it has pursued a systematic policy of protection of children at work from undesirable working conditions. The activities of the ILO in this area fall under three main headings: (1) Prohibition and limitation of child labour in the framework of international instruments concerning minimum age of admission to employment. (2) Protection of children at work through regulation and supervision of working conditions. (3) Development of fitness for work through pre-vocational training. One of the principal ways of ILO has-been to adopt international labour standards. In addition ILO has also contributed to the cause through study and research as well as technical assistance.

The ILO has adopted several conventions and made special recommendations concerning minimum age, working conditions, and medical examination of child labour. There are several others relating to health and safety of workers also.

1. Minimum Age

The supplementary convention on the abolition of slavery and the Slave Trade (1956) prohibits the use of child labour as slaves. The convention, suggests that each state should take appropriate practicable and necessary legislative and other measures to bring about complete abolition of trading of children below the age of 18 years. The convention on Economics, Social and Cultural Rights imposes a general prohibition on such employment of children which leads to their economic and social exploitation. When their employment is harmful to their morals or health, or dangerous to life or likely to hamper their normal development, it should be punishable by law. States should also let age limits below which children should not be employed.

The first instrument setting a minimum age for admission to employment was in Convention 5 (Industry) adopted at the first session in 1919. This convention prohibited employment of children under 14 years of age in industry. ILO subsequently adopted several other conventions/ recommendations fixing minimum age standards for admission to employment in various occupations such as on sea (1920), agriculture (1921), trimmers and Strokers (1932), non-industrial employment (1936 and 1953), coal mines (1953), fisherman (1959) and underground work (1965).

In 1973, the ILO adopted the Minimum Age Convention No. 138 with a view to achieving the total abolition of child labour and aimed at replacing the existing instruments applicable to limited sectors. This convention requires each state "to pursue a national policy designed to ensure the effective abolition of child labour and to raise progressively the minimum age for admission to employment or work to a level consistent with the fullest physical and mental development of young persons." The members are called upon to specify a minimum age for employment which should not be less then the age of completion of compulsory schooling, that is, 15 years and gradually not less than 18 years. The convention, provides that these age limits may be lowered where the economic and educational facilities are insufficiently developed, but such countries are required to report their gradual progress in the matter. The convention also provides that a country may allow employment in dangerous work from the age of 16 years if the health, safety and morals of the young persons are fully protected and that the young persons have received adequate training.

In 1973, the ILO also adopted the minimum age Recommendation No. 146, to supplement the Convention No. 138. This recommendation invites states to give high priority to planning for meeting the needs of children and youth in national development policies and programmes and recommends progressive raising of the minimum age to 16 years. The recommendation also requires that the types of employment or work should be reexamined periodically in the light of advancing scientific and technological knowledge to determine the types of employment or work to which the convention applies.

2. *Working Conditions*

The abolition of child labour is a long-term objective. In the meantime, it is necessary to protect child labour against abuse and exploitation. The ILO has therefore adopted a number of conventions and recommendations which regulate the working conditions of children when it is not possible to ban their employment altogether. These are: (a) conventions prohibiting night work by children and young persons in industry (1919; 1948), agriculture (1921), non-industrial occupations (1946), and on sea (1958) as well as corresponding recommendations; (b) conventions prohibiting the employment of children and young persons in certain categories of hazardous work such as, lead poisoning (1919), white lead painting (1921), radiation (1960), ground work (1965), maximum weight convention (1967), and benzene convention (1971), and, (c) instruments making provision for stricter standards for young workers with regard to hours of work, weekly rest, paid holidays and apprenticeship, such as, utilisation of spare time recommendation (1924), holidays with pay recommendation (1936, 1952 and 1954), apprenticeship recommendation (1939), weekly rest recommendation (1957), and reduction of hours of work recommendation (1962).

3. *Medical Examinations*

Convention No. 77 concerning medical examinations of young persons industry (1946) lays down that young persons under 18 years of age shall not be admitted to employment unless they have been found fit through a medical examination. This fitness shall be subject to regular medical supervision.

In occupations which involve high health risks, medical examination and re-examination for fitness for employment shall be required until at least the age of 21 years. The convention also requires that appropriate measures be taken for vocational guidance and physical and vocational rehabilitation of children who are found medically unsuited for certain jobs. There are similar provisions about medical examination in the convention for non-industrial occupations and the convention for underground work in mines. Recommendation No. 125 requires that young persons employed or to be employed underground in mines should be given practical and theoretical instructions: (1) in the health and safety hazards of the work, (2) in hygiene and first aid, and (3) in the precautions to be taken to safeguard health and safety. This recommendation also requires that young persons under 18 years of age working underground in mines should be entitled to an uninterrupted weekly rest which should be for at least 36 hours, and to an annual holiday of not less than 24 working days excluding public and customary holidays, and they should also be entitled to sick leave.

Recommendation No. 4 concerning the protection of women and children against lead poisoning requires that pregnant women and women under 18 years of age should be excluded from employment in certain specified processes. Convention No. 13 prohibits the employment of young persons under 18 years of age and all females in any painting work of an industrial character involving the use of white lead sulphate of lead or other products containing these pigments. Convention No. 115 requires that children under 16 years of age shall not be engaged in work involving radiation, and for other workers appropriate levels of radiation should be fixed. Convention No. 127 requires that no worker shall be permitted to engage in the manual transport of lead which is likely to jeopardise his health or safety. It also requires that the women and young persons shall be banned from manual transport of lead other than light lead. Convention No. 136 lays down that young persons under 18 years of age shall not work in processes dealing with benzene or products containing benzene. Recommendation No. 21 concerning utilisation of spare time requires institutions to be established for the physical development of children and for encouraging initiative and the spirit of emulation. Recommendation No. 47 concerning annual holidays with pay recommends holidays with pay for young workers under 18 years of age. Recommendation No. 103 concerning weekly rest (commerce and offices) requires that children under 13 years of age should be granted a weekly rest of two days. Recommendation No. 116 states that while reducing working hours priority should be given to industries and occupations which involve physical and mental strain and health risks for women and young persons.

Limitations of ILO Endeavors

Adoption of these conventions and recommendations does not mean that these are enforced in all the member countries. These conventions can come into force only after their ratification by the concerned national governments. If a convention is not ratified its status is that of a recommendation which by its very nature is not mandatory. A state may enforce it fully or partly or may not enforce it at all. Table 1 shows the number of countries who have ratified the various conventions concerning child labour (as on 1-1-1986). Table 1 shows that out of the total of 162 member countries only a small number has ratified most of the conventions. The Committee of Experts on the application of conventions and recommendations has aptly noted the application of Convention No. 138 and Recommendation No. 146 that: "it is an inescapable fact that children work in most countries and in most regions, and that too many in violation of international standards and of national law .... of the total of 55 million child labour majority violate the international standards and national laws." It is also argued by experts that this figure of 55 million is a gross underestimation of the real size of the phenomenon. It seems that there is a great distance to be travelled before the objectives stated in Article 1 of Convention No. 138 are realised: "To ensure effective abolition of child labour and to raise progressively the minimum age for employment to a level consistent with the fullest physical and mental development of young persons.

In fact, the Committee of Experts was struck by the fact that the goals laid down in Convention 138 are still very distant goals. In many cases the governments are simply unable to arrest child labour because of the extreme poverty of these countries. What measures can be taken to abolish child labour from these poor countries? It is apparent that there are certain sectors and areas where the incidence of child labour is high. These areas should be identified by investigations and specific efforts should be made, with the assistance of the ILO and other international agencies to undertake development programmes there. It will be necessary to conduct pilot programmes to determine what measurers are most effective. In addition, and equally important, national government should not delay the adoption of legislation, in accordance with international standards wherever possible, until they consider that the problem has already been resolved in practice. The ILO's experience demonstrates that the adoption of standards can in itself serve as an important impetus to the achievement of the objectives they represent. As economic development continues, and as labour administrations gradually are able to extend their effectiveness, these laws can be applied to wider areas and to more sectors of the national economy.

The Committee has emphasised the crucial importance of consultations with the organisations of employers and workers in formulating measures to achieve the goals of these ILO instruments. Their involvement and acceptance of the aim of eliminating child labour will both lessen the burdens of government supervision and provide another example of the great potential in responsible tripartism. Voluntarism is no substitute for government responsibility; it may however be an effective supplement and spur to such action.

TABLE 1

Convention No.	*Name*	*No. of ratifications*
5.	Minimum age (industry)	50
6.	Night work of young persons.	48
7.	Minimum age (sea)	34
10.	Minimum age (agriculture)	32
15.	Minimum age (trimmers and stokers)	47
16.	Medical examination of young persons (SEA).	70
13.	Minimum age (non-industrial employment).	19
59.	Minimum age (industry revised).	20
60.	Minimum age (non-industrial employment).	1
77.	Medical examination (young persons) industry.	38
78.	Medical examination-young persons (non-industrial occupations).	34
79.	Night work of young persons (non-industrial employment).	16
90.	Night work of young persons (industry) (revised).	41
123.	Minimum age (undesired work).	32
138.	Minimum age.	33

Undoubtedly there are been a great deal of legislative activity with respect of child labour for which the ILO with the large number of conventions and recommendations on the subject has given a lead. But there is not enough information about the utility and effectiveness of the legislations. It has been recognised that applied research is urgently needed to determine whether or not these legislations had much impact on the extent and type of child work. It is said that an effective policy design in general requires an understanding of the roles of children within a broad social framework.[1]

There have been few analyses of the economic role of children in the process of socio-economic transformation and economic development, that is, attempts to understand the causes, functions and consequences of child work as opposed to descriptions of its manifestations. The very failure of legislation to reduce child labour substantively in much of the world raises basic questions about the effectiveness of a purely legislative approach.

Types of Child Labour

Child labour falls broadly under the following types: (1) domestic work, (2) non-domestic, non-monetary work, (3) tied or bonded labour, (4) wage labour, (5) marginal semi-economic activities, and (6) others. The conventions and recommendations adopted by the ILO concern mainly wage labour although bulk of the children at work are employed in other types of activities. Some of the conventions also specifically exclude children's work in domestic occupations or in school as a part of the school curriculum. The scope of the conventions is therefore very limited.

The conventions and recommendations are concentrated mainly in the minimum age for employment and conditions of work for child labour. However, there is no instrument regarding social security for child labour. A child goes or is sent to work either because he or she has no one to look after him or her, or, because his or her parents or guardians are not able to look after the child. In the circumstances, the only consequence of abolition of child labour without providing an alternative means of livelihood and education would be starvation and death. While the "declaration of the rights of the child" requires that the child be protected against all forms of neglect, cruelty and exploitation, the measures adopted by the ILO, if strictly enforced without complimentary measures, are only likely to subject the child to greater neglect, cruelty and exploitation. It does not seem that such possible consequences of implementing the international standards in the developing countries have been given due consideration. It seems therefore necessary that before abolishing child labour the state should consider the need to provide an alternative means of livelihood to the children. One such means would be to establish orphanages, homes or hostels at state expense for the maintenance of the destitute and delinquent children and to provide them adequate nutrition, housing, recreation and medical facilities through such institutions. This is the basic function of social security.

It is a moot question in considering the magnitude of child labour in the developing countries whether they can be maintained at the state expenses. At the same time considering that a large proportion of the population in these countries live below the poverty line it should also be realised that the poor families find it necessary to send their children to work and to supplement their income. In the circumstances total abolition of child labour may not be a practical proposition in the third world and it is also not enough to protect child labour against unsatisfactory work conditions. It is necessary therefore to provide adults with employment and minimum living conditions.

Gerry Rodgers and Guy Standing have stated: "Where child labour does have adverse effects—and in terms of personal development and social differentiation these are often serious—they can usually be traced to the socio-economic framework within which children work as much as to the work itself. Thus the suppression of child wage labour opportunities is unlikely to increase the welfare of the children concerned unless substitute income sources and alternative possibilities for personal development are developed at the same time. Action towards child work must be sympathetically oriented towards the need and perceptions of the children themselves. It must also be based on a thorough understanding of the motivations behind child work, its functions, and the individual gains from it, whether for the children themselves or for others who benefit from their work."

REFERENCES

"Economic roles of Children Issues for Analysis. *In* Gerry Rodgers and Gay Standing (eds).*Child Work Poverty and Underdevelopment.*

Child Labour, *International Labour Review*, Sep.-Oct., 1979.

Rodgers Gerry and Gay Standing, (eds.) *Child Work, Poverty and Underemployment.*

ANNEXURE-1

DECLARATION OF THE RIGHTS OF THE CHILD

Proclaimed by the United Nations General Assembly on 20 November 1959 (Resolution XIV)

Preamble

Whereas the people of the United Nations have, in the Charter, reaffirmed their faith in fundamental human rights and in the dignity and worth of the human person, and have determined to promote social progress and better standards of life in larger freedom.

Whereas the United Nations has, in the Universal Declaration of Humans Rights, proclaimed that everyone is entitled to all the rights and freedoms set forth therein, without distinction of any kind, such as race, colour, sex, language, religion, political or other opinion, national or social origin, property, birth or other status.

Whereas the child, by reason of his physical and mental immaturity, needs special safeguards and care, including appropriate legal protection, before as well as after birth.

Whereas the need for such special safeguards has been stated in the Geneva Declaration of the Rights of the child of 1924, and recognised in the Universal Declaration of Human Rights and in the statutes of specialised agencies and international organisations concerned with the welfare of children.

Whereas mankind owes to the child the best it has to give, Now therefore,

The General Assembly

Proclaims this Declaration of the Rights of the Child to the end that he may have a happy childhood and enjoy for his own good and for the good of society the rights end freedoms herein set forth, and calls upon parents, upon men and women as individuals, and upon voluntary organisations, local authorities and national governments to recognise these rights and strive for their observance by legislative and other measures progressively taken in accordance with the following principles:

Principle 1

The child shall enjoy all the rights set forth in his Declaration. Every child, without any exception whatsoever, shall be entitled to these rights, distinction or discrimination on account or race, colour, sex, language, religion, political or other opinion, national or social origin, property, birth or other status, whether of himself or of his family.

Principle 2

The child shall enjoy special protection, and shall be given opportunities and facilities, by law and by other means, to enable him to develop physically, mentally, morally, spiritually and socially in a healthy and normal manner and in conditions of freedom and dignity. In the enactment of laws for this purpose, the best interests of the child shall be the paramount consideration.

Principle 3

The child shall be entitled from his birth to a name and a nationality.

Principle 4

The child shall enjoy the benefits of social security. He shall be entitled to grow and develop in health ; to this end, special care and protection shall be provided both to him and to his mother, including adequate pre-natal and post-natal, care. The child shall have the right to adequate nutrition, housing, recreation and medical services.

Principle 5

The child who is physically, mentally or socially

handicapped shall be given the special treatment, education and care required by his particular condition.

Principle 6

The child, for the full and harmonious development of his personality, needs love and understanding. He shall, wherever possible, grow up in the care and under the responsibility of his parents, and in any case, in an atmosphere of affection and of moral and material security a child of tender years shall not, save in exceptional circumstances be separated from his mother.

Society and the public authorities shall have the duty to extent particular care to children without a family and to those without adequate means of support. Payment of state and other assistance towards the maintenance of children of large families is desirable.

Principle 7

The child is entitled to receive education, which shall be free and compulsory, at least in the elementary stages. He shall be given an education which will promote his general culture, and enable him on a basis of equal opportunity, to develop his abilities, his individual judgment, and his sense of moral and social responsibility, and to become a useful member of society.

The best interests of the child shall be the guiding principle of those responsible for his education and guidance ; that responsibility lies in the first place with his parents.

The child shall have full opportunity for play and recreation, which should be directed to the same purposes as education; society and the public authorities shall endeavour to promote the enjoyment of this right.

Principle 8

The child shall in all circumstances be among the first to receive protection and relief.

Principle 9

The child shall not be protected against all forms of neglect, cruelty and exploitation. He shall not be the subject of traffic, in any form.

The child shall not be admitted to employment before appropriate minimum age; he shall in no case be caused or permitted to engage in any occupation or employment which would prejudice his health or education, or interfere with his physical, mental or moral development.

Principle 10

The child shall be protected from practices which may foster racial, religious and any other form of discrimination. He shall be brought up in a spirit of understanding, tolerance, friendship among people, peace and universal brotherhood, and in full consciousness that his energy and talents should be devoted to the service of his fellow men.

ANNEXURE-2

RESOLUTION CONCERNING THE INTERNATIONAL YEAR OF THE CHILD AND THE PROGRESS OF ELIMINATION OF CHILD LABOUR AND TRANSITIONAL MEASURES

The General Conference of the International Labour Organisation, Recalling resolution 31/169 adopted by the United National General Assembly, proclaiming 1979 as the International Year of the Child, with the general objectives of promoting the well-being of children, drawing attention to their special needs and encouraging national action on behalf of children particularly for the least privileged and those who are at work.

Noting the activities that were undertaken at the national, regional and international levels in preparation for the International year of the child and the Progress made since.

Convinced that the International Year of the Child provides for all members states an opportunity to review their economic and social policies concerning the child welfare and to formulate guidelines in this sphere.

Considering that a new and fair international economic order would greatly contribute towards genuine economic and social development, primarily of benefit to children.

Recalling the endorsement by the ILO of the aims of the International Year of the Child and its pledge to make every effort and lend all support to members states for their earliest possible fulfilment.

Recalling the United Nations Declaration of the Right of the Child, 1959 and particularly Principle 9, which, stipulates that the child should be protected against all forms of neglect, cruelty and exploitation; that he should not be admitted to employment before an appropriate minimum age ; and that he should in no case be caused or permitted to engage in any occupation or employment which would prejudice his health or education, or interfere with his physical, mental or moral development.

Concerning that since its foundation the International Labour Organisation has sought to eliminate child labour and to provide protection for children.

Noting with approval the Director General's Declaration on the International Year of the Child, deeply concerned that child labour still remains widespread in many parts of the world and that working children frequently work under conditions including those of exploitation detrimental to their health and welfare; recognising the need to ensure that the health and strength and the tender age of children are not abused and that children are not permitted to enter avocations unsuited to their age or strength, considering that the International Year of the Child should be an occasion to raffirm with practical measures and deeds the well-being of today's children, is the concern or all people everywhere.

Recalling the decision of the governing body of the International Labour Office, taken at its twentieth session (November 1978), to request the member states to supply a report in 1980 under article 19 of the Constitution on the extent to which effect has been given or is proposed to be given to the Minimum Age Convention (No. 138) and Recommendation (No. 146) of 1973:

1. Calls upon member states to strengthen their efforts for the elimination of child labour and for the protection of children, and in this context:

a) to implement the provisions of the Minimum Age Convention, 1973 (No. 138), and, where they have not already done so, to ratify this convention as early as practicable;

b) to ensure in particular full recognition of the principle that any work undertaken by children who have not completed their compulsory education shall not be such as would prejudice their education or development;

c) to apply the Minimum Age Recommendation, 1973 (No. 146), and the Minimum Age (Underground Work) Recommendation, 1965 (No. 124);

d) to report in detail in 1980 under the procedure of article 19 of the Constitution on the progress reached in the implementation of the Minimum Age Convention (No. 138) and Recommendation (No. 146), 1973;

e) pending the elimination of child labour, to take all necessary social and legislative action for the progressive elimination of child labour and during the transitional period until the elimination of child labour, to regulate and humanise it and to give particular attention to the implementation of special standards for children relating to medical examination, night work, underground work, working hours, weekly rest, paid annual leave and certain types of hazardous and dangerous work embodied in a number of ILO instruments;

f) to make every effort to extend the provisions of appropriate educational facilities, in order fully to apply compulsory education and to introduce it where it does not exist and where education is compulsory, to make it effective;

g) to ensure that appropriate protective labour legislation applies to all children at work in the sectors of activity in which they are employed;

h) to ensure that special attention is given to the provision of fair remuneration and to its protection for the benefit of the child;

i) to strengthen, where appropriate, labour inspection and to undertake all other measures conducive to the elimination of child labour;

j) (i) to identify the special needs of children, to strengthen efforts to improve the general economic and social well-being of the family, and to launch a national campaign aimed at creating awareness among the general public of the adverse effects of child labour on his/her development; and (ii) to develop international solidarity and cooperation with the developing countries and to activate efforts to establish a new and fair international economic order so as to respond more effectively to the basic measures undertaken by each state for better child protection.

2. Calls upon governments and employers and workers organisations to assess the situation of child work and to assist the competent bodies and the ILO to strengthen their action programme for children.

3. Invites the governing body of the International Labour Office to instruct the director-general to continue and reinforce the ILO's action through such means as factual surveys of national situations and practices for the elimination of child labour and for the protection of children at work, and to make the necessary preparations for the global revision of the relevant ILO instruments.

Chapter 7

Child Labour: A European Experience (18th & 19th Century)

In order to manage children well, we must borrow their eyes and their hearts, see and feel as they do, and judge them from their own point of view.

I pray God to make parents reasonable."

—*Eugene de Guerin*

Child Labour in Germany During 1750-1850

Historically, child labour has been prevalent in Germany in:

(i) Workshops as well as factories of the Proto-industrial and Early Industrial Phases between 1750-1850.

(ii) Factories during the peak phase industrialisation.

As early as in the 16th and 17th centuries, child labour was in vogue in orphanages and work houses. In 1667, for instance, children worked together with convicts at the loom in the orphanage of Basel, in order to turn out products of sale.

"One of the first to criticise the cruel exploitation of children in workshops, particularly in the workshops run for orphans, was Christian Gotthilf Salzmann, a representative of the Enlightenment Movement. His criticism is voiced in his novel "Carl von Carlsberg or on Human Misery" which appeared in 1783. The portrayal of the scene wherein five children are "tortured" in a workshop for orphans because they had not "spun up all the wool and cotton given to them," though ficticious, probably does bear some degree of authenticity since surrogate parents at the orphanages were often discharged because they were torturing the children too much during work or because the mortality rate in the orphanages had risen too high as a result of child labour." (Arno Herzig)

To a great extent, the entrepreneurs who ran workshops employing orphans had a free hand where their access to child labour was concerned. However the attempts to develop workshops for orphans into independent enterprises failed due to inadequate profits. *A system of "renting out" cheap child labour* developed next, with the entrepreneurs working in conjunction with feudal political authorities (kings") here. As a result of this, the spheres of life and work of the children were duly separated from each other. The cottage industry had gradually broken away from the agricultural sector in the 16th and 17th centuries and itself grown into an independent sector. Textile workers constituted the largest section of those carrying on a cottage industry. Besides, they could also be found in areas with iron industries. In the second half of the 18th century, middle-men, putting out work to cottage industry began gaining an increasingly stronger hold over these cottage industry workers, resulting in negative economic consequences for the latter. The cottage industry manufacturers then began to rent out their children to other manufacturers in the cotton industry, or to manufacturers of silk, lace, thread, needles cotton and chains. A report of the factory commissioner Eversmann dating back to 1797 corroborates, by way of example, this link between the subsistence crisis of manufacturers of thread who worked at home and child labour. With this, the separation of the spheres of life and production took place here as well.

It is significant to note here that in the 18th century, orphans and beggar children (of whom there was an abundance after the 7 Years War) played a significant role.as a cheap wage factor in mercantilist-economits policy.

The setting up of production centres offered itself as a possibility of overcoming mass poverty. The establishment of production centres was regarded as a most effective way of eradicating pauperism. The establishment of government-run poor houses especially served this cause. But the state, of course, preferred to be relieved of this task by having entrepreneurs erect workshops, followed by proto-factories.

Governmental entrepreneurial and pedagogic interest converged at the expense of (beggar) children. Even so-called 'enlightened' economic theorists and pedagogues justified child labour. Requests of manufacturers for state privileges—whether it was for the granting of a monopoly status for subsidies for a workshop or for sustaining a whole branch of industry—therefore never failed to refer to the "benevolence" of the workshop concerned in getting children off the streets.

The Napoleonic system had led to the liberalisation of the economies in the Western territories. Prussia followed suit by promulgating the Hardenberg Legislation in 1810. There remained only a few small territories in which efforts were being made to restore the economic system of the Ancient Regime. The change-over to the liberal system triggered off an economic crisis which was especially marked in the textile sector which found itself competing with the more advanced sectors in Great Britain. The idea of balancing out production costs with low labour costs and of achieving this primarily by engaging child workers, suggested itself. As during the Ancien Regime, pointing to child workers as providing a cheap source of labour grew to be the favourite line of argumentation of entrepreneurs in the liberal phase as well. The gradual intesification of the development of proto-factories made work in workshops appear to be mere "child's play." The reference to the subsistence level of the lower classes being assured as a result of this, provided yet another reason for politicians and the general public alike to view child labour in factories as a completely natural phenomenon.

A description of the region of Wuppertal drawn up in 1809 by an official of the Napoleonic Age states yet the consequences which child labour brought in its wake:

"The great majority of the inhabitants of the Arrondissement of Elbersfeld are in an extremely wretched condition. This state of degeneration can probably be ascribed to the practice of sending children to work in factories too early in life which is characteristic of this region. Herded together in great numbers in the factories and confined to a sedentary occupation which requires them to sit in a bent position for long spells at a time, these children cannot but remain physically underdeveloped." (Arno Herzig)

Efforts Towards Child Protection in 19th Century Germany

A point of interest is the fact that the Protective Labour Legislation enacted in the wake of the industrialisation of Europe was the outcome of efforts to protect child labour. The first measures towards child protection were initiated in England in 1802, sparking off a controversy in Germany about the pedagogic value of child labour, its deleterious effects on health and its economic benefits. The protective clauses for labour embodied in the statutes of guilds dating back to the Middle Ages were either no longer in keeping with changes in reality or were forgotten. It was not altruistic but rather socio-political considerations which led to Legislation for Child Protection. Here, the statement made by General von Horn in 1828 that as a result of child employment for night work in factories the army was being deprived of sufficient stand-by recruits, induced suitable legislation.

Individual entrepreneurs—as for e.g. the manufacturer Schuchart from Barmen—, the English Laws and warnings from teachers induced the Rhineland Diet, in the face of the miserable plight of children, to petition for official factory inspectors. The Law of 16.5.1953 stipulated that factory inspectors be engaged for the well-being of young labourers—the objective being to lay down afresh conditions of work at factories requisite for the protection of health and the prevention of accidents, and to regulate anew the hours of work and night work for children. As in several developing countries, factory inspectors had often to fight opposition from manufacturers, political authorities and even from politically unconscious parents. According to the statement made by the future Chancellor of the German Reich, Bismarck, in the Reichstag (Imperial Diet) in 1869, the law remained a 'dead letter' in those branches of industry in which there were no factory inspectors: It was only with the new social and economic policies pursued by the State that opposition from liberal industrialists and conservative landed gentry could gradually be overcome.

But, Chancellor Bismarck dismissed the idea of protective labour legislation and, above all, the regulation of the hours of work as well as the restriction of women and child labour which had long since formed the base and core of social legislation in England.

On the other hand, the laws initiated by Bismarck—the Sickness Insurance Act (1884) and the Old Age and Disablement Insurance Act (1889)—helped Germany attain the world lead in social reform by a generation.

Industrial pedagogics proceeded on the assumption that the disciplining of child factory workers could be combined with the development of creative skills. However, no specific line of teaching was developed for this purpose. Today, against the background of prevailing standards, here the polytechnique approaches could be a possibility or even a "political line of teaching" for working children. Equally it is necessary to raise the awareness of their parents through means of adult education.

In the "Communist Manifesto," Marx and Engels already defend the parents of working children against these accusations. But they seized on a realisation which was to surface later when they formulated the following question addressed to the bourgeoisie: "Are you accusing us of wanting to put an end to this exploitation of children by the parents?", to which they replied: "We admit to this crime." Marx lashed out at the "pharisaicalness" behind these accusations in 1863 in his "Das Kapital."

Education in the workshop—that is, if individual lessons were conducted regularly at all—was secondary to the entrepreneurs' interest in profit-making. In 1872, the world renowned "bourgeois" pedagogue F.A.W. Diesterweg criticised the utilitarian standpoint of industrial pedagogics for the very first time in his study "On the Utilisation of Children as Factory Workers—A View from the Pedagogic Angle." However, he did not at the same time question the phenomenon of "capitalist exploitation." (Arno Herzig, p. 350). In Diesterweg's opinion, children under 10 should not be allowed to enter a factory and should only work for a maximum of 4 to 6 hours there. He pleads for socially corrective state intervention in economic life through the education system.

Social Democrats Speak Out Against Exploitation of Children in the State Parliament of Saxony

With the emergence of the Proletarian Movement in the "Fraternity of Workers" ('Arbeiterverbruederung') official protests against child labour were articulated for the very first time by the workers themselves. Accordingly, the Congress of Workers which convened in Berlin between 23.8.1948 and 3.9.1348 resolved that no child should be engaged in industrial work of any sort which prevents regular and full attendance of school before completing 14 years of age; however, the recruitment of children in factories and for peddling is not permitted on any grounds whatsoever before the child completes 14 years of age."

In opposition to the representatives of the bourgeois parties the Social Democratic members of Parliament attacked child labour during the last quarter of the 19th century and questioned their ideological justification that child labour "has educational value." They also voiced strong criticism on "the transformation of immature human beings into mere machines" (Karl Marx) and pointed out the harm this was causing to the mental, physical and moral development of these. Child labour—"social assassination" as Engels termed it—was an expression of the prevalent bougeois form of society. Despite legislation against child labour, the number of children working in factories doubled between 1880-1886. According to a census on working children in Germany in the year 1898, 532.238 children were registered as being employed. This figure corresponds to 6.5% of all children of school going age. In the kingdom of Saxony, however, 137.831 children of school going age were counted who were working against wages of factories and other enterprises, a figure which corresponds to 22.8 per cent.

As a result of a shifting of child labour into the areas of cottage industry and agriculture after 1890, the Social Democrats demanded a safety and health control which the representatives of the "bourgeois" parties denounced as an interference into "holy family life."

The rejection of exploitative child labour did however not imply that Social Democrats did not realise that children and juveniles had to be instructed and educated through productive work. Children were to be inducted gradually into different practical activities such as horticulture, fruit-growing and apiculture, as well as farming, factory work and processes of production. They were guided by the observations of their party chairman of many years, August Bebel, made in 1879 in his most important book: *"Women and Socialism"* ("Die Frau under Sozialismus").

"Child labour today is the most infamous form of

exploitation which in Socialist society should only be allowed as a means of education commensurate with the strength and capability of the individual and in course of time should be reduced to a point where it can only be beneficial and not detrimental to health and well being."

The Social Democratic education movement of the "Friends of Children" ('Kinderfreunde'), since 1908 in Austria and 1923 in Germany became the largest non-professional paedagogical and child movement of its time. Co-educational, a religious child education and self-managed children's groups formed an alternative to bourgeois and clerical institutions of education and followed the thoughts of August Bebel.

Some Consideration and Questions

In which historical period of time ("historische Zeit") did child labour prevail in Europe and when was it finally abolished? To what extent can this "veritable" historic period of time spanning several decades, even centuries, be realistically curtailed under changed socio-economic conditions and through the partial integration of the public/private sector of a national economy into the world market?

Germany serves an interesting case in point to observe how acute social problems, like child labour, for instance, were handled by the rulers under specific conditions of rule and finally "resolved" ("the Social Question").

The suppression by the State (the Anti-Socialist Law of 1878) of the proletariat emerging under social democracy, with its Marxian Eisenach Programme, was simultaneously or soon after supplemented by the positive role played by the State through Social Legislation in moulding social conditions.

Is child labour necessarily an integral part of certain early stages of development of the capitalist mode of production or was it to a considerable extent dependent on socio-cultural and religion-based values as well?

Child labour served to assure the lower classes their means of subsistence—and was a means of depressing wages—, a role not confined to Germany alone.

A retrospective glance at European or German history in the light of the problem of "child labour" throws open the possibility of gaining a clearer perspective of the stage of social and economic evolution attained in countries with developing societies despite the many socio-cultural differences between the developed and developing world. The study of the subject of child labour constitutes one of the key instruments to a sound, value-based social analysis of any nation-state. What do the tremendous proportions assumed by child labour reveal about the inner fabric of a society and to what extent does it—alongside social malconditions and contradictions—threaten even the international credibility of expressions of legitimation articulated by political, economic and trade union elites?

Transnational corporations are the basic acting units in the International Economic System, challenging or at least-relativising the very existence of newly independent nation-states in the historical perspective. To what extent does their role in national economies impair the independent development of these economies and release uncontrolled entrepreneurial forces which, amongst other things, for reasons of a competition increasingly exploit the factor of labour, and with that child labour as well, thereby indirectly initiating the very practice of child labour?

Many other than historical examples illustrating the overcoming of child labour in developed industrialised countries, are there known examples of success in the drastic reduction or elimination of child labour in the various countries of Asia, Africa or Latin America?

Though the possibility cannot completely be ruled out, Europeans as generations born in the wake of the Industrial

Revolution are not exactly preeminently legitimised to point an accusing finger at conditions prevailing in developing countries, on account of their own history of child labour. How could European trade union fedrations, industrial unions or non-governmental organisations contribute in a non-interventionist manner within the framework of the efforts made, for instance, by Indian trade unions or voluntary agencies to protect children.

The subject of child labour can be dealt with in didactic texts at various levels of schooling, or explicitly made a subject of education for unionised labour, with examples, even historical references to child labour and its abolition during the Industrial Revolution in Europe, to serve as illustration.

Chronology of Child Labour, Child Protection Measures/ Laws and Workers' Resistance Against Child Labour in Germany

16th/ 17th century onward	Child labour introduced in orphanages to ensure economic survival. It existed in commercially oriented workshops for orphans.
From approx. 1750	"Lending out" of orphan children as cheap labour to entrepreneurs from outside, as a result of which the spheres of work and daily life of children are separated.
1988	The Poor disposition of Hamburg with financial incentive (the so-called "Sitzgeld" or "attendance allowance") for attending Poor School.
1821	Evening school for child factory workers in Iserlohn.
1827	The celebrated bourgeois pedagogue F.A.W. Diesterweg questions the permissibility of child labour and the utilitarian standpoint of industrial pedagogues in his study "On the Use of Children

for Factory work—an Observation from the Pedagogic Angle."

1827 The Government of Arnsberg promulgates school regulations for children employed in factories. Factory schools, however, only remained episodic.

1827 General Heinrich Wilhelm von Horn complains of the inability of the industrial areas to adequately complement the ranks of the Army.

1828 The King of Prussia prohibits night work for children in an Order on Council.

1839 Regulation on Child Labour in Factories, the first Supervisory Law for the textile industry;

— Prohibition of Child labour in the case of children below 9 years of age.
— Proof of three years school attendance.
— Maximum hours of work fixed at 10 hours, with a two hour break at noon.
— Prohibition of work on Sundays, holidays and at night.

1840 First Labour Protection Ordinance of favour of children promulgated in the Kingdom of Bavaria.

1840 First Child Protection Ordinance in Baden.

1842 Prohibition of female labour and the employment of children below 10 in mines.

1848 The Congress of Workers in Berlin denounces the employment of children below 14.

1849 State inspection of steam boiler plant in the Kingdom of Saxony.

1853 Law on the engagement of factory inspectors for the well-being of young workers.

1853 The Prussian Government prohibits factory work for children below 12.

Factory control by industrial inspectors. Child

labour continues in agriculture and the cottage industry for decades on end.

1961 Legislative protection for child labour in factories in Saxony.

1862 First statutory regulation (Factory Act) for child labour in Wuerttemberg.

1866 The First International condemns child labour and calls for solidarity on this issue.

1870 Introduction of honorary factory inspection in Baden.

1978 Compulsory factory inspection with obligatory annual submission of reports introduced by a majority of the "Reichstag" (Imperial Diet) against the will of the government.

1891 Amendment of the Industrial Regulation of 1878: Prohibition of factory work for children of school-going age.

Lower age limit for child workers in factories raised from 12 to 13 years.

1895 According to Kaete Dunker's interpretation of the results of the enumeration of the employed, about 2 million, i.e. 25% of the children of school-going age, were engaged primarily in agriculture and as domestic servants.

1903/04 Child Protection Law: Prohibition of child labour in those branches of industry having pernicious effects on health and in smaller industrial establishments; agriculture and as domestic help, however, being excluded here.

1904 1.7 million children employed in the agricultural sector.

1904/05 The formation of social democratic Child Protection Commissions by women in order to enforce existing laws and improve protective legislation.

1908 Extension of protective Legislation to cover cottage industrial units with a minimum of 10 workers.

1911 Extension of the Cottage Industry Legislation to cover even workshops in which only members of the family worked.

1910 The Child Protection Commission of the Social Democratic Party (SPD) and the Trade Union Commission of Berlin call for a ban on children of school-going age being recruited for any kind of wage employment.

1913 The Social Democratic Faction in the Reichstag calls for an improvement in the Child Protection Law.

4.8.1914 Beginning of the First World War: Almost all Laws for the Protection of working children were annulled. The ban on recruitment of children below 13 years is repealed. Children under 14 may once again work more than 6 hours.

Selected Documents

(1) The Path to Protective Legislation for Child Workers in Factories

In order to comprehend the inordinate delay in the development of Protective Legislation for children and the slow tediousness of the path leading to the promulgation of the first law—the regulation of 1839—, one has to be clear on the reasons for industrial child labour being taken for granted at that time. The most important reasons are stated in the following:

(2) Reasons for Industrial Child Labour Being Regarded a Natural Phenomenon

1. Firstly, child labour was not invented by the Industrial Age but had always existed, for instance in agriculture or in the cottage industry. "The child grew up by the

spooling wheel." According to Robert Alt, there were many workers in the factories who "as a result of their own habitual practices during adolescence or their former occupation, found the induction of children as wage labour most natural...." —in other words, to utilise children as factory labour. It can, therefore, be said that the second phase of child labour started with industrialisation.

2. In the 19th century child labour was not only prevalent in England and Prussia but all over the world. "The over-exploitation of children as labour is not peculiar to individual kingdoms, provinces or regions. It can be found in varying degrees in all countries of Europe: from the tobacco plantations of Bessarabia to the sulphur pits of Southern Italy, in the industrial and agricultural sectors of Germany, England, Austria, France, Belgium, Spain and Switzerland."

   Ellen Key draws attention to the magnesium mines of Spain employing children between 6 and 8 years of age, to the bast-mat weaving centres of Russia, with three year olds and the sulphur pits of Sicily where even children between 12 and 14 were rendered unfit for work.

3. The laws already in existence were considered adequate to protect children from exploitation; particularly the Provisions of the Universal Law of the Land of 1794, the codification of all laws in force in Prussia:

   (a) Parents who could not prove that their child was receiving the necessary level of education at home could be compelled, by the use of coercive means and threat to punishment, to send their child to school after completion of 5 years.

   (b) Regular schooling was to be continued as long as the pastor was satisfied that the child had procured sufficient knowledge to assume his growing into a rational being.

(c) A child could be exempted from attending school over a longer period only with the permission of the authorities and clerical members of the school governing body.

4. The emergence of mass poverty (pauperism) as a transient, if not even permanent state of affairs resulting from industrial development, made even child labour appear natural. The "commonly portrayed picture" of early industrialisation is characterised by long hours of work, female and child labours, low remuneration, insufficient security, lack of safeguards at the place of work and miserable living conditions.

   Robert Alt draws attention to the vicious circle inherent in this situation, namely that the parents on the one hand needed the additional income accruing from children's wages and on the other contributed to depressed ages and increased unemployment amongst themselves by accepting child labour.

5. The new machinery employed initially permitted the engagement of workers with low muscle power. "To the extent to which machinery makes physical strength dispensable, it becomes the means of employing workers without muscular strength or of immature physical growth, albeit with greater suppleness of limb. Female and child labour was thus the primary outcome of the capitalist employment machinery."

6. The nascent industry was faced with severe competition and needed cheap labour. This is found in industrial child labour. This motive has, time and again, been brought to attention during conflicts between industry and law enforcement authorities and even in the struggle to enforce overtime for adolescent workers.

7. Industrial child labour was at the time considered to be a pedagogic value—a view which the industrial schools helped create. The educational value of industrial labour was considered to lie in its training the children to acquire the qualities of diligence, perseverance, self-discipline, conscientiousness and dexterity. Keller, Privy Councillor to the Administration made precise observations on the educative value of child labour during his journey across the Rhineland in 1834.

   He was particularly impressed by the educative effect of production with division of labour in a needle factory in Aachen. The work allotted to the children employed there, who numbered about 100, was, in his opinion, indeed exhausting and not exactly free of danger, but at least it was not too difficult and the "deftness, agility and dexterity displayed by the children while executing all these tasks is astonishing. The tools and machines they handle are ingenious; the children themselves sitting side by side in a row while working, at times bending forward and at times back-ward, all synchronising almost perfectly in the rhythm of their movements, remind the observer of machines. But they are strong, healthy, cheerful and bright and even mischievous and lively.... There is certainly some truth in the assumption that the educative value of industrial work was only recognised for child workers in factories at the time and not for pupils of the "Gymnasium."*

8. The so-called social question did not exist at all during the early phase of industrialisation. There were, at the time, still no social reformist movements which could have balanced out the social and techno-economic demands against each other. The top priority and objective of the state at that time was to assure itself power and privileges so much so it did not

interfere in economic life. The reluctance of the state to concern itself with social issues, and with that the emergence of industrial child labour as well, can be attributed to this. It is also true that the rapidly developing industrial sector held the fascination of entrepreneurs and statesmen to such an extent that the latter were initially blind to accompanying social problems.

Excerpt from Report Compiled by a Privy Councillor, 1834

"Children are made to work every day from 5 o'clock in the morning till noon, and then from 1 o'clock in the morning till noon, till late in the evening; in winter naturally as long as there is light. These children have never known the benefits of schooling, neither in their younger days nor during the time when they are employed. They have never even attended Sunday school which is practically unknown in Bonn.

Those who did work in factories, therefore, were still considered the most well behaved and decent. The others perished from begging, from being exposed to the rigours of the weather or due to the vagaries of the lives they led. However, although children working in factories have to put in 12 to 15 hours of work per day, it is only through this that they regularly earn their daily bread and are treated to that indispensable disciplining. The urchins who crouched by roadside ditches all day in the hope of pitifully whining their way to a few pennies from the next traveller through pretence and false-hoods, and who interspersed this with thefts in fields and gardens are in my opinion too hardened for and unaccustomed to any form of disciplining. They will probably only die in the open of poverty and want or put an end to their lives in the provincial penitentiaries and workhouses near Werden or Brauweiler."

(3) Accident of a Child Worker

"I wish to give yet another example. I have a brother

who is 8 years old. My mother was persuaded by a spinner into sending him to work in a factory where he earned 10 Reichsgroschen every week as a piecer operating a new mill spinning machine. One day he was asked to clean the machine which is generally done while the machine is still running. This meant that one had to be very careful for the piecer has to crawl in quickly during the run-out of the carriage, do some cleaning and again crawl out quickly before the run-in. A delay of a few seconds could result in death, as was the case in 1862 in the joint-stock spinning factory at Chemnitz where a live child was reduced to a corpse in just two minutes."

(4) Child Workers During Famine Years

The following account of a worker in the cotton spinning factory of Himmelmuehle in Saxony provides vivid depiction of the situation of child workers in factories during the famine years of 1846/47:

"It was simply frightful in the scarce years of 1846/47 when the poor young workers at the tender age of 9, 10 to 14 and 15, had to brave the fiercest of storms and blizzards early in the morning and late in the evening to set out for work; often lean and hungry, heart broken when their weekly wages were consumed for buying dry bread right in the beginning of the week, for the cold, metallic air from the power driven machines sapped one of all energy and made one hungry. The spinner could give them nothing; he himself had to go hungry during those years, with just dry bread to eat, while continuing to work all the time in this state. His heart bled as he watched his piecers make their way hurriedly during the lunch break in the last few days of their week, over the hill to the farmers in villages lying a good half hour away, to beg for a few pieces of bread, for they had to be back at the stroke of 1. A factory owner could frown down despotically upon this with characteristic lack of empathy when told—upon asking where the children hurried off to every afternoon towards the end of the week, whilst they always stayed behind in the dining hall during the first few days of the week—that these children had gone to beg for a few pieces of bread.

The workers lived within the narrow confines of their lodgings, crowded together. The rooms were hardly aired out for fear of losing any heart. Generally the living quarters were far off from the factories so that apart from working for 14 hours at a stretch, the workers also had to spend a great deal of time walking to and fro.

In winter this meant wading through slush and snow without adequate clothing. Most of the time the children arrived at the factories completely drenched, whereby their chest and lung ailments, which they had developed due to the unhealthy air in the factories, were only further aggravated. The children could hardly resist as they were "dragged away crying and protesting to such a prison by their mothers, early in the morning at 5 o'clock, even in cold or wet weather." Everyone stood against them: the authorities, the manufacturers, the parents and even the workers with whom they worked in the factories. The right of disciplining the children wielded by the overseer formed part of the control system in proto-factories. The worst cases of child abuse" by overseers were recorded in 1824 by the Provincial Administrative Counsellor of Iserlohn. The factory workers of the cotton spinning factory of Himmel-muehle also confirmed that the chief overseer, Schuessler, administered slaps to the "poor hungry children for the slightest mistake they committed" and dug his fist into their sides and ribs. The "fraternisation" (Verbruederung") recorded similar instances in 1849: Children were kept awake and attentive at work by being beaten with whips, lashes and canes. Their helplessness, especially that of the female child workers, before the overseers were revealed in a recent on the conditions in Elbersfeld,. presented in the Rhineland Provincial Diet of 1843. Here, it was revealed that an overseer had passed on syphilis to the young girls working in the factory, causing great misery and hardship to their families.

Friedrich Engels on "The Condition of the Working Class in England

"In the coal and iron mines which are worked in pretty much the same way, children of four, five, and seven years are employed. They are set to transporting the ore or coal loosened by the miner from its place to the horse-path or the main shaft, and to opening and shutting the doors (which separate the divisions of the mine and regulate its ventilation) for the passage of workers and material. For watching the doors the smallest children are usually employed, who thus pass twelve hours daily, in the dark, alone, sitting usually in damp passages without even having work enough to save them from the stupefying, brutalising tedium of doing nothing. The transport of coal and iron-stone, on the other hand, is very hard labour, the stuff being shoved in large tubs, without wheels, over the uneven floor of the mine; often over moist clay, or through water, and frequently up steep inclines and through paths so low-roofed that the workers are forced to creep on hands and knees. For this more wearing labour, therefore, older children and half-grown girls are employed. One man or two boys per tub are employed, according to circumstances; and, if two boys, one pushes and the other pulls. The loosening of the ore or coal, which is done by men or strong youths of sixteen years or more, is also very weary work. The usual working day is eleven to twelve hours, often longer; in Scotland it reaches fourteen hours, and double time is frequent, when all the employees are at work below ground twenty-four, and even thirty-six hours at a stretch. Set times for meals are almost unknown, so that these people eat when hunger and time permit.

The children and young people who are employed in transporting coal and iron-stone all complain of being over-tried.

It is constantly happening that children throw themselves down on the stone hearth or the floor as soon as the reach home, fall asleep at once without being able to take one bite of food, and have to be washed and put to bed while asleep; it even happens that they lie down on the way home, and are found by their parents late at night asleep on the road. It seems to be a universal practice among these children to spend Sunday in bed to recover in some degree from the over-exertion of the week. Church and school are visited by but few, and even of these the teachers complain of their great sleepiness and the want of all eagerness to learn."

REFERENCES

Dahrendorf, Ralph (1967), Gesellschaft und Demokratie in Deutschland (Society and Democracy in Germany), Muenche.

Ebeling, Hans/Birkenfeld, Wolfgang (1972), Die Reise in die Vergangenheir. Ein geschichtliches Arbeitsbuch. Band 3, Das Werden der modernen Welt. Lehrerausgabe, Braunschweig.

Engels, Friedrich (1973), The Condition of the Working Class in England, *From personal observation and authentic sources,* Moscow.

Gebhardt, Bruno (1965), Handbuch der deutschen Geschichte. Band 3: Von der Franzoesischen Revolution bis zum Ersten Weltkrieg. (Handbook of German history. Vol. 3: From the French revolution to world war I). Stuttgart.

Herzfeld, Hans (1961), Die Moderne Welt, 1989-1945. Teil I: Die Epoche der buergerlichen Nationalstaaten. (The modern world, 1789-1945. Part I: The era of the bourgeois nation states). Braunschwei.

Herzig, Arno (1983), Kinderarbeit in Deutschland in Manufacture und Proto-Fabrik (1950—1850), S. 311-375, in: "Archiv fuer Sozialgeschichte," herausgegeben von der Friedrich-Ebert-Stiftung in Verbindung mit dem Institut fuer Sozialgeschichte. Braunschweig—Bonn. XXIII, Band 1, Bonn.

Hug, Wolfgang (1985), Unsere Geschichte. Band 2: Vom Beginn der Neuzeit bis zum ende des 19. Jahrhunderts. (Our history. Vol. 2 : From the beginning of modern times to the end of the 19th century.) Frankfurt/Main, Berlin, Muenchen.

Jenss, Harro (1980), Jugendarbeitsschutz. Von den Anfaengen der Industrialisierung bis zur Gegenwart. (Legislation on Juvenile labour. From the beginning of industrialisation to the present. Frankfurt/New York.

Lesanovsky, Werner, Die Bemuehungen der Sozialdemokratischen Abgeordneten im Saechsischen Landtag um die Verbesserung der proletarischen Familienerziehung und der Kampf gegen die kapitalistische Kinderausbeutung (1877-1900). In: "Saechsische Heimatblatter," 28. Jahrgg, Heft 3/1982.

Meyer, Thomas/Klaer, Karl-Heinz/Miller, Susanne/Nory, Klaus/ Timmermann, Heinz (1986) Lexikon des Sozialismus. (An Encyclopaedia of Socialism), Koeln.

Quandt, Siegfried (1978), Kinderarbeit und Kinderschutz in Deutschland, 1783-1976. Quellen und Anmerkungen. (Child labour and legislation in Germany, 1783-1976. Sources and Notes). Paderborn.

Stark von der Haar, Elike and Heinrich, Kinderarbeit in der Bundesrepublik und im Deutschen Reich. Eine Bestandsaufnahme ueber Ausmass und Folgen der Beschaeftigung von Kindern und ueber den gesetzlichen Kinderschutz. Mit zahlreichen Dokumenten und einer Unterrichtseinheit.

Chapter 8

The ILO Perspective on Child Labour

[The information gathered in this chapter is substantially based on ILO: Report of the Director General, Part I: Child Labour, International Labour Conference, 69th Session, Geneva, 1983. We gratefully acknowledge this. —Ed.]

1. The Nature of the Problem

It is now over 81 years since the International Labour Conference adopted the Minimum Age (Industry) Convention, 1919 (No. 5) — the first in a long line of such Conventions—which fixed a minimum age of 14 for admission to employment in industry. It is ten years since the adoption of the more comprehensive Minimum Age Convention, 1973 (No. 138), a general instrument aimed at the total abolition of child labour. Over all this time, the progress made towards the elimination of child labour has been in many ways impressive. Yet the situation remains disquieting.

Child labour is still a widespread and perhaps even growing phenomenon in much of the world today. While many of the children who are working are engaged in activities permitted by national and international standards, many more are working in violation of these standards. Such is the case, for example, of;

- Young girls working in small industrial enterprises in tasks that involve handling microscopically fine wires, finally resulting in loss of the eyesight within five to eight years;
- shepherd boys subcontracted to owners of large estates to work for as long as 15 hours a day;

— children working underground in mines;
— bonded children;
— children employed as seasonal and cheap labour in pesticide-soaked fields;
— children working in numerous small industrial workshops and service establishments;
— children in street trades practically ubiquitous in the developing world.

That is child labour. Not teenagers working for a few hours to earn additional pocket money; not children helped on family farms; not youngsters doing household chores. But children prematurely leading adult lives, working long hours for low wages under conditions damaging to their health and to their physical and mental development, sometimes separated from their families, frequently deprived of meaningful educational and training opportunities that could open up for them a better future. Child labour of this kind is the object of national and international concern.

2. Causes and Forms of Child Labour

Children in almost all societies do one kind of work or another. But the extent and nature of their work are influenced mainly by the structure of the economy and the level and pace of development.

In agrarian societies work by children is an integral part of the socialisation process and a means of transmitting traditionally acquired skills from parent to child. Moreover, in societies at low levels of technological development the participation of all those who can contribute to domestic or non-domestic production is essential for meeting the consumption requirements of the household. Child work is therefore in essential part of the farm household's survival. This situation is still prevalent in many parts of rural Africa and Asia and, to some extent, Latin America. In such societies the division of labour is largely based on sex, age and physical capacity. Children, until they reach a certain age, are involved in light and time-intensive activities while adults usually take up effort-intensive activities.

To some extent, comparable patterns may be found in artisanal workshops and small-scale services. Children assist their parents in ancillary tasks, acquire skills and gradually become fully fledged workers in family establishments or trades.

Work of this kind is not without its problems, especially in relation to the health and safety of the children and to their schooling. But it is not what we usually mean by child labour.

Wage or quasi-wage employment is another matter altogether.

Historically, the growth of wage labour and industrial expansion are associated with a decline in child employment. The early stages of industrialisation, however, are marked by a high incidence of child employment, often under extremely poor and indeed exploitative conditions. This is the case in much of the developing world today.

Thus, in many developing countries, children are found working in all types of industrial and service establishments in urban areas in both the formal and the informal sectors and also in commercial agriculture. Often they are working for low wages and for excessively long hours. Vulnerable, flexible and unorganised child workers are used for reducing labour costs and maintaining competitive advantages and as a means of adapting and responding to economic uncertainties and fluctuations in demand.

The subordination of child workers to such pressures has been aggravated in many developing countries by the slow growth of urban employment. Urban unemployment rates of 20 to 25 per cent are not uncommon in many countries.

In these circumstances, the employment of children becomes an essential means of generating or supplementing family income. The poverty or unemployment of their parents therefore forces children to work in households as domestic servants or in small enterprises or in street trades. At worst, they are drawn into such activities as beggary and prostitution.

The situation in the rural areas is in many respects similar. In a large number of developing countries technological innovations in agriculture have been accompanied by increasing landlessness and rural differentiation. This has led to the search for wage employment in commercial farms, especially plantations, as well as to a rapid migration way from rural areas. Children, especially from poor families, are forced into the labour market to work either individually or as part of contracted family labour. Given the need to met subsistence requirements on the one hand and growing pauperisation resulting from land alienation on the other, the pressure on rural households to find alternative sources of survival by all means, including the labour of their children, whether under family control or under contract to prospective employers and labour recruiters, becomes almost insurmountable.

A particularly disturbing situation may arise in agrarian societies where land tenure patterns impose on tenants, sharecroppers and similar categories of workers obligations over and above household consumption requirements. In some cases, these obligations may take the form of providing the landlord a share of the farmers' produce. But in others they might involve the provision of labour services, including those of children. The prevalence of such relations is known to lead to a severe and high incidence of debt bondage, giving rise to the phenomenon known as "bounded" labour which, while generally prohibited by law, is still found, for example, in parts of south and south-east Asia.

In short, the problem of child labour in both rural and urban areas is principally one of poverty and unemployment, themselves a result of unequal and low levels of development.

3. The Two Planks of ILO Policy

For the ILO, the abolition of child labour and more generally the protection of children and young persons against work of a character or under conditions unsuitable to their age have been constant concerns since its foundation.

A major part of the ILO's work in this area has been the adoption by the International Labour Conference of a series of Conventions and Recommendations dealing with the employment or work of children and young persons.

The first such Convention was adopted at the first session of the International Labour Conference, 1919. This instrument—the Minimum Age (Industry) Convention, 1919 (No. 5) — fixed at 14 years the minimum age for admission of children to industrial employment., Subsequently, many international labour Conventions and Recommendations were adopted prohibiting the employment of children under a certain age and regulating their conditions of work in particular sectors or occupations—the most recent instruments on the subject being the Minimum Age Convention (No. 138) and Recommendation (No. 146), adopted by the Conference in 1973.

A further policy statement was issued by the Conference in 1979, the year designated as International Year of the Child, in the form of a resolution concerning the International Year of the Child. This resolution called on member States to ratify and implement the relevant international labour standards and, above all, to take measures to ensure the proper protection of children with regard to work. Recognising that the abolition of child labour in practice will take time, the resolution stresses the need—during the transitional period until its elimination — for measures to regulate and humanise it.

This affirmation of the elimination of child labour as an objective coupled with a commitment to action, pending its attainment, to improve the conditions of working children are the two planks of ILO policy. In the long run, the progressive elimination of child labour requires a general improvement of living standards, a reinforcement of the educational infrastructure and, perhaps most basically, a greater consciousness of the need for change. In the short run, the protection of working children requires practical measures that can improve their working and living conditions.

4. A General Framework for Policies on Child Labour

Effective policies aimed at the protection of children at work and the gradual elimination of child labour must be adjusted to the socio-economic situation of each country. Child labour cannot be approached as an isolated problem; its reduction and elimination will require a set of direct and indirect, albeit inter-related, measures.

Where work by children is truly part of the socialisation process and a means of transmitting skills from parent to child, it is hardly meaningful to speak of child labour. Nor can such work be divorced from the poverty and underdevelopment and the absence of alternatives to child work which together generate and sustain it. For the overwhelming majority who assist and work with their parents at home or on the farm, it is almost impossible to address their situation through formal measures as such; nor would such measures, if successful, necessarily be in the interest of many child workers and their families. Child labour is rooted in poverty: the progressive elimination of unacceptable labour by those too young to undertake it requires a general improvement in the economies of the countries concerned. In this context, the impact of policies or measures which may not be specifically addressed to children but which do try to bear on the causes of poverty and inequality can have a significant and even decisive impact on the incidence and extent of child labour. Such policies may include agrarian reforms, employment creation schemes, greater access by the poor to improved technologies, informal sector promotion policies, creation of co-operatives and social security programmes. These and similar measures can lead to broad-based growth, a more egalitarian structure and asset and income distribution and, consequently, a reduction in the incidence of child labour.

Another set of policies which can have a bearing on the incidence and extent of child labour relates to education, training and apprenticeship. The extension and application of universal compulsory education and the provision of training and apprenticeship schemes can have significant potential because they could not only reduce the number of children out of school but also provide opportunities for skill acquisition and later employment.

In addition, there is a third set of complementary policies which needs to be conceived parallel to these medium to long-term macro-economic and educational policies. This consists of measures which address the worst forms of child exploitation and lead to better working conditions.

Pending the improvement of economic conditions to the point where it will no longer be necessary or profitable for children to work, efforts must be made to complement long-term employment and development policies with progressive measures aimed at regulating and humanising child work so that children are provided with some protection against conditions that jeopardise their normal physical and mental development, deny them educational and skill development and block their lifetime opportunities. Such measures include the adoption and enforcement of protective labour laws, the implementation of improvements at the worksite and the provision of welfare facilities.

At this juncture, we should like to stress some points in

respect of the role of labour laws in preventing or suppressing child labour, since they have been a subject of misunderstanding and even distortion in recent years.

The aim of such measures is not to supplant long-term structural reforms and anti-poverty-oriented policies but to reinforce and complement them wherever possible, to deal with the worst forms of child labour wherever they exist, and to provide minimum levels of protection where such labour is unavoidable. There is a risk that labour legislation, especially child labour laws, without supporting socio-economic changes may lead to greater Clandestine work and more exploitative work situations. Such laws must therefore never be conceived or implemented in isolation from the socio-economic setting.

By the same token, the dynamic character of child labour laws must also be recognised. Standards and laws must be based on specific country situations and must therefore taken into account the socio-economic realities of each country. At the same time, these standards should be raised progressively over time; hence, laws must be revised accordingly as the countries concerned develop their economies and institutions.

Yet it must also be stressed that there are certain absolutes arising from the inherent dignity of the human person and recognised in international convenants which nations, irrespective of their level of development, have accepted and should therefore adhere to both in the formulation of labour laws and in their subsequent enforcement. Every effort must be made at the national and international level to persuade and assist governments to adopt and enforce labour laws that can protect children at least from the worst forms or exploitation and dangerous working conditions. Such laws need not and should not await structural changes or significant improvements in general standards of living. To dismiss in a cavalier way, as some do, the potential role of child protective laws, or to invoke the pretext of poverty and underdevelopment for the continued transgression of universally accepted values is to accept the perpetuation of universally condemned abuses.

Child labour laws can play a catalytic and supportive role in efforts aiming at the establishment of a more humane socio-economic order. That is why the ILO, and indeed national governments, attach so much importance to the setting and implementation of international and national labour standards.

5. International Labour Standards

As we said earlier, the International Labour Conference has over the years adopted a series of Conventions and Recommendations dealing with the employment or work of children and young persons, starting with the adoption in 1919 of Convention No. 5, which fixed at 14 years the minimum age for admission of children to industrial employment. Since then, many such Conventions and Recommendations have been adopted regulating the employment of children in particular sectors and occupations. In 1973 the Conference re-examined the problem in depth and adopted the comprehensive standards laid down in Convention No. 138 and Recommendation No. 146 concerning minimum age for admission to employment.

Due to the fundamental importance of Convention No. 138 and Recommendation No. 146 as the basis for ILO policy aimed at the protection of working children and the gradual elimination of child labour it is worthwhile to spell out what, in the light of the provisions of those instruments, are the major elements that should inspire national policy and legislation.

First and foremost is a strong commitment to pursue a national policy designed to ensure the effective abolition of child labour and to raise progressively the minimum age for admission to employment or work to a level consistent with the fullest physical and mental development of young persons.

The elements of such a policy may vary from country to country but should in general include:

(a) firm national commitment to full employment and measures designed promote employment-oriented development in rural and urban areas;

(b) the progressive extension of other economic and social measures alleviate poverty wherever it exists and to ensure family living standards and income which are such as to make it unnecessary to have recourse to the economic activity of children;

(c) the development and progressive extension of social security and family welfare measures aimed at ensuring child maintenance;

(d) the development and progressive extension of adequate facilities for education and vocational orientation and training appropriate in from and content to the needs of the children and young persons concerned;

(e) the development and progressive extension of appropriate, facilities for the protection and welfare of children and young persons, including employed young persons.

Secondly, national laws or regulations should specify a minimum age for admission to employment or work. This minimum age should not be less than the age of completion of compulsory schooling and, in any case, according to the Convention, should not be less than 15 years. However, countries whose economy and educational facilities are insufficiently developed may initially specify a minimum age of 14 years.

The minimum age set for employment or work must also be linked to the nature of the work. Thus it is necessary to specify the ages of admission to heavy and light work. The Convention fixes at 18 the minimum age for admission to employment or work which is likely to jeopardise the health, safety or morals of young persons. However, this may be lowered to 16 on condition that the health, safety and morals of the young persons concerned are fully protected and that they have received adequate, specific instruction and training in the relevant branch of activity.

On the other hand, national laws or regulations may permit the employment or work of persons 13 to 15 years of age (or 12 to 14 if the basic minimum age is 14) on light work which is not likely to be harmful to their health or development and will not prejudice their attendance at school or their participation in vocational training programmes.

A third element that needs to be given special attention in legislation and indeed as a focus for national action relates to coverage. Although every effort must be made to provide protection in as many sectors as possible, the existence of serious constraints and hence the need for flexibility in coverage must be recognised. For these reasons, it may well be, and often is, necessary for national laws and regulations to exclude certain categories of employment or work where there could be special and substantial problems of application. Moreover, where the economy and administrative facilities are insufficiently developed, the scope of application of national laws and regulations may be initially limited to certain branches of economic activity or types of undertakings. Which activities or sectors should be included depends once again on the country's situation. But national laws should cover, as a minimum mining and quarrying , manufacturing, construction, electricity, gas and water, sanitary services, transport, storage and communication, and plantation and other agricultural undertakings mainly producing for commercial purposes. The Convention also provides for the possible exemption, under certain conditions, of work done in educational establishments for vocational training or won in undertakings if it is part of a training, guidance or orientation course.

A fourth important area for national policy is conditions of work. Given the fact that the total abolition of child labour is unattainable in the short run in many developing countries and that therefore millions of children will continue to be working, the conditions under which they work should be a focus of policy. Special efforts should be made to ensure that children are not employed under conditions involving use of dangerous substances, agents or processes, the lifting of heavy weights and underground work. Special attention should also be paid to the provision of fair remuneration and its protection, the strict limitation of daily and weekly hours of work and the prohibition of overtime, the granting of a minimum consecutive period of 12 hours' night rest and of customary weekly rest days, the granting of an annual holiday with pay of at least four weeks and, in any case, not shorter than that granted to adults, coverage by social security schemes, including employment injury, medical care and sickness benefits schemes, and the maintenance of satisfactory standards of safety and health.

Finally, an area that deserves to be conceived of as an integral part of national efforts is that of enforcement. Laws and regulations, if they are to be effective, must be backed by effective enforcement machinery. This therefore calls for the strengthening of labour inspection and related services, for instance by the special training of inspectors, so as to detect and correct abuses in the employment or work of children and young persons, especially in respect of employment in hazardous types of work. In order to facilitate the verification of ages, it is necessary (a) that the public authorities maintain an effective system of birth registration, (b) that employers be required to maintain registers and documents indicating the names and ages of all employed children and young persons and of all those receiving training, and (c) that children and young persons working in the streets, in outside stalls, in public places, etc., be licensed.

These are some of the elements that are at the heart of the international labour standards on minimum age of admission to employment and should serve as a guideline in the setting of national standards.

6. Conclusion

Although its extent and nature vary among countries and regions, child labour remains a widespread phenomenon. The magnitude of the problem, especially in developing countries, is great and the task of attacking it is urgent.

Not all work is harmful for children. Some types of activities under regulated conditions can have positive effects for the child and for society. Work experiences of the right sort can be a means of acquiring skills, of learning responsibility, of becoming a full member of the community-in short, a valuable part of growing up.

What gives cause for concern is work that places too heavy a burden on the child; work that endangers his safety, health or welfare, work that takes advantage of the defencelessness of the child, work that exploits the child as a cheap substitute for adult labour, work that uses the child's effort but does nothing for his development, work that impedes the child's education or training and thus prejudices his future.

Child labour of this kind must be the target of national and international action.

To be effective, such action must be realistic. Children in the developing world work out of necessity. Without their earnings, however small, the already low living standards of their families would be still lower. Large numbers of them do not even have families or cannot count on their families for support: they must rely on their own efforts. For many children in the developing world the chances of receiving serious education and training are minimal. The facilities are inadequate, the direct and indirect costs are prohibitive and, perhaps most discouragingly, the relevance and practical value of the education offered are doubted by parents and by the children themselves. Many children do not go to school; many drop out very early; and many more attend but only sporadically and without drawing much benefit. In these circumstances, the alternative to work might be idleness, beggary or crime.

Thus the elimination of child labour and the progressive raising of the minimum age for admission to employment must be regarded as objectives to be attained gradually and as an integral part of a process of development designed to overcome the scourges of unemployment and destitution. Formal measures alone will not work; if applied in isolation from overall measures to improve the economic and social context, and especially in the absence of alternatives to work, they may even be harmful. Child labour is embedded in poverty and it is through sustained increases in standards of living that it will be abolished.

But recognition of this reality must not serve as a pretext for inaction. The problem of child labour is so grave and is often manifested in forms so unacceptable that it cannot be left aside until economic conditions and social structures are fundamentally improved.

We are convinced that, under existing conditions, direct action can be taken and significant progress can be made. Long-term development policies can be complemented by immediate measures aimed at regulating and humanising work by children so as to protect them against practices or conditions that jeopardise their normal physical and mental development, deny them the possibility of acquiring knowledge and skills and block their opportunities for the future.

We urge giving priority to:

— the review of existing legal standards on minimum age for admission to employment or work with the aim of identifying any significant gaps in coverage and, where possible, adopting laws or regulations for some or all of the sectors concerned;

— the adoption and strict enforcement of laws or regulations prohibiting the employment or work of children in hazardous activities;

— the promotion of occupational safety and health and the improvement of the physical environment at the workplace in sectors where children are known to be engaged;

— The regulation and improvement of other conditions of work of children, especially in respect of hours of work, night work, weekly rest and holidays;

— the regulation of levels and methods of remuneration and the protection of wages;

— the strengthening of labour inspection and other enforcement measures for the regulation of child labour;

— the provision of welfare facilities and services for children at or near the workplace;

— the expansion of educational facilities to permit the extension or more effective implementation of compulsory education;

— the introduction of schemes by which children who are obliged to work can combine remunerative activity with education or training;

— the encouragement of action by employers, trade unions and voluntary organisations to promote child welfare;

— the exposure of particularly abusive or exploitative practices;

— the dissemination of information designed to create greater public awareness of the adverse effects of child labour.

We reiterate the appeal made by the Conference during the International Year of the Child for member States to ratify the Minimum Age Convention, 1973 (No. 138), if they have not already done so, and to apply the provisions of that Convention and its supplementary recommendation (No. 146).

The protection of children at work and the ultimate abolition of child labour require concerted action by governments along many fronts, but they are not tasks for governments alone. They also require the commitment and the active co-operation of employers' and workers' organisations and indeed of the world community as a whole.

II. Child Labour: Questions and Answer

I. The Nature and Extent of the Problem

1. What is "child labour"?
2. Where do children work?
3. How many child workers are there in the world today?
4. Where are they mostly found?
5. Has it been decreasing or increasing?

II. What is to be done?

1. Why do children work?
2. What do they need?

III. ILO's Policy

1. Is the ILO opposed to all types of work?
2. What is ILO's policy on child labour?

IV. International Labour Standards: Principles and Relevance

1. Are there international norms and standards on child labour and the protection of working children?

2. What are Conventions and Recommendations?
3. What is the relevance of these international labour standards (or Conventions and Recommendations)?
4. What is the most important international labour Convention on the subject?
5. What are the major provisions of the Minimum Age Convention of 1973?
6. Does the minimum age limit of 15 apply for every country and for all types of work?
7. What is the real value of these international labour standards and for that matter national laws on child labour since, given the poverty of their families, children will continue to work at any rate?

I. THE NATURE AND EXTENT OF THE PROBLEM

1. What is "Child Labour"?

The concept of child labour is not as simple and straightforward as it may appear. Childhood can be defined in terms of age, but then different societies may have different age thresholds for demarcating childhood and adulthood. In some societies, age may not be a sufficient basis for defining "childhood." The fulfilment of certain social rites and traditional obligations may well be important requirements in defining "adult" and "child" status. In still others, the integration of children into socio-economic life may begin so early and the transition from childhood and adulthood may be so smooth and gradual that it may be virtually impossible to identify clearly the different life phases. We must therefore recognise that we are dealing with a concept which could mean different things in different societies and at different times.

However, in the context of child labour, a working definition of a "child" may be a person below the internationally agreed age limit of 15 years. We will come back to this point later in discussing international labour standards on the subject.

How about "labour"? Labour too can be a controversial concept to define, especially in the case of children. Children assist their families, for example, at home from early years on; they also assist in farms, in shops, etc. But this is not what we call child labour. Rather, we have in mind work or employment situation where children are engaged on a more or less regular basis to earn a livelihood for themselves or their families.

In short, the notion of child labour is intended to cover children under the age of 15 engaged in work or employment with the aim of earning a livelihood for themselves or for their families.

2. Where do Children Work?

On the land and in the village; in and around the home; on the streets; in crafts and trading; in plantations, in mines and factories. They are found almost everywhere under varying forms and terms of employment. Many work as unpaid family labour, but a growing number are also found working as wage labourers, casually hired, just as casually fired.

3. How Many Child Workers are There in the World Today?

Who knows? The honest truth is that nobody really knows. And this is not for lack of interest but because, among other reasons, child workers are statistically hidden even in the modern sector. Governments and employers deny that they exist—not everywhere but nearly so. We know, however, that it is a huge problem. Some years back, the ILO estimated the number of child workers at around 50 million. This is a significant figure but it is generally considered to be a serious underestimate. By some, it is felt that there are probably at least 100 million working children today and quite possibly nearly twice as many. All of this indicates that we know that the number is big, but how big it is, we don't know. But we need to know, and governments need to know if they, as well as the international community, are to respond effectively to the needs of children and child labourers.

4. Where are They Mostly Found?

Nearly everywhere. In Asia, Africa, Latin America, and, even in Europe and North America. Although we cannot rely too much on existing statistics, available estimates indicate that:

— child workers constitute as much as 7 per cent of the population under 15 years of age and as high a proportion as 11 per cent of the overall labour force in some Asian countries;

— in some African countries, as many as 20 per cent of the children are reported to be working, and child workers make up as much as 17 per cent of the workforce;

— as high a proportion as 12 to 26 per cent of children in some Latin American countries may well be working;

— in some industrialised countries hundreds of thousands and, by some accounts, millions of children under the age of 15 are known to work.

5. Has it been Decreasing or Increasing?

It is quite difficult to give a definite answer one way or the other. Statistics, as we said earlier, are quite difficult to come by and, even when available, are not altogether reliable or comparable. Moreover, the trend varies form one region to another and form one country to another.

But some tentative generalisations can be made:

— Firstly, in the industrialised countries the spread of

compulsory schooling, the rapid and considerable improvement in levels of living and the enforcement of anti-child labour laws have all lead to a significant decline in child labour in both absolute and relative terms. In fact, in the vast majority of the countries in the industrialised countries, child labour has been virtually abolished, though it is still found in some.

— Secondly, in a large number of developing countries also there has been, say over the last five decades or so, a decline in the proportion of child workers, mainly because of the considerable expansion of schooling opportunities.

— Thirdly, the progress in many countries notwithstanding, the deterioration in living standards in some developing countries over the last decade or so is likely the have resulted in an increases both in the incidence and the number of child labourers.

Having said this, however, it should be recognised that the problem of child labour should be looked at not only in quantitative terms but also qualitatively. Unlike the pre-industrial period when children worked with their parents on farms or in family craft shops, today however many child workers are employed in wage or semi-wage employment in mines, factories, plantations, etc. Children are thus found working increasingly outside the orbit of the family. As a result, they are subjected to exploitative practices and, worse still, forced to work under conditions dangerous to their health, physical and mental development. As the Director-General said in his report to the 1983 International Labour Conference, "it is this radical transformation in the nature and forms of children's work with its concomitant harmful effects on the children concerned that makes child labour and even more pressing problem and a compelling cause for international concern."

II. WHAT IS TO BE DONE?

1. Why do Children Work

The are several reasons.

Is it because of the lack of legislation? This may be so in some exceptional cases. But as noted before, in the overwhelming majority of countries, legislation concerning minimum age for admission to employment and regulations on the employment of children do exist.

Is it then because of the ineffectiveness of enforcement of such legislation? Certainly, "yes," for in many countries the inspection system is not adequately developed; legislation often excludes traditional workshops, quasi-family undertakings, petty commerce, street trades and agriculture where the majority of children work and where the enforcement of legislation, if any takes place, is extremely difficult.

However, while part of the problem certainly derives from inadequate legislation and insufficient enforcement, a far more basic cause for child work is poverty. A child goes out to work in order to contribute to the family income. Also, another widespread cause for child labour is the low level of development of the countries concerned and the lack of educational facilities. The only alternative left for children in work in subsistence farming or fishing and petty commerce in which the family is engaged.

In some cases, ignorance, negligence or indifference towards the question of child labour could still be an explanation. It may be noted in this respect that reforms in the past, in many countries, originated in the recognition of the ill effects of child labour and the mobilisation of public opinion for the elimination of child labour and the protection of working children.

2. What Do They Need?

If children work, and they do, policies must be planned

on how to meet their needs. What are their needs?

Firstly, they should certainly be protected from exploitation and from hazardous conditions of work which are likely to endanger their physical and mental development. They should be ensured of safety and health in their working place; they should be kept from night work; they should not carry heavy loads; they should be protected from excessively long working hours; they should have sufficient weekly rest periods and holidays. These call for adequate provisions in national legislation, in conformity with the standards set by the ILO, and their effective enforcement.

Children should also have access to educational opportunities, to get at least basic education and, it is to be hoped, basic vocational education to develop their potential as capable workers and responsible citizens. Where there are schools, the working hours should be so regulated that the children are able to attend classes. Where there are no schools, provision for some informal education should be made. Provision of such educational facilities falls naturally under public authorities but the responsibility for ensuring that children use such facilities naturally rests with parents and employers as well.

Further, there should be programmes to bring about a proper recognition of the needs of children among parents and the general public.

III. ILO's POLICY

1. Is the ILO Opposed to All Types of Work?

The simple answer is No. After all, child work takes many forms. In some cases, such as traditional agricultural or handicraft production, it is carried out under the supervision of parents. Work of this type is often an integral part of the socialisation process. It is a means of transmitting traditionally acquired skills from parent to child. Such work could also be a source of pride and satisfaction to the children themselves. This type of economic involvement is occasionally observed even in modern industrial societies where children may assist their families on a part-time basis or where teenagers may work for a few hours to earn additional pocket money. That is not what we are concerned about. Rather, the ILO is concerned about those situations where children are compelled to work on a regular or continuous basis to earn a living for themselves or for their families, and as a result are disadvantaged educationally and socially; where they work in conditions that are exploitative and damaging to their health and to their physical and mental development; where they are separated from their families, often deprived of educational and training opportunities; where they work as bonded labourers; where children are forced to lead prematurely adult lives, condemned to a cruel present and to a bleak future.

2. What is ILO's Policy on Child Labour?

The ILO's policy in the field of child labour derives from two inter-related but distinct objectives. The first is the effective abolition of child labour. The attainment of this objective requires countries to carry out a series of legal and socio-economic measures. Laws prohibiting admission to employment below a certain minimum age should be adopted and enforced. Socio-economic measures leading to improvements in living standards, fuller or higher levels of adult employment, and the application of compulsory schooling should be adopted in order to make child work economically unnecessary and to enhance the moral force and practical application of the law.

But the ILO recognises that the adoption and successful implementation of legal and socio-economic measures that could lead to the effective abolition of child labour will take time and that child labour will continue to be a persistent problem in large parts of the world. For this reason, its second policy objective is the protection of children at work. It therefore encourages countries to regulate the conditions under which they work, e.g. shorter hours of work, improved wages and remuneration, safer and less hazardous working conditions, etc.; it also encourages countries to provide working children with welfare facilities and services so that they can have minimum levels of education, nutrition and health protection.

IV. INTERNATIONAL LABOUR STANDARDS: PRINCIPLES AND PROTECTION OF WORKING CHILDREN?

1. Are There International Norms and Standards on Child Labour and Protection of Working Children?

Yes, there several norms and standards set up by the United Nations General Assembly as well as the International Labour Organisation to abolish child labour and to protect working children.

In 1959, for example, the United Nations General Assembly adopted the Declaration of the Rights of the Child which stressed that "mankind owes to the child the best it has to give." It also specified that "the child shall not be admitted to employment before an appropriate minimum age" and that "he shall in no case be caused or permitted to engage in any occupation or employment which would prejudice his health or education, or interfere with his physical, mental or moral development." These same principles were later reaffirmed in the International Covenant on Economic, Social and Cultural Rights adopted by the General Assembly in 1966.

But certainly the most extensive standards on the subject are those adopted by the International Labour Organisation in the from of Conventions and Recommendations defining the conditions, terms and areas of employment and work. These go as far back as 1919 and there are today well over 20

Conventions and Recommendations on the subject, the most recent and comprehensive being the Minimum Age Convention, 1973 (No. 138), and the accompanying Recommendation, 1973 (No. 146).

2. What are Conventions and Recommendations?

Conventions are comparable to multilateral international treaties: they are open to ratification by member States and, once ratified, create specific, binding obligations. A state that has ratified a Convention is expected to apply its provisions by legislation or other appropriate means as indicated in the text of the Convention. The Government is required to report regularly on the application of ratified Conventions; the extent of compliance is subject to examination and public comment by ILO machinery; complaints about alleged non-compliance may be made by the governments of their ratifying States or by employers' or workers' organisations and procedures exist for investigating and acting upon such complaints. Conventions that have not been ratified have the same value as Recommendations.

Recommendation are intended to offer guide-lines for action by member States. Often, a particular Recommendation will elaborate upon the provisions of a Convention on the same subject. Member States have certain important procedural obligations in respect of Recommendations — namely, to submit the texts to their legislative bodies, to report on the action result and to report occasionally at the request of the Governing Body on the measures takes or envisaged to give effect to the provisions. But no specific substantive obligations are entailed.

3. What is the Relevance of These International Labour Standards (or Conventions and Recommendations)?

ILO standards (i.e. Conventions and Recommendations) have a moral (political) and practical value, it is fair to say that ILO standards have exerted considerable influence on the laws and regulations of member States. Many texts have been modelled on the relevant provisions of ILO instruments; drafts of new legislation or amendments are often prepared with ILO standards in mind; trade unions use ILO standard to support arguments in bargaining and in promoting legislation; governments frequently consult the ILO, both formally and informally, about the compatibility of proposed texts with international labour standards.

The ILO's role is, however, more than that. It also exercises a supervisory role. The Office has the constitutional mandate to prepare detailed reports on the application of international standards and summarising national law and practice on specific subjects. Although the process can be slow, its observations often lead to changes in laws and regulations.

The extent to which national laws and regulations themselves are applied in practice is a more difficult question. The ILO's supervisory machinery does inquire as far as possible into practice as well as law. Governments must supply information on the practical implementation of ratified Conventions. Moreover, national employers' and workers' organisations have the right to participate in the supervisory process by receiving copies of reports sent to the ILO and submitting comments on the application of ratified Conventions. These comments often relate to the way in which the Conventions are applied in practice. On several occasions, pursuant to complaints or Conference resolutions and with the agreement of the government concerned, the ILO has sent special missions to various countries.

Clearly, a country's economic and social conditions, the government's material capacity for enforcement, the value that government places on national laws and regulations, and the vigilance of employers' and workers' organisations determine how those laws and regulations are applied. Even so, this qualification does not diminish the importance of ILO standards: they are a strong normative force; they have widely been reflected in national laws and regulations; and their implementation at least at the statutory level is effectively supervised by ILO machinery.

4. What is the Most Important International Labour Convention on the Subject?

As is said earlier, there are a number of ILO Conventions on the abolition of child labour and the protection of working children. But the most important of these is the Minimum Age Convention, 1973 (No. 138) and the accompanying Minimum Age Recommendation, 1973 (No. 146).

5. What are the Major Provisions of the Minimum Age Convention, 1973 (No. 138)?

The major elements of this Convention are described in Chapter 10 and 11. Briefly, however, the two most important ones are those that require member States:

(a) to specify a minimum age for admission to employment and to raise it progressively to a level consistent with the fullest physical and mental development of young persons; and

(b) to ensure that the minimum age for admission to employment shall not be less than the age of completion of compulsory schooling and, in any case, shall not be less than 15 years.

6. Does the Minimum age Limit of 15 Apply for every Country and for all Types of Work?

No. The Convention makes provisions for differences in levels of development and the nature of the work in which children are engaged. For example, a country whose economy and educational facilities are insufficiently developed may specify a minimum age of 14. In addition, the Convention sets a lower minimum age for light work, while it sets a higher age limit for heavy work. So while the Convention sets a minimum age of 15 for admission to employment, it has sufficient flexibility to accommodate the needs of countries at various levels of development and of children in different types of work situations.

7. What is the Real Value of These International Labour Standards and of National Laws on Child Labour Since, Given the Poverty of Their Families, Children will have to Continue to Work?

The first part of this question has already been answered indirectly under question IV. 3 above, where it was said that international labour standards provide both a common basis for international dialogue and a framework for drawing up national laws, regulations and programmes of practical action on labour and social matters. Take, for example, international standards on child labour. A survey of 107 countries conducted by the ILO, as part of its supervisory duties, concerning the application of the Minimum Age Convention, 1973 (No. 138), and Recommendation, 1973 (No. 146), showed that the principle of minimum age for admission to employment or work had been universally recognised. There was not a single State among all those which provided information which had not set some standards in this field. A number of countries have incorporated the ILO's Conventions on various aspects of the subject in their legislation.

But, even so, it may still be asked what the value of national laws and regulations is, given the poverty in large parts of the Third World and the difficulties of enforcing laws and regulations.

It must be stressed that child labour laws are not intended to supplant, or be carried out apart from, socio-economic changes; they are intended to reinforce and complement them wherever possible, to deal with the worst forms of the exploitation of children wherever they exist and to provide minimum levels of protection wherever such labour is unavoidable.

National legal standards also serve as a benchmark against which progress can be assessed. Far more importantly, they serve to provide minimum standards of protection. There are, after all, certain absolutes arising from the inherent dignity of the human person and recognised in international convenants which nations, irrespective of their level of development, have accepted and should adhere to, both in the formulation of labour laws and in their subsequent enforcement. Minimum standards enshrined in national laws help to provide the minimum protection to the human person; and such laws need not, or should not, await structural changes or significant improvements in general standards of living. As the Director-General said in his Report to the 1983 International Labour Conference, "To dismiss in a cavalier way, as some do, the potential role of child labour protective laws, or to invoke the pretext of poverty and underdevelopment for the continued transgression of universally accepted values, is to accept the perpetuation of universally condemned abuses."

Chapter 9

Social Implications of Child Labour

"Children not only make the home—they subject it to constant alternations."

—Herb Nelson

"A baby is an angel whose wings decrease as his legs increase."

—Early French Saying

Child is not only the future of a nation and its aspirations but also, and mainly, its strength in reserve. The future of nation is best insured if its children are healthy and active, educated and informed, disciplined and trained, as well as free from social prejudices, having a scientific outlook. It is, therefore a duty cast on the society at large to protect this crop of nation from the damaging effects of excessive exposure to vagaries of climate, as well as, from social oppression and injustice.

The childhood is the most significant period of one's life. It is considered, and rightly so, to be the very foundation of life on which depends the entire structure-the whole personality as such. Child—the father of man—is the natural future leader of the nation in every walk of life, may it be industry, education, politics, social services, administration, defence, civil services or anything else. It is during this formative period of moulding that the life begins to acquire shape and substance, and the attitudes, behaviours, manners and emotions do get developed.

The over-all and long ranging consequences of the practice and tradition of child labour that it deserves to be placed high on the list of our priorities. Then comes the question of ways and means by which this problem should be tackled, and they would, and should, very from situation to situation. However, in each and every case it is imperative that it should be preceded by collection of facts and figures, dissemination of information, understanding of the nature of the problem and a reasonably high level of social concern for mitigation of this centuries old.

The term 'child labour' is, at times, used as a synonym for 'employed child' or 'working child.' In this sense it is co-existensive with any work done by a child for profit or reward. But more commonly than not, the term 'child labour' is used in a derogatory sense. It suggests something which is hateful and exploitative. Thus, child labour is recognised by the sociologists, development workers, educationists and medical professionals as hazardous and injurious to the child, both physically and mentally.

Homer Folks, the Chairman of the United States National Child Labour Committee, has defines child labour as "... any work by children that interferes with their full physical development, their opportunities for a desirable minimum of education or their needed recreation."

Wage labour is rather too narrow a criterion. For the wider connotation we have to include in it the notion of income earning activities which is beset with problems. The main difficulty lies in determining as to what constitutes contribution to the income of families and households. We have to include in it the usual household duties, such as, cooking, fetching water, looking after the kids, etc., as indirect contribution to household income for the wider and more useful definition.

It would be pertinent to add that in the case of a child, the labour is specially harmful to him because the energy that should have been expended on the nurturing of his latent powers gets consumed for purposes of bare survival. Child labour, therefore, assumes, the character of a social problem in as much as it hinders, arrests or distorts the natural growth processes and prevents the child from attaining his full bloom manhood.

As such child labour, in a restricted sense, means the engagement of children in gainful occupations which are often hazardous to their health, and deny them the opportunities of development. Three factors should, therefore, be necessarily present in employment/engagement of a child so as to bring it within the concept of child labour. Firstly, the child should be engaged in some gainful activities; secondly, the work to which he is exposed, must be detrimental to his natural growth; thirdly, it must deprive him of the opportunity for development. Hence, obviously, any work taken by a father from his child on his field or at his business place for long hours also gets covered by this definition, but any work done by the students at school workshops cannot be termed as 'child labour.'

Unfortunately, in India, there is no such statutory provision which defines the term 'child labour' in precise terms. Even the numerous legislative provisions which prescribe the minimum age for employment in different vocations do not fix any uniform age, presumably, for reasons of multiplicity in the nature of activities in which children are employed. The minimum age for entrance into the labour market has not been precisely fixed by law or convention, either at the national or the international level. Hence, child labour should be understood in the context of given circumstance and the nature of occupation. According to generally prevalent conceptions, the child labour normally constitutes children between the age group of 14 to 17 years.

The accurate and precise estimate of the overall magnitude of child labour, either from a qualitative or quantitative point of view, is virtually not possible due to the predominance of informal and unorganised nature of the labour market. The problem of estimating the child labour force becomes all the more complicated and complex on account of the multiplicity of concepts, modes of measurement, methods of research and the sources of information for data collection.

A report published by the Director General of International Labour Organisation in 1960 says:

"Children and youth make up a fifth, or a fourth or even a third of the total labour force in many of the industrialising countries. Young people between 15, to 19 make up 20 per cent of the labour force of the Egyptian Region of the United Arab Republic, and a higher percentage in many of the less developed Asian and African countries; and it should be noted that in most of the less developed areas the great bulk of children seek to enter the labour force by the time they are 12, 13 or 14, if they have not begun to work at a much earlier age."

The Report IV (1) of the 57th Session of the International Labour Conference, Geneva, 1972, indicates that 90 per cent or more of the child population was engaged in the employment market in the developing regions of the world. The report has also indicate that 4,11,25,000 children of these regions, making 5.1 per cent of the whole of 0-14 age group, were engaged in 1960; and in 1970 the number was reduced to 3,99,75,000 which formed 4 per cent of all children. In the industrialised areas the number of child workers in the year 1960 was 40,85,000 which formed 1.4 per cent of all children and in 1970 the number was 33,43,000, constituting 1.1 per cent of the total number of children. Geographically, the 1960 and 1970 figures given in Table-1.

Since the 1960s, considerable progress has been made in the reducing child labour, largely due to the expansion of primary education in developing countries. But, it is still widespread in the Third World's agricultural sector, the informal urban sector and domestic services. However, this improvement has been uneven and far from universal, leaving many millions of children exposed to premature death or maiming in dangerous occuapations.

TABLE 1: PERCENTAGE OF CHILD WORKERS TO CHILD POPULATION IN DIFFERENT REGIONS OF THE WORLD IN 1960 AND 1970

Regions	*1960*	*Percentage*	*1970*	*Percentage*
Africa	60,55,000	5.2	59,92,000	4.0
North America	2,82,000	0.5	3,11,000	0.5
Latin America including Caribbean	31,59,000	3.6	31,22,000	2.6
East Asia	83,05,000	2.9	58,30,000	1.9
South Asia including India	2,39,85,000	6.8	2,53,71,000	5.4
Europe	20,70,000	1.9	16,00,000	1.4
Oceania excluding Micronesia and Polynesia 26,000			33,000 0.5	0.7
U.S.S.R. 10,66,000			13,21,000 1.5	2.0

According to a recent International Labour Organisation study on the exploitation of young children in hazardous industries in the developing world, as many as 200 million children, under the age of 15, are workers, excluding those who help on family farms and small holdings.

The data available from the International Labour Organisation's *Year Book of Labour Statistics*, 1988, indicates that in absolute terms the number of child labour is the highest in India but percentage-wise it is not so.

In respect to India, a general idea can be had from the census of 1971, which shows that 10.7 million children were engaged in employment. Out of them only 0.7 million, constituting 7 per cent, were working in urban areas, the remaining 10 million, that is, 93 per cent were employed in rural areas. 36.1 per cent of the child labour was employed as cultivators and 42.7 per cent as agricultural labourers. The remaining 8.2 per cent were employed in animal husbandry, forestry, fishing, hunting, plantation and horticulture, etc., 6.1 per cent in house-hold and industries, 2.4 per cent in trade, commerce, transport, storage and communication, and the rest in construction work, mining and other types of services. The Indian States and the Union Territories with proportions higher than the national average of child workers are Andhra Pradesh, Karnataka, Madhya Pradesh, Meghalaya, Nagaland, Orissa, Rajasthan, Arunachal Pradesh and Dadra and Nagar Haveli.

A non-governmental organisation, named as, Concerned, for Working Children (CWC), claims that 1,000 million children are at work in India, but the Operations Research Group (ORG) Baroda, puts the figure at 44 million only. However, the findings of the ORG have gained more credibility in the welfare circles since they are based on a nation-wide survey.

Nature of Child Labour

From time immemorial it has been the practice that children were to engage themselves in some sort of work or the other, both in home and in the field. In olden days, children of tender age performed even toilsome work alongwith adult agricultural and other workers. In the mediaeval period, children used to be engaged as trainees under the guidance of their parents to learn traditional crafts of the family.

The earlier reports of the Royal Commission on Labour, the Labour Investigation Committee on working conditions of children and a number of surveys conducted by the Labour Bureau and other non-governmental agencies-all invariably focus on one point that children do light work in comparison to adult workers. But, it is no more true now. These days they do not less a hard work than their parents in order to earn enough for their family's survival.

The social scenario, according tot he report of Gurupadaswami Committee on Child Labour, changed radically with the advent of industrialisation and urbanisation. The Committee further says: ".... The family members no longer worked as a team and in caste sanctioned occupations. The child had to work as an individual person either under an employer or independently without enjoying the benevolent protection of his guardian. His work place was divorced and totally dissimilar from his home. His job exposed him to various kinds of health hazards emanating from the extensive use of chemicals and poisonous substances in industries and the pollutants discharged by them. His work was reputitive, monotonous and unpromising. His hours of work stretched long but his earnings were meagre. His employer, in most of the instances, maltreated him and exploited him unscrupulously. His work environment thus endangered his physical health and mental growth."

Alone, in agriculture, children are employed not only in agricultural operations but in non-agricultural operations also. They are employed in such diverse agricultural operations as ploughing, sowing, transplanting, weeding, harvesting threshing and guarding the crops, etc.

In plantations, child labour is a part of family labour. They assist their parents in plucking of leaves and coffee berries, or collecting of latex, or they do some secondary jobs, such as, weeding spreading of fertilisers, the care of nurseries, digging of drains, etc. They are also employed to pick out stalks and coarse leaves of tea spread over the green leaves in the shadow.

There is also an increasing concern about the accident and disease incidence among child agricultural workers. Controls on hazardous insecticides and pesticides are deficient and neither the children nor their parents receive any instruction as how to use them safely. The same is true of mechanical operations.

Children in cities per form much larger varieties of activities than those in village because of the extensively diversified structure of urban economies. Often, children are employed for packing, labelling, etc., in the factories. Other industries in which children are engaged are match factories, bidi manufacturing, mica cutting, wood and cork, furniture and fixture, printing, publishing and allied trades, leather products, rubber and rubber products, machinery, transport equipment, lock, factories, gem cutting and polishing, potteries, glass bangle industries, brass work, carpet industries and personal services like laundries, dyeing and cleaning.

Millions of small boys and girls are engaged in the unorganised sector, comprising hotels, restaurants, canteens, wayside 'dhabas,' shops, repair workshops, and establishments of various types. They also work as hawkers, coolies, shoe-shine boys and venders. In big cities, children can be seen cleaning and washing automobiles just for a tip. The bigger the city, the higher is the persistent demand for teenagers to work as domestic servants and it is there that they are often subjected to worst types of exploitation without any means of protections-legal or social. Thee young servants are malnourished, often made to sleep on the kitchen floor and are, as a rule, not permitted to attend school. Frequent reports are there of Sexual abuse.

The most nefarious, rather barbarian form of child exploitation is the practice of bonded labour. The child is handed over by the parents to the loaner as security or collateral security against small sums of loan obtained at an exorbitant rate of interest. The bonded child usually gets only a handful of coarse grain for his subsistance. He has to toil very hard and exist at the mercy of his lord for the whole of his life without the least hope of redemption. The mortgagee is usually some big landlord, money-lender or the village businessman, and the mortgager is the poor landless labourer. Though this practices is prevalent in many parts of rural India, it is predominant in Vellore district of Tamil Nadu but with a distinguishing feature that there the bonded child is allowed to stay with his parents on the condition that he must present himself at work daily at 8 a.m. The practice of bonded labour is still prevalent despite stringent laws against it which provide for imprisonment of, and imposition of fine on, the guilty. Though strange, but it is true that the owners or managers of the lock industry of Aligarh also take in orphans as "purchased labour" and when their premises are inspected by the law enforcement authorities they try to get away on the plea that the orphan is no other a person than his own son.

It has been also discovered that a sizable number of children ranging between 5 to 12 years of age had actually been kidnapped from different places to weave carpets and were forced to work for as long as 22 hours a day. These children treated like virtual slaves, were found to bear scar marks of torture. They were, reportedly, severely beaten even with iron rods, if they were difficient in work or committed errors in weaving. Thus, a closer look would go to show that child labour far from being uniform in pattern and magnitude, is by and large concentrated in certain specific activities and industries. Moreover, there appears to be considerable variance in the form, quantum and intensity of exploitation.

Juvenile Delinquency

Due to rapid growth of industrialisation and urbanisation, a fairly large number of people migrate from rural to urban areas in search of gainful employment or vocation. This situation greatly hampers and disrupts the stability of the traditional family life and its basic structure, and also diminishes the capability of the family to discharge effectively its responsibilities towards children. In order to supplement the meagre and irregular income of the family, children of the migrated families are left with no choice but to go to the market to sell their labour power. It not only adversely effect their physical and mental health and natural growth, and, side by side mars their future economic prospects, but also creates manifold problems of delinquency which is more frequent among children who work in street shops and as domestic servants. The child gets paid some money, howsoever meagre, for his services. It develops a feeling of independence, though wrongly in the mind of child labour. As the child is not well capable of differentiating between the good and the bad, he is likely to mis-spent the money which he had earned at a very heavy cost.

The parents and other family members fast lose the control, nay, even the moral authority, over the child labour, who soon begins to imitate his adult fellow workers, mistaking them to be their ideals. The illiterate child, having freed himself from the family ties, becomes susceptible to all sorts of evil influences which may turn him into a heavy smoker, a drug-addict, a gambler, a smuggling operator, a film addict, a thief, a pick-pocket, or even a hard criminal. Such children are often seen to be in the habit of using filthy and abusive language. Some of them soon leave their home for good to live with their gangs. These children, as a rule, leave their home very early in the morning and return to their parental shelter after sunset. The parents also return home from their work almost at the same time. Consequently, they hardly have sufficient time at their disposal to be with their children. This results into neglect of the children, and lack of supervision of, and control over, them. Guidance is conspicuous by its absence in such homes, and all the more so when the parents happen to be illiterate.

This is the sage how grows a whole race of children, bodily and mentally ill-equipped, in a psycho-socio environment of privation and desperate struggle for existence, face to face with the predatory demands of the exploiting world. Their efforts at preparation for adult-hood are cruelly shattered and crumbled by the tentacles of the monster of greed, oppression and inhumanity and by the time they acquire maturity, they are a lot of bruised and impaired individuals.

Obviously that the child labour is fruitful neither for the child himself, nor his family or the society. Therefore, in dealing with the problem of child labour and delinquency, the cost benefits, resource constraints and other considerations should not be allowed to dampen the spirit of the status because they aim to serve the larger interests of the society as such.

Desirability of Work for Children

According to *Encyclopaedia of Social Sciences:*

> "Every child labourer is a called with all the needs of other children. He needs opportunity for growth not only physical, but in mind and personality, through all the activities and experiences, which properly belong to childhood, when the business of wage earning, or of participation in self or family support, conflicts directly or indirectly, with the business of growth and education, the social evil of child labour becomes evident."

Some claim that child labour has certain welcome implications, such as, transmission of skills, evolution of attitude to work, industrial discipline, socialisation, class consciousness and operation of labour market. In addition to this, the advocates of child labour assert that "some types of work are a source of pride, status and perhaps independence for the children themselves."

The Report on "Child Labour in Indian Industries" says: "Taking a global view of the situation in which India features prominently, the International Labour Organisation came to the conclusion: The problem with child labour is that it can hardly be legislated away, for its roots lie in abject poverty.

Where social and economic conditions have improved, children go to school and child labour has virtually disappeared. So any society which wants its children to be free to learn and play must first free the entire population from fear of want. This means ensuring basic human needs of all people.".

The International Labour Organisation, in its report of 1980, also holds that child labour in general should be gradually eliminated because of:

(i) the physical and mental havoc wrought by it;

(ii) the displacement of adult workers in effect by child workers; and

(iii) the lowering of adult earning power due to its prevalence.

However, in the prevailing economic conditions of India, the total eradication of child labour does not appear to be feasible though much desirable. Though the ultimate aim of every society must,, undoubtedly, be complete eradication of child labour, the least we can do is to try our level best to minimise the evils of child labour and prohibit it in hazardous occupations in view of the fact that, under present circumstances, total eradication of child labour, at one stretch, would amount to inflicting unbearable sufferings on the poverty-ridden families.

Supporters of child labour argue and, perhaps, believe also that children who go to work at a very early age tend to acquire the habit of being industrious and labourious which is profitable for them in the long run because they become well trained workers at an early age. Many employers, exhibiting benevolent pride in their child labour force, assert that the child who starts working at a very early age soon gets to know his work and the value of money which takes him to higher success in his later life.

The National Commission on Labour was told by some

of the employers that unless the fingers get trained at a very early age when they are nimble, there adaptation later on to the requirements of work would be indeed difficult. The employers also agrued that handicrafts, like carpet weaving, cannot do without the child's nimble fingers, and so is the case with cottage industries like that of match sticks and fire works which save so much of foreign exchange for the country.

It is also argued on behalf of the supporters of child labour that the children of master-craftsmen get to learn their skills from their parents and then themselves develop into master-craftsmen.

The employers often advance the argument that by employing children they help them to increase the income of their families. The employment also saves them from becoming indolent and vagabonds or anti-social. Thus, they argue, it is the sympathy for the poor and the needy, rather than the desire to exploit them, which motivates them to employ children. When the employment of children increases the earnings of the family, it keeps the children away from mischief, they argue. No civilised nation can afford to take the risk of destroying the lives of its children who are the embodiment of all the hopes and aspirations for the country's future prosperity and progress. They represent the destiny of the nation itself.

Protection Against Exploitation

One of the most weighty arguments against child labour is that it accelerates and quantifies adult unemployment, and is indirectly instrumental for under-scaling of their wages. It has been estimated that if the children engaged in gainful occupations are ejected totally then it will, to a great extent, cure the country, automatically, of the inimical problem of unemployment, because atleast 15 million vacancies would be created thereby for the adult unemployed persons.

Karl Marx had observed that the result of buying children

and young persons of under age by the capitalists is physical deterioration and moral degradation. Some of the social thinkers see the source of the problem of delinquency in child labour. They say that this practice not only effects the health of children but also creates the problem of delinquency which must be paid for by the society.

S.W. Woodward, criticised the child labour by saying that, "Employment at too early an age belighted a child's economic prospects; it may be stated as a safe preposition that for every dollar earned by a child under fourteen years of age ten fold will be taken away from its earning capacity in later years."

Thus, so far as the projects for development of human resources are concerned, the programme for welfare of children must be given top priority. It is only in this way that children can be trained to be good future citizen, mentally alert and prosperous. We should aim at providing proper and equal opportunities for development to all children in the light of the above mentioned constitutional directives. It is only then that we can fulfil our aspirations, and achieve objectives of social justice and equality enshrined in the Constitution of India.

REFERENCES

Agnivesh, Swami, in his Public Interest Litigation before the Supreme Court in Bandhua Mukti Morcha vs. Union of India, AIR 1984 SC 802.

Chandra, Ramesh (1961), "Effect of Law Income on the Size of Labour Force and Unemployment in India," *Indian Labour Journal*, p. 1164.

Encyclopaedia of Social Sciences, Vol. III, pp. 412-413.

Giri, V.V. (1958), *Labour Problems in Indian Industries*, Asia Publishing House, Bombay, p. 360.

Government of India (1954), "*Child Labour in India*".

Hull, Terence (1981) "Perspectives and Data Requirements for the Study of Children's Work," *Child Work, Poverty and Underdevelopment*, ed. Rodgers and Standing, 49.

International Labour Organisation's Report (1990) published in *The Hindustan Times*, May 2.

Jain, S.N. (1982), "Preventive Legal Measures in the Area of Child Labour," read at the National Seminar on Child and the Law, Organised by National Institute of Public Co-operation and Child Development, New Delhi.

Karl Marx, *Das Kapital*, Ch. XV sec. 3-a.

Mathur, Deep (1984), While They Should Have Been Playing. *The Hindustan Times*, August 19.

Report IV-1 of the 57th Session of the International Labour Conference (1972), Geneva.

Report of National Commission on Labour (1969), p. 386.

Report of the Committee on Child Labour (1979), p. 7.

Report of the Director General (1960), International Labour Organisation; Youth and Work (Part I).

Report on Child Labour in Indian Industries (1981), p. 7.

Schindkrout, Enid (1981), The Employment of Children in Kano (Nigeria), *Child Work, Poverty and Underdevelopment*, ed. Rogers and Standing, 95.

Sengupta, Padmini: *Child Labour as a Social Problem*, (Unpublished).

Woodward, S.W.: "A Businessman's Views on Child Labour," *Charities and the Commons*, XV (1905-6) pp. 800-1.

Chapter 10

Impact of Child Labour

'We sow our thoughts and reap our actions.
We sow our actions and reap our habits.
We sow our habits and reap our characters.
We sow our characters and reap our destiny."

—*C.A. Hall*

Asia is thought to have the largest child worker population in the world. India alone of officially said to have 17.36 million child workers, more than anywhere else, comprising 5.9 per cent of the total labour force—some 93 per cent of these child workers are in the rural areas (UN Seminar, 1985); and yet, other estimates for India talk of 54 million and 100 million. In Africa, 20 per cent of children under 15 are said to be working and in some African cities, children constitute 17 per cent of the total work-force. In Latin America, estimate between 12 and 26 per cent have been put forward for some countries (ILO Paper, UN Seminar, 1985).

Obviously much more rigorous work needs to be done in this area, but it is in no state's interest to have an accurate picture of the extent of child work, and only recently has the subject attracted social scientists. If we are to attain a better understanding of child work then we shall need to place it within the broader framework of the institution of childhood which has attracted the attention of historians, sociologists and anthropologists. Here one is reminded of Anna Freud's depiction of childhood as a phenomenon which taxed of defied our understanding. Nevertheless, it would be useful to explore childhood in an historical context, at least to begin with, in order to obtain a view on how we have arrived at the various perceptions of what is desirable or undesirable for children.

It was Philippe Aries in his classic *Centuries of Childhood,* who first put forward the thesis that childhood is a modern Western invention. According to Aries, 'there was no place for childhood in the medieval world' (Jenks, 1982, p. 31). The infant who could not participate in the adult world simply did not count. Only gradually in the sixteenth and seventeenth centuries do we witness, in the art of the times, the child or infant of the upper strata depicted in special dress and thereby distinguished from adults. By the eighteenth century everything to do with children's health and education had become established as a concern worthy of serious attention. By the end of that century childhood had been established by Blake and Wordsworth as a major literary theme, something which was to continue well into the nineteenth century with Dickens, Mark Twain and Tolstoy.

The seventeenth century appears then as a watershed in the evolution modern institution of childhood. 'Baby,' 'child' and 'youth' were interchangeable terms prior to the modern age. The child in medieval society was fully integrated from the earliest age into all aspect of daily life including education, work and play, Children were treated as if they were expendable, as indeed they were. Even in the early nineteenth century the English essayist Charles Lamb could remark in a letter to a friend '..... we have had a sick child, who, sleeping or not sleeping, next to me, with a pasteboard partition between, killed my sleep. The little bastard is gone' (Schorsch, 1979 p. 11). At the end of the fifteenth century the numbers seven and fourteen were already associated with childhood. Seven was the beginning of the rite of passage for boys, when apprenticeship contracts were drawn up, and by 14 schooling in reading, writing and religion was over, as was apprenticeship. Girls were even less likely to survive infancy and were regarded as a liability by medieval parents until married off as early as 12 (if a sufficiently attractive dowry could be provided). Girls were less likely to have been schooled and would remain subordinated to men throughout life. The Reformation, with its encouragement of individualism, also helped to establish the individuality of the child. By the end of the seventeenth century each child was regarded as having a soul of its own and was given its own name. This separation had its price in the growing institutional constraints on the child's freedom. Parents, the Church, moralists, and educators all came to circumscribe the world of the child, who was deemed to need both protection and a prolonged period of training.

Today we have come a long way from the romantic view of innocent childhood in which children were depicted as 'little angels' who are 'close to God.' Today childhood in industrialised countries is problematic, protracted, ill-defined, and the centre of vehement claims and counter-claims concerning 'what is best for the child.' Childhood has spawned an army of child-care professional experts in the new sciences of pedagogy, paediatrics, psychology and psychoanalysis (Ennew, 1986a). The modern conception of childhood, invented and sustained by adults, has two key features. Firstly, a rigid age hierarchy which separates children from adults. This institutionalisation of childhood is marked by special dress, games, language and literature. Secondly, the myth of childhood innocence where the child must be both happy and separated from the corrupt adult world. This becomes expressed in the child-cared family which is determined materially if in no other way to make these the best years of life.

These adult modes and prescriptions have been codified into international standards expressed in Declarations, Covenants and Charters. These date back to the early part of this century and express a protective view of childhood. In such instruments the child cannot by definition be a worker in the formal economy, but requires a protracted period of socialisation in which schooling becomes the acceptable from of 'work' for the child. Children have become in these circumstances economic dependents and liabilities. And school-days are seen as a golden age.

Nevertheless, there are physiological criteria which provide clear broad stages in childhood and its separation from adulthood. These are: infancy (0-5), pre-pubertal childhood (6-2), and post pubertal childhood (12 to adulthood or majority). The age of adulthood is now expressed by the Draft UN Convention on the Rights of the Child as 'being eighteen unless, under the law of his/her state he/she has reached his/her age of majority earlier.' In the end one returns to the simplest of all definitions of a child by chronological age which itself differs from state to state.

Children have always worked and today where families need help, in developed and developing countries, children will and do continue to work. Work has always been part of a wider set of childhood activities which is the starting point for any classification and analysis of children's economic role. Here the most comprehensive conceptual framework to date is that of Rodgers and Standing. The authors distinguish ten childhood activities: domestic work; non-domestic work; non-monetary work; tied or bonded labour; wage labour, marginal economic activities; schooling; idleness and unemployment; recreation and leisure; and reproductive activities (Rodgers and Standing, 1981, pp. 2-11).

Typically, cooking, cleaning, child care and other domestic duties are under taken to some extent by children in all societies. Such duties form part of the socialisation process and cannot, according to the International Labour Organisation, be termed child labour (Blanchard, 1983, p. 18). But domestic work, as it has been defined, becomes 'social exploitation' if it denies children their right to play, to learn and to enjoy a normal childhood. Many children, especially girls, do miss educational and recreational opportunities because of a heavy domestic work burden. Though domestic work does not of itself produce in income it is economically important because it facilitates adult work, freeing parents to go out to earn money, Such domestic work can begin very early, especially in developing counters, where the starting age can be as low as five or less. Though girls often carry the heaviest burden of preparing food, cleaning the house, washing the clothes and looking after younger brothers and sisters, boys too, in countries as diverse as Peru, Jamaica and India, play their part.

Nevertheless, boys tend to do less, particularly in the case of child care, though there are examples where pre-pubertal boys share domestic duties with girls. But not all domestic work takes place within the child's own family. There are the 'maids-of-all-work' in developing countries, whom professor Boudhiba described as virtual slaves (Boudhiba, 1982, p. 46). These girls tend to come from rural areas to the home of an urban 'relative' who undertakes to look after them and provide them with an education. But they are usually being framed out to distant, if not fictional, relatives where they need not be paid for being on call virtually 24 hours a day. Being strangers to the city and isolated from their parents, they are powerless to change their position. Domestic work is not only an unrecognised form of economic contribution, it remains unappreciated as a from of child labour.

Non-domestic, non-monetary work forms a continuum with domestic work, especially in subsistence economies. It encompasses such time-consuming activities as looking after animals, protecting fields from pests, weeding, etc. Analytically, this category can be broken down depending on whether the production is for the family's consumption or for the market, and whether the child is working for its own benefit, or for parents, for relatives, or for strangers. This form of child work for no pay of widely viewed as the largest sector of child work in the world. At the first UN Seminar on Child Labour, delegates from developing countries stressed that this type of work expressed family solidarity and therefore was not subject to exploitative relationships. Exploitation occurs, they contended, when third parties are involved, usually in an urban context. Thus, logically, child labour cannot be a major problem. The anthropological evidence, though non-quantitative, tends to undermine this blithe assumption. The idea that rural children learn as they work and are, therefore, experiencing a traditional form of socialisation rather than exploitation, ignores the extent to which even simple societies are not integrated into cash economies and are subject to agricultural capitalism. In reality, children are involved from the age of five or six in hard labour in agrarian communities. One study of family labour among pastoralists in the Sahel has shown that children often perform much harder work than adult and such work often express a sexual division of labour: 'The boys look after the sheep, gather wood, collect fodder, draw water, sow and reap. The girl milk, cook, spin, look after the younger children. The country child is invariably a working child and work is a fundamental part of his/her existence' (Mendelievich, 1979, p. 128).

The term 'cottage industry,' in which the child works at home, should not obscure the real costs to healthy child development that it often entails. In the Indian glassware industry in Moradabad, Uttar Pradesh, nearly one-quarter of the work-force are children who work in all but one of the processes, either at home, or in workshops. Long hours, heat, gases and dust, leave many children with eye injuries and lung diseases. Working as part of a family unit is, therefore, no protection if the family is subject to exploitation, as for example within plantation labour or crafts manufacture. Children working outside of their parental home on a fostering, adopted, godchild, apprenticeship basis, find themselves even more the hostages to fortune in the face of isolation and powerlessness. To be a slave is to reach the limits of powerlessness. In Indian some children work for either a money lender or landowner as bonded labour to pay off he debts of parents or even grandparents.

But this can easily become a contract for life: 'Sometimes, his parents or, when he grows older, he himself may take further loans, get deeper into debt and continue to work as a bonded labourer without any possibility of release,' (Blanchard, 1979, p. 55). This form of intergenerational debt resembles a feudal landlord-tenant relationship in which the child is pledged to work for the landlord or money lender, in order that a debt be paid off, or to obtain a loan or some other benefits. It continues in India despite attempts to outlaw it, most notably by the Bonded Labour System (Abolition) Act 1976.

Child-wage labour exploitation is the easiest to document and, therefore, to campaign and legislate against. But there is ample evidence that child-wage labourers continue to work even when minimum age legislation exists. It is small-scale enterprises or 'sweatshops,' often operating as subcontractors to larger enterprises, that are most adapt at avoiding the usually inadequate factory insepectorate. Child-wage labour is a feature of developed and developing countries, and one which increases adult unemployment and lowers overall wages. Children are the most subordinate and cheapest form of labour, thus highly attractive to some types of employer, be they in Britain or Bangladesh. The child-wage sector can, according to Rodgers and Standing (p. 7), be analysed in terms of the following criteria: family or individual basis; method of payment—time rate or piece—share cropping system; work with a training component and without; regular or casual work and seasonal work; legal or illegal work; work compatible with schooling and work competitive with schooling. The most difficult cases to document are those in which children earn an income in the informal (marginal) non-waged sector, such as car washing, shoe shining, market trading and garbage collecting. It also includes such illegal activities as begging, petty theft and prostitution. Economists have been reluctant to analyse the informal, as opposed to the formal, sector of the economy, and yet the two are intertwined and their activities are vital to the survival of poor people, especially in urban areas. Many of these activities take place on the street, leading to the exotic phenomenon of 'street children.' This category has been notoriously difficult to define, covering as it does children who retain contact with a family and a home to those relative few who appear totally abandoned to their 'mother the street'—the true outcasts.

The Minority Rights Group Report of 1985 suggested that it was through work that most child exploitation takes place. But when does child work become explorative? There have been many attempts at defining exploitation in this context, however the most comprehensive formulation has been put forward by UNICEF in its 1986 Executive Board Paper (UNICEF, 1986c, pp. 3-4):

1. *Starting full time work at too early an age*
   This happened historically in the earlier stages of industrialisation in Europe where children began work in factories from nine, eight or even five years., This is still the case today in many developing countries.
2. *Working too long* within or outside of the family so that children are unable to attend school, where it is available, or to make the most of school due to fatigue or lack of time. In some cases children still work 12-16 hours a day.
3. Work resulting in *excessive physical, social and psychological strains* upon the child as in the case of sexual exploitation in prostitution and pornography, work in sweatshops, as well as such dangerous work as military service and mining.

4. *Work and life on the streets* in unhealthy and dangerous conditions.
5. *Inadequate remuneration* for working outside of the family as in the case of child workers in carpet weaving who are paid US$ 3.00 for a 60-hour week.
6. *Too much responsibility too early* as in the domestic situation where children under ten may have to look after young brothers are sisters for a hole day thereby preventing school attendance.
7. *Work that does not facilitate the psychological and social development* of the child as in dull and repetitive tasks associated with industries like handicrafts.
8. *Work that inhibits the child's self-esteem* as in bonded labour and prostitution, and in a less extreme case the negative perception of 'street children.'

This framework accommodates the traditional view that the term exploitation has something to do with a third party who extracts a profit for instance, via exploiter/employer and exploited/employee relationships. But, more importantly, it goes beyond it to embrace a 'social exploitation' dimension by acknowledging work in the informal sector (where the family can be the exploiter), as well as the human rights dimension recognising children's subordinate position in society.

The analysis of indices of exploitation is crucial to distinguishing child work from child labour, and therefore to the setting of priorities and policies. There has been an almost universal tendency hitherto in the literature to use child work and child labour almost interchangeably as if they were synonymous. In fact, child labour is a sub-set of child work, denoting that work which is exploitative of the child. Child work becomes child labour when it threatens the health and development of children. It is child labour, and not all child work, that one is trying to root out. After all, child work can be a positive experience and, in the best circumstance, children's work can prepare them for productive adult life. Through their work they can gain increasing status as family members and citizens. They can learn the skills of their parents and neighbours. Therefore, children's work can be an integral part of family life and can contribute to their healthy development. It can also build their confidence and self-steem. Child work can then be a painless and gradual initiation into adult life.

Child labour has implications for the individual, the group and the wider society. It was in early industrial Britain that social investigators first associated child work with poor health. The health of exploited child workers in still being endangered today, some hundred years later. A WHO/Defence for children (DCI) joint report on child labour states that: 'Normal growth spurts during puberty and adolescence are adversely affected by the poor nutrient intake and increased manual work' (Shah, 1985, p. 39). In 28 countries, the average per capita intake of calories is 73 to 89 per cent of what is required, but it is lower for the poorer segments of the population, from which most working children come, even though their work raises their nutritional requirements. Working children also become more susceptible to infectious diseases, including tuberculosis, if they suffer from malnutrition, anaemia, fatigue and inadequate sleep. The report cities other physical health hazards, including bone lesions and postural deformity due to working doubled-up in carpet factories and lifting heavy weights. In modern industries other health, problems occur: 'The eyesight of young girls working for 12-14 hours a day in micro-computer factories is reported to be damaged within a period of 5-8 years' (Shah, 1985, p. 39).

Children often work with poorly maintained and dangerous machinery and in intrinsically dangerous works situations such as mining. Even on the streets, children can be subject to the constant threat of traffic accidents and street violence. Exploitative sweatshops often have an especially pernicious effect on children's health. Excessive noise can lead to hearing loss, and hot, damp or dusty conditions to the transmission of communicable diseases. In manufacturing, children can be exposed to toxic substances, such as glue in shoe production. Even being outdoors is not necessarily an escape as many children in modern agriculture are often exposed to lethal chemical pesticides.

Child prostitution and pornography are increasing worldwide, as is the incidence of sexually transmitted diseases. The drug trade also uses children, both as intermediaries and countries and the children themselves often become addicted. In many cities glue-sniffing and the abuse of soft and hard drugs is endemic among street children. In developing countries large numbers of working children face the unhappy reality of increasing separation from their natural families. Poverty produces its own stress to the point that marriage and less formalised adult relationships break down. One parent or guardian leaves, or is forced to leave to find work, placing an additional burden upon the remaining single parent—often the mother — as well as the children who may be forced to work for the family's survival., Home relationships and the economic situation may continue to deteriorate to the point where the child abandons the family, or is abandoned by it. As children's contracts with their families weaken, they lose even their limited access to basic services, such as health, education and recreation. In urban areas, children who work daily no the streets may experience a freer and more adventurous lifestyle than at home, but at the same time they encounter much higher level of risk and less access to services and support.

Street children habitually faced with negative behaviour towards them have serious problems in maintaining healthy self-esteem and miss out on play and recreation essential for their social and emotional development. The opportunity cost of working for children is often a reduction in their chances of any kind of schooling. Formal education takes place during the day and during working hours. Therefore, a large proportion of working children do not attend school. Other constraints on regular school attendance include the cost of fees, books and uniforms as well as the often inappropriate nature of the curriculum. Meaningful apprenticeship might at least compensate for some of these disadvantages, but it can also be a form of exploitation in which the child acts as a servant to the craftsman on very low ay, running errands and performing menial tasks which bear no relation to the trade.

Children in rural areas can make an early work contribution. This, in turn, can positively influence fertility as the family views children as more hands rather than more months, as well as a form of social security in old age. The extent of child work in rural areas also has implications for rural emigration. As noted before, the parental use of child workers in domestic and farm activities may well allow other family members to migrate in search of seasonal or longer-term employment. Such migration usually involves male heads of households often leading to an increased work burden for the children. Conversely, lack of opportunities for child work, or a lack of adequate schooling and recreational facilities can encourage the emigration of children themselves.

Unemployment may be increased by the participation of young workers and high unemployment increases labour-force divisions. In urban industrial labour-markets, high and rising youth unemployment encourages the more affluent families to invest more in schooling, as higher qualifications are necessary to secure highwage and high-status jobs. By contrast, among the working class, high unemployment may have the perverse effect of discouraging school attendance, not only because their labour is needed to supplement family income, but due to the perception that the amount of schooling their children could obtain would be insufficient to secure a reasonable job (Rodgers and Standing, 1981, p. 35).

Child labour is not accidental. Many children are hired because they can be paid at much lower rates than adults. In certain industries like carpet-making or electronics assembly, children are more skilful because of the dexterity of their small fingers. But children, because of their dependent position, are the most easily exploited of all workers. They are the cheapest from of labour and their situation is analogous to that of other relatively powerless groups, such as women workers and new immigrants, who accept lower wages and poor conditions of work because of the lack of organisation and their need to work. Not all child labour is therefore the result of poverty.

We have already seen the extent to which children are absorbed into the more time-intensive tasks in agrarian societies. Children are a from (perhaps the only form) of capital investment open to peasant farmers. Additionally, continuing rental obligations may force peasant families to employ all their domestic labour resources. Debt is a common mechanism that encourages this feudal-like situation and children may be the commodity traded to meet debt repayments. The growth of wage labour and capitalist relations of production has been associated in the industrialised societies with a decline in child labour in the long run. In the early stages children were used in many contexts to help further capital accumulation. It was common for whole families to b employed for a 'family wage,' especially, but not exclusively, in agriculture. In developing countries today, large industrial firms and other sizeable capitalist enterprises do not seem to make extensive use of child work, perhaps because of the skill factor or the need to respect legislation, or because of the abundant supply of youth and adult workers. Nevertheless, there is one notable exception, and that is the use of child workers in small manufacturing enterprises where it is probably under reported because of its illegality. In such enterprises children are used as cheap 'sweated' labour, frequently alongside older relatives. Such industrialised and developing countries. Here, too, child work can be a way of circumventing the potential power of trade unions as well as substituting cheap labour for higher adult wage employment.

Another correlate of capitalist relationships is the need for a wage income to pay taxes or to purchase new consumer goods, forcing many youths and children to migrate. Where farming is dominated by male workers, as in Latin America and the Caribbean, there may be a considerable amount of migration of girls and young women. Where men have been the first to move into the wage labour sector women and children have taken over domestic and subsistence work or lower forms of wage employment, such as cotton picking and weeding (Rodgers and Standing, p. 17). Landlordlessness, which itself forces children into the labour-market, is another correlate of capitalist relationships. With the growth of capitalist relations the labour-market becomes increasingly differentiated and the participation of child workers can be conducive to the formation of a subordinated workers' group.

The situation of child workers is also affected by economic changes, such as the world-wide recession of the early 1980s. Unemployment rates rose to 51 per cent of the urban labour force in some African countries. Latin America in particular has been significantly affected by the Debt Crisis and the harsh repayment policies advocated by the International Monetary Fund turning the 1980s into the decade of debt rather than development. The effects of these trends, including increased poverty, inequitable distribution of income, and adult unemployment directly affect children. Child work in paid-wage employment outside the family has increased as children are forced to work for their own and their families survival. This qualitative change in child work has opened up more opportunities for exploitation (ILO, 1983).

It is remarkable to note that the cild work is not only a response to economic processes, it also reflects the culturally determined roles and functions of children, the values by which the activities of children are judged, and the nature of the socialisation process. These two sets of factors—economic and cultural — indeed go together, though the nature of the relationship has been much debated. Child labour, then, remains a seriously neglected issue in relation to the magnitude of the problem, and though the study of child labour is hampered by several particular research problems, the real constraint lies in the universal perception of it as a low-priority concern.

Chapter 11

Child Labour: Economic View

"Grief is the agony of an instant, the indulgence of grief the blunder of a life."

—*Benjamin Disraeli*

This chapter is intended to focus on some of the dimensions and determinants of the economic activities of children in rural areas with special reference to India. Evidence is presented with regard to the magnitude, intensity and the nature of activities performed by children. Information regarding wages earned is also given. Selected socio-economic indicators are used to analyse the possible causes of child work participation.

Data on economic activities of children are rather scarce. Data on the size of child population, dependency ratios and those children who wee reported as engaged in any gainful activity is obtained from the decennial censuses of India. Nevertheless, problems arise while comparing these data for different census years because of the definitional changes particularly on work. Problems are also encounted with respect to the reporting of age, occupational classification of children, etc. Labour Enquiry Survey Reports, National Sample Survey Tabulations and Publications of the Bureau of Economic and Statistics are the other major sources of data. A few micro level studies also have been conducted in the country, but they are all area specific and the scope of these enquiries varies from one to the other.

Roughly, about 40 per cent of the population in India comprises of children in the age group 0-14. This young age structure is a consequence of relatively higher levels of fertility and declining mortality. The dependency burden is thus higher especially in the rural areas. The census classification to categorise a person as worker or non-worker does not prescribe any minimum age limit. However, it may be assumed safely that no child under age five is entered as working. Among the child population in rural India nearly one-third are dependents as they belong to the age group of 0-4. Another third of the child population or about half of those aged 5-14 are entered as dependents as shown in Table 1. These are the persons who have no activity of their own, but are dependents on other members of the family for their living. Remaining children either go to school or work. It is rather difficult to estimate those who combine schooling and work. The conditions in rural areas are conducive for school-going children to work either by withdrawing from school for a couple of days or intermittently or after school hours. During the last several years the number of children entering school has increased, and as a consequence, the percentage of children working has declined. However, we are not sure whether the proportion of children combining work with schooling has changed over years.

The 1971 Census data show that 11.5 per cent of males and 4.6 per cent of females of 5-14 years were full-time workers in rural areas. Considering children performing household duties as those who were engaged in useful activities, the child work participation rate in rural India is estimated to be 13.3 per cent and 22.4 per cent for males and females, respectively. Child work participation rate for girls was thus higher than that for boys. Reciprocally, proportion of full-time school attending girls in the female child population (5-14) is lower than the proportion of full-time school attending boys in the male child population (5-14). The ratio of school-going children to the non-school going children is higher for male than for females in both 1961 and 1971 Census.

The 1961 and 1971 Census data on students, dependents

TABLE 1: SIZE AND DISTRIBUTION OF CHILD POPULATION IN RURAL INDIA

Sex		*Child population (0-14) in thousands*	*Per cent of child population to total population*	*Per cent of children (0-4) to the total child population (0-14)*	*Per cent distribution of children (5-14) as*					
					Child workers	*Students*	*Children performing household duties*	*Dependents**	*Other***	*Total*
1971	Males	96,867	43.0	65.9	11.4	36.6	2.0	49.4	0.6	100.0
Census	Females	90,884	42.5	64.3	4.6	19.0	17.8	58.3	0.3	100.0
1961	Males	76,585	41.8	63.9	16.6	35.4	0.3	47.5	0.2	100.0
Census	Females	72,719	41.2	62.1	12.3	14.7	13.2	59.8	0.1	100.0

* Dependents include all non-workers, even if able bodies, who have no other activity coming under any of the above classification and who are not seeking any work, but are purely dependent.

** Persons who are not engaged in any activity but are seeking work and those who are with independent means, beggars, vagrants, etc. inmates of penal, mental and charitable institutions are categorised as 'others.'

Sources:
1. Census of India, 1971, *Series 1, India, Part II—B(i), General Economic Tables*, Controller of Publications, Delhi, 1977:18-21.
2. Census of India 1971, *Series 1, India, Part II-B(ii), General Economic Tables*, Controller of Publications, Delhi, 1978: 417-423.
3. Census of India 1971, *Series 1, India, Part II—C(ii), Social and Cultural Tables*, Controller of Publications, Delhi, 1977: 106.
4. Census of India 1961, *Volume 1, India, Part II—B(i), General Economic Tables*, Manager of Publications, Delhi, 1965: 86-87.
5. Census of India 1961, *Volume 1, India, Part II—B(iii), General Economic Tables*, Manager of Publications, Delhi, 1965: 590-593.
6. Census of India 1961, *Volume 1, India, Part II—C(i), Social and Cultural Tables*, Manager of Publications, Delhi, 1965: 408.

are not strictly comparable due to definitional differences. It is more so with regard to data on work. The 1961 Census data includes marginal workers in the work force whereas the 1971 census data is based on main activity only. Assuming no substantial change in the actual work participation rate of children over 1961-71, the marginal child workers can be estimated to be roughly about 5 per cent for males and 7 per cent for females. Looking at the statistics given for students, children performing household duties, dependents and others in both the censuses, one gets the impression that a bulk of the female marginal workers were children performing household duties and the male marginal workers were students and dependents in 1971 Census. The dependent children (5-14) of 1961 Census refer to those who neither work nor go to school. They perform no other economic activity and are not seeking any work either. The dependent children of 1971 Census on the other hand may be consisting of some marginal workers. However, according to both the censuses 47 per cent of male children and nearly 60 per cent of female children are reported as dependents (see Table 1). But we are not sure whether children who neither work nor go to school are absolutely idle. It is possible that a substantial proportion of these children are performing activities which do not come under the purview of the census definition of work or household duty. It is also possible that non-school going marginal workers are under-reported and are counted as dependents. In bot the cases certain activities performed by children are concealed.

A meaningful indicator of the incidence of child labour is the child work participation rate. It indicates the magnitude of child labour in relation to the child population. The age-specific child work participation rate (child workers to the population 5-14 years of age, with the assumption that children blow five years are not working) shows that according to 1971 Census, the highest participation rate is found in Sikkim (30.7 per cent). Among the major states Andhra Pradesh stands first (16.3 per cent) followed by Karnataka (11.5 per cent), Madhya Pradesh (11.1 per cent), Maharashtra (9.3 per cent), Rajasthan (9.1 per cent), Tamil Nadu (8.6 per cent), Orissa (8.4 per cent), Jammu and Kashmir (6.0 per cent) and so on. Among all the major states child work participation of male children is found to be higher than that of female children.

TABLE 2: INDUSTRIAL CLASSIFICATION OF THE CHILD WORKERS IN RURAL INDIA, 1971 CENSUS

Industrial classification	*Number of child workers*		*Per cent of child workers to the total workers in each category*	
	M	*F*	*M*	*F*
1. Cultivators	3,092,973	748,455	4.6	8.2
2. Agricultural labourers	2,928,901	1,544,584	9.7	10.2
3. Livestock, Forestry, Fishing, hunting, Plantations, orchard and allied activities	716,424	138,245	23.5	19.3
4. Mining and quarrying	12,133	7,436	2.4	7.7
5. Household industry	150,520	108,919	4.0	10.9
6. Other than household industry	92,704	48,442	3.1	11.0
7. Construction	24,453	11,172	2.4	10.2
8. Trade and Commerce	73,459	8,906	2.9	3.2
9. Transport, storage and communications	10,534	2,481	0.9	5.1
10. Other services	182,560	74,154	2.7	7.8

Source: Census of India, 1971, *Series I, India, Part II-B (ii) General Economic Tables*, Controller of Publications Delhi, 1978, 417-423.

The sectors engaging children in various economic activities vary from country to country, but child labour is most common in agriculture followed by services and industry. Agricultural child labour constitutes nearly 10 per cent of the total agricultural labour force in the country. In livestock, forestry, fishing, hunting and plantations, they constitute nearly 21 per cent of the total labour force. Children work in all sectors of the economy. In rural areas, about 91.9 per cent of the child labour is found in agricultural sector. Secondary sector makes up 4.6 per cent and service sector 3.5 per cent of the total child workers.

On the basis of 1971 Census data, fourteen groups of occupations are identified in rural areas as child labour concentrated occupations. Occupations in which more than 25,000 children are engaged-in and which have a child worker-adult worker ratio of more than 3 per cent are considered as child labour concentrated occupation.

As was seen in the case of sectoral concentration of child workers, the occupational concentration of child workers also shows the child worker-adult worker ratio, generally, in favour of girls than of boys. This is true for All India as well as for Karnataka and Kerala states. The pattern of occupational concentration of child labour of Karnataka is almost similar to that of All India pattern for both the sexes. For Kerala, however, higher concentrations is found only in four groups of occupations, viz., other farm workers, maids and other house-keeping service workers, cooks, waiters, bar-tenders and related workers and tobacco prepares and tobacco product makers. Thus, unlike All India and Karnataka patterns, the highest concentration of child workers of Kerala is found in service sector. Generally, wage employment and schooling are competitive for children both in agriculture and non-agricultural occupations. In the case of self-employment or working at home to help other members of the household, schooling and work can be combined. In beedi rolling, for

TABLE 3: RATIO OF CHILD WORKERS TO ADULT WORKERS IN CHILD LABOUR CONCENTRATED OCCUPATIONS* IN RURAL AREAS—1971 CENSUS

Occupational groups (as given in census of India)	*Occupation*	*Per cent child workers (0-14) to adult workers (15+)*					
		India		*Karnataka*		*Kerala*	
		M	*F*	*M*	*F*	*M*	*F*
52	Cook, waiters bar tenders and related workers (Domestic and Institutional)	10.8	25.8	10.5	13.7	11.0	33.1
53	Maids and other housekeeping service workers	25.7	21.5	20.8	22.6	30.8	28.4
55	Launders, dry cleaners and pressers	7.1	10.0	5.8	8.1	1.6	1.3
62	Farmers other than cultivators	75.2	123.6	98.4	135.8	1.7	2.0
64	Plantation labourers and related workers	3.0	5.0	6.7	13.4	1.1	2.7
65	Other farms workers	57.3	102.6	101.8	142.8	35.3	26.7
75	Spinners, weavers, knitters, dyers and related workers	4.4	10.0	5.5	12.3	2.3	6.3
77	Food and beverage processors	3.0	5.0	3.8	4.5	1.6	3.1
78	Tobacco prepares and tobacco product makers	10.7	28.4	23.0	41.4	6.4	41.2
79	Tailors, dress makers, sewers, upholderers & related workers	3.9	6.8	4.7	6.7	1.6	2.1
89	Glass formers, potters and related workers	4.1	8.5	4.6	6.0	2.0	5.1
94	Production and related workers without specific classification	5.6	8.8	7.4	11.3	2.3	4.2
	Cultivators	4.7	8.9	5.7	8.9	0.4	0.8
	Agricultural Labourers	10.7	11.3	14.3	13.9	1.5	2.0

* Occupations in which more than 25,000 children are engaged and which has a child worker-adult worker ratio of more than 3 per cent of All India are considered as child labour concentrated occupations.

Sources:
1. Census of India, 1971, *Series, I, India, Part II-B(v), General Economic Tables*, Controller of Publications, Delhi, 1978: 393-692.
2. Census of India, 1971, *Series, 14, Mysore, Part II-B (iii), Economic Tables*, Controller of Publications, Delhi, 1979: 425-610.
3. Census of India, 1971, *Series, 9, Kerala, Part II-B (ii), Economic Tables*, Controller of Publications, Delhi, 1977: 262-367.

example, working and schooling can be combined as beedi rolling work is usually carried out in the household itself and there are no rigid working hours or working norms that have to be met. Similar is the case in occupations such as spinning, weaving, dress making, etc.

A major concentration of working children in rural areas is in livestock rearing. Though not proportionate, generally in areas where relatively larger number of livestock are raised the child work participation is found to be high. In states like Rajasthan, Karnataka, Madhya Pradesh, Andhra Pradesh, Orissa, and Jammu and Kashmir, both the number of livestock raised and the number of children working per household are much higher compared to Kerala, Tamil Nadu, Uttar Pradesh, West Bengal, Assam and Tripura.

The Report of the Rural Labour Enquiry Survey (Government of India, 1965) conducted during 1963-65 provides information for the number of days worked per annum by children in the agricultural labour households and all rural labour households. When the major portion of the household income was derived from the wage paid manual labour they were categorised as rural labour households. According to this report children in rural labour households were working on an average for 267 days per year out of which 187 days were accounted for by wage employment. In agricultural labour households separately, the corresponding figures were 280 days and 202 days. Non-agricultural child labourers were found to be working more number of days than the agricultural child labourers and self-employed and salaried children.

With respect to educational variables that affect participation of children in different kinds of work we have to consider literacy and educational levels of population, schooling of children, school drop-outs and wastage and availability of schooling facilities. The Literacy levels of adult population is a good indicator of the levels of enrolment of children in schools. Illiteracy among the population particularly among females acts as a major deterrent to school enrolment of children. When schooling is denied they are usually forced to work.

The Survey Report provides state-wise statistics for the intensity of child work. Data show state-wise variation in the intensity of work performed by children in terms of number of days employed per annum. In West Bengal agricultural and non-agricultural child labourers of both agricultural labour and all rural labour households worked for about 320 days in a year. In Gujarat, Punjab-Haryana and Jammu and Kashmir, children who were working as agricultural labourers worked for about three-fourth of a year. Karnataka, Kerala, Punjab-Haryana and West Bengal are bracketed for the highest number of days worked by non-agricultural child labourers among agricultural labour households and Assam, Bihar Punjab-Haryana, Kerala and West Bengal among all rural labour households.

Since Independence school enrolment of children has been improving for both sexes in the country. School enrolment ratio which stood at 65 per cent for boys in 1953 -54 rose to 76 per cent in 1958-59, further to 96 per cent in 1968-69, and 100 per cent in 1975-76. The corresponding figures for girls were 28, 38, 59 and 66 per cent respectively (Government of India, 1962: 300; Government of India, 1980:20-22). However, school enrolment may not be uniform among all sections of the population. School enrolment of children among weaker sections in the rural areas are definitely on the lower side. The difference between the school enrolment ratios of scheduled population and general population widened from primary school to high school (Rayappa and Grover, 1980: 27-28). Enrolment ratios of male and female children are also not the same. Even though school enrolment ratios may be high, school retention rates may not be so. This has been amply demonstrated by the amount of wastage in school education particularly in rural areas. The wastage rate which was as high as 60 per cent for primary state in the country in 1958-59 (Government of India, 1962:301) has not shown any improvement even after more than ten years. In fact, it has worsened to 66.9 per cent in 1970-71 (Government of India, 1977: 20). The higher the school wastage, the higher the chance of children participating in economic activities.

Chapter 12

Against the Child Labour

"It matters not how small the beginning may seem to be; what is once well done is done for ever."

—Henry David Thoreau

Child labour is absolutely the outcome of poverty and underdevelopment and campaigning against it is not going to lead to its elimination over-night. Neither can the United Nations put the world to right by simply passing declarations and conventions in this field or any other. Action against child labour, if it is to be significant, must come from within states and be supported from outside.

Campaigns are not new to the developing world. Both the Green Revolution in the 1960s and 1970s and the Universal Child Immunisation Campaign of the 1980s are good examples of externally inspired development initiatives. In the latter case, UNICEF was able to inspire a massive immunisation campaign in Colombia over the summer months of 1984. All media channels were utilised and some 120,000 volunteers were mobilised to achieve three-quarters coverage of the child population against five of the major childhood diseases. And the President fired the first shot in the campaign! (UNICEF, 1984 pp. 159-79) Columbia has inspired other examples of social mobilisation behind child immunisation. Could the same be achieved for child labour? One doubts it. Child immunisation is self-evidently a good thing that most, if not all, governments find it in their interest to support. Not so with child labour, which is far more political in its implications. The political sensitivity of child labour is reflected in the poor take-up of the chief international instrument in the field — ILO Convention 138. Few governments have ratified this convention which prohibits all work under 15 years. Many governments in the development world find the instrument too ambitious given their economic reality. Indeed, many see child work in a family context as a naturally good thing—an expression of family solidarity. Besides, why should the state interfere with parental wishes? A clear echo here of nineteenth-century Britain. Not surprisingly, then, there is as yet no internationally orchestrated campaign against child labour though the ILO has called for such systematic action at this level (Blanchard, 1983, p. 37). But there have been a number of international initiatives, and the potential does exist to construct more integrated programmes in support of government action using in part lessons drawn from past campaigns. Let us now examine the main potential actors in such campaigns.

The ILO is widely viewed as the lead international agency concerned with child labour. Funded in 1919 as part of the League of Nations, it is now a unique agency within the United Nations system because of its tripartite representation of governments, employers' and workers' organisations. It is comparable to a ministry in a medium sized country with a staff of 2,000. In a startling disclosure its Director-General, Francis Blanchard, claimed that it consumed 22,000 pencils a year, 354 tonnes of paper and a million envelopes (*Gaurdian*, 15 August 1987). How many forests were destroyed on behalf of the child workers of the world must remain another little known development statistic! From the outset the ILO has attempted to regulate child labour in the short term without losing sight of the long-term goal of elimination. Its regulating and protective work has been expressed in terms of international standard setting. These international standards, or conventions, are only binding on those member states who ratify them. Once ratified, article 22 of the ILO's Constitution requires signatories to provide annual reports on their compliance, while articles 24 and 26 allow for the consideration of complaints against a state for failure to live up to the instrument in question. Perhaps an additional reason for a lack of enthusiasm for Convention 138.

The first child work convention was passed in 1919, setting the minimum age for regular industrial work, excluding family enterprise and technical schools, at 14. This Convention no. 5 was revised in 1937 when the minimum age was raised to 15.

From 1920 to 1965 minimum age conventions were adopted for the areas shown in Table 1.

TABLE 1: ILO MINIMUM AGE CONVENTIONS: 1920-65

Occupation	Convention	Minimum age
Seamen	No. 7 1920	14
	No. 58 1936	15
Agriculture	No. 10 1921	14 (except out of school hours)
Mining	No. 123 1965	16
Non-Industrial	No. 33 1932	14 (out allows children over 12 to be employed outside of school hours on light work)

ILO conventions are usually flexible, allowing for gradual implementation and the facility for a state to grant exceptions (so called 'saving clauses'), particularly in the case of family enterprises. In 1973 the ILO replaced these conventions with Convention 138 which applies to all areas of economic activity. Convention 138, coupled with Recommendation 146, is the most comprehensive international instrument and statement on child labour:

CONVENTION 138

CONVENTION CONCERNING MINIMUM AGE FOR ADMISSION TO EMPLOYMENT

Article 1

Each Member of which this Convention is in force undertakes to pursue a national policy designed to ensure the effective abolition of child labour and to raise progressively the minimum age for admission to employment or work to a level consistent with the fullest physical and mental development of young persons.

Article 2

3. The minimum age specified in pursuance of paragraph 1 of this Article shall not be less than the age of completion of compulsory schooling and, in any case, shall not be less than 15 years.

Article 3

1. The minimum age for admission to any type of employment or work which by its nature or the circumstances in which it is carried out is likely to jeopardise the health, safety or morals of young persons shall not be less than 18.

RECOMMENDATION NO. 146

(i) National Policy

..... high priority should be given to planning for and meeting the needs of children and youth in national development policies and programmes......

(ii) Minimum Age 7(1)

Members should take as their objective the progressive raising to 16 years of the minimum age for admission to employment or work specified in pursuance of Article 2 of the Minimum Age Convention 1973.

As with previous conventions, no. 138 contains flexible

provisions and saving clauses. The ratification of Convention 138 has been disappointing. By 1979 only 13 countries had ratified it and by 1988 this figure had risen to 36.

There are those, like the UK delegate to the UN Seminar, who assert that this paltry number overstates support for Convention 138. It was Professor Boudhiba who pointed out in his report that states often seemed to ratify conventions without having the means to implement them. So, as the UK delegate asserted, what is the point of ratifying conventions one cannot implement, and then hectoring others for not doing so? At the seminar. The Netherlands took a different view, asserting that ratification of such instruments is an indication of the political will to broadly comply with their provisions, and that it was necessary to show support for the principles they embody.

Whether for or against, all that states need do as members of the ILO is to bring conventions to the attention of their relevant authorities. In the case of no. 138, the UK Government did so in 1974 by publishing a White Paper setting out general support for the convention but claiming that it could not ratify it as yet. This has remained the official UK position ever since. Indeed the UK delegate to the UN Seminar stated that UK regulations on child work complied with, if not exceeded, the provisions of Convention 138. So why not ratify? Perhaps the most telling argument against is the reporting provision — why have your country held up to international scrutiny if you can avoid it?

Nevertheless, the ILO finds consolation in the fact that most member states have adopted a minimum age standard of 14 or higher, although a smaller group of countries have set the minimum age at between 12 and 13. Additionally, more than 100 countries have ratified one or more of the ten convention prior to 197. These conventions regulate industrial employment and dangerous work much more rigorously than family enterprise and agriculture.

The ILO has hardly been zealous in following up on Convention 138. IYC (1979) provided the first real opportunity for the ILO and other agencies to focus world attention on the issue of child labour. In his declaration concerning IYC, the Director-General stated that:

(a) a child is not a 'small adult' but a person entitled to self-fulfilment through learning and play so that his adult life is not jeopardised by the having to work at an early age;

(b) governments should... take all necessary social and legislative action for the progressive elimination of child labour;

(c) pending the elimination of child labour, it must be regulated and humanised.

A number of important publications emerged from the IYC, but the ILO's attention did not become re-focused on the issue until 1983, when the Director-General's Report made a special feature of child labour. The reality behind the exhortation has meant that the ILO has not been able to obtain major donor support for its child labour activities. This state of affairs was openly pointed to by an ILO delegate to the UN Seminar who virtually pleaded with the government delegates to reverse the low priority given to the issue by member states. Understandably, then, the sensitivity with which governments view child labour has encouraged a cautious approach by the ILO. Despite its tripartite structure, it is governmental who really count. They pay the bills and they count for more in difficult economic times.

There were NGO observes at the UN Seminar who held that UNICEF ought to be the principal agency for child labour because of its specific responsibility for child welfare. In looking ahead to the adoption of a UN Convention on the Rights of the Child, some NGOs saw UNICEF as the chief regulatory agency for this instrument. Despite these lofty ambitions (flattering in one sense, but utterly naive) the political realities facing UNICEF are no less constraining, while its operating budget is less than that of Hampshire Country Council in Britain. UNICEF, unlike ILO, was established in 1946 on a voluntary basis. It began as a temporary relief operation mainly in Europe, and it was not until 1953 that its mandate to work exclusively in the developing world became firmly established. Each year UNICEF has to go to governments for support, and in particular to the US government, its largest donor. This economic reality may account for the public relations style and strategy adopted by UNICEF's Executive Director from 1982. Under James Grant, UNICEF has made the Child Survival and Development Revolution (CSDR) its main campaigning thrust. CSDR refers to a package of low-cost child health measures which UNICEF claims could have infant mortality rates if adopted world-wide. Emphasis on CSDR, and latterly on the universal immunisation goal for 1990, tends to obscure the more broadly-based development work UNICEF continues to support.

Nevertheless, at its 1984 Executive Board, UNICEF was asked, mainly at the insistence of its Scandinavian members, to review its policy on Children in Especially Difficult Circumstances. This reflected a concern that UNICEF was neglecting important child development issues in its emphasis on child survival. The report presented to UNICEF's 1986 Executive Board covered a review of working and street children; children in armed conflict and in situations of natural disaster; and those subject to abuse. The final draft paper observed:

> UNICEF, within the context of existing programmes of support and in co-operation with other agencies, should advocate and support the progressive abolition of child exploitation, the protection of working children and street children, the amelioration of working conditions and the analysis of the impact of national policies on these children.

While the underlying causes are basically structural – widespread poverty, underdevelopment and gross inequality—society must do more than wait for the long-term results of structural changes that it may be seeking to effect. Through extending the child survival and development strategy in response to the special needs of these children and youth, families and communities can be strengthened to decrease and/or prevent the exploitation of child work and the growth of numbers of street children. (UNICEF, 1986a, p. 11).

In a rather confused final debate, what emerged was the recognition that UNICEF should play a major role within the UN system for street children, but in terms of actions should, 'concentrate mainly one advocacy and rely primarily on governments and voluntary agencies for implementation; (UNICEF, 1986d, p. 3). Advocacy was therefore seen as UNICEF's natural role and advantage while the more sensitive campaigning work should be left to NGO's. On the funding side, the expansion of programmes would have to be left to the initiative of field offices and secure supplementary funding for 'noted projects' (projects funded not out of UNICEF's mainstream budget, but by National Committees).

The outcome of the 1986 Board was more positive than many had hoped. It was a flexible and realistic response to the situation facing UNICEF. In the child labour field, UNICEF's intention was to build on what it knew best, i.e., non-institutional programmes for street children, and gradually extending the lessons of Latin American to the new challenges of Africa and Asia. The emphasis on the 'noted projects' mechanism again builds on past policy. Some $ 2 million was raised in this way in the early 1980s, with only a small $ 500,000 commitment from UNICEF's stretched general resources. But will UNICEF campaign against child labour? Given the realities of a threatened annual budget of some $ 400 million which UNICEF has to raise each year, campaigning is too politically sensitive to contemplate. Child Survival brings in the money while UNICEF quietly goes on with its broad-based field programmes.

Many see child labour as a human rights issue so, finally, it is worth pointing to a number of United Nations pronouncements on human rights which relate to child labour:

1. The Universal Declaration of Human Rights, 1948.
2. The international Covenant on Human Rights, 1966.
3. The Supplementary Convention on the Abolition of Slavery, 1956.
4. The Convention for the Suppression of the Traffic in Persons and of the Exploitation of the Prostitution of others, 1949.
5. The Declaration of the Rights of the Child, 1959.

Additionally, regional organisations such as the Council of Europe, the Organisation of African Unity and the Organisation of American States, have their own instruments.

Since the International Year of the Child, NGOs have become an increasingly powerful force, lobbying the UN system to adhere to the principles enshrined in these instruments, and to take more effective action against child labour. NGOs like the Anti-Slavery Society, have produced some of the best documented country studies of child labour. Others, like the Geneva based Defence for Children International have taken up the human rights dimension of child labour and effectively lobbied UN agencies (particularly UNICEF) to pay more attention to the issue.

But of all the NGOs, it is perhaps the trade unions who have the greatest untapped potential for action, both at the national and international level. The Trade Union Congress of Britain produced its own educational resource on child labour in 1985, and subsequently lobbied the ILO Governing Body to follow this example by doing more in the field of public education (see Fyfe, 1985). In *Breaking Down the Wall of Silence* the ICFTU resolved that 'free trade unions all over the world will pave the way for the eventual abolition of child labour' (ICFTU, 1986, p. 34). But the same organisation faces its own constraints in acting upon this commitment. Its resources are limited and have only permitted small-scale projects, such as a vocational education initiative in Bombay. More fundamental, though is the reality that many of its developing world affiliates are lukewarm at best, given their member's dependence on child work. The ICFTU has, therefor, gone along with the humanising strategy, which the TUC has often opposed, of ameliorative actions which deliver services, like health and education, to the child at work, or attempts at loosening the rigidities of the school system so that working children can fit education around their work schedule.

These pragmatic projects and programmes recognise the need for children to work. But to change that reality, to eliminate the necessity for children to work, is a radical shift which requires a long-term integrated international effort, and virtually everyone agrees that public education campaigns are the first necessary, but not sufficient, steps along a very long road. The Report of the Director-General of the ILO in 1983 provides the essential rationale:

> The role of information gathering and dissemination in raising public awareness of the evils of child labour and in exposing the sectors of activities where it is prevalent should not be under-estimated. In many developing countries there is a surprisingly high degree of ignorance about the consequences of child labour in general and the ill-effects of unsafe working conditions in particular. Child work is often accepted as part of the natural state of things, and the rights and needs of the child are not always fully appreciated. A great deal of effort, therefore, needs to be made to generate and promote public awareness of the consequences of child labour and the rights of the working child and to expose unacceptable conditions wherever they exist. (Blanchard, 1983, p. 23).

The Anti-Slavery Society in a report commissioned by UNICEF as part of its preparation for the 1986 Executive Board suggested that, 'Trends in the use of child labour could be reversed by public education on the needs and the rights of children' (ASS, 1984b, p. 49). The trade union movement has an enormous potential role to play in this area. As Professor Boudhiba has pointed out: 'the unions ..... would still seem not to be clearly aware of the magnitude of the question. They should be requested to include specific activity on this matter in their programmes. They are active pressure groups that can have a decisive effect on governments, employers, enterprises and public opinion (Boudhiba, 1982, p. 71).

The ICFTU in recognising the need to respond to the challenge and child labour, and in its own report to its members early in 1986, observed that: '.... public opinion was largely ignorant of the problem and must be made aware of the dangers of child labour, the damage it can cause to family life and to entire societies and economies.' UNICEF's Draft Working Paper for its 1986 Executive Board recommended that UNICEF should work to enhance government and public awareness of children in especially difficult circumstances and of possibilities for preventive and ameliorative actions (UNICEF, 1986a, p. 14). Finally, the UN Seminar on Child Labour called on governmental, international and non-governmental organisations '.... to increase awareness amongst children, parents, workers and employers of the causes and the adverse effects of child labour and the measures to combat its exploitation' (UN, 1986, p. 28).

If everyone is agreed that the raising of public awareness is the first essential step in the child labour campaign, there is little in the way of guidance on how best this can be done. Perhaps the past is our only guide. The question of whether it is possible to derive lessons from the past has, of course, long exercised historians. Many historians would now clam that this is a futile endeavour, however, for the student of child labour campaigns, the past is virtually the only reference point. And as long as one avoids attempts at drawing crude parallels between nineteenth-century Britain and the contemporary developing world, the past can provide important pointers for those wishing to conceptualise, and contruct, child labour campaigns.

The first campaigns against child labour took place in Britain just over 200 years ago over the issue of chile chimney sweeps. Prior to the 1780s, child work was taken for granted in Britain and Europe. It was philanthropists like Jonas Hanway who turned child labour into a public issue. Hanway's aim, like those of the early nineteenth century philanthropists, was not to abolish child labour but to regulate it through parliamentary action. Then, in 1803, with the foundation of the Society for Superseeding the Necessity of Climbing Boys we witness the first attempt to abolish a from of child labour. According to Hugh Cunningham, the early reformers had to overcome four major obstacles (Cunningham, 1985, p. 1). There was, firstly, the traditional assumption that it was natural for children to work and to contribute to the family economy. Secondly, that the problem was too little work for children rather than too much. Thirdly, a belief that parents had the right to do what they wished with their children, and finally the *laissez-faire* belief in the value of free labour. That these obstacles were gradually surmounted is now part of the romance which has stuck in English history textbooks for over 50 years and become as universal as the story of 1066.

What was the reality of these first campaigns and what lessons can be learnt from them? It is a long story, for it is only gradually that we witness in nineteenth-century Britain an awakening of social conscience. Then in the latter half of the century 'a veritable fury of compassion" (Thompson, 1984, p. 384) produced 'an extreme sensibility to human suffering' (Bagehot in Collins, 1965, pp. 178-9). But how was this transformation achieved? The movement to protect children from the new impersonal and systematic exploitation under industrial capitalism took over a century to achieve its goal. This campaign was never broadly based, comprising as it did a handful of enlightened professional men from the industrial north, the workers' own Short-Time Committees, and the parliamentary skills of Lord Shaftesbury. At the centre of the campaign was the task of building the evidence which proved so effective in persuading the nation of the iniquities of child labour. The first step was the raising of awareness; many people were simply unaware of the conditions of child work around them. Richard Oastler, who become one of the lading factory reformers, had to be told about child labour abuse even though he lived alongside it. As E.P. Thompson observes, 'we forget how long abuses can continue unknown until they are articulated; how people can look at misery and not notice it, until misery itself rebels' (Thompson, 1984, p. 377).

Oastler founded the Short-Time Committees which collected evidences for the Parliamentary Committees. These in turn allowed working people to speak for themselves about the abuses of child labour. The children themselves gave testimony, particularly to the Royal Commission which in 1842 examined women's and children's work in the mines. A public accustomed to the horror stories of factory work was unprepared for the stories of child miners of seven working 14 hours a day in conditions that disabled and deformed them. Victorians were particularly susceptible to accounts of sexual depravity and exploitation, which working naked down the mines encouraged—it was this more than any other feature which shocked contemporary opinion.

For the Victorians it was the potential for sexual exploitation in the expanding industries which moved them into action. The Mines Act of 1842 was passed virtually overnight. In the end it was not factory legislation, but free compulsory education, which proved the most effective child labour law. The campaign for universal schooling was much more popularly based on culminated in the passing of the Education Act of 1870. This act expressed both a changing view of childhood and the belief that the future of the nation was ultimately served best not by making children work, but by educating them.

Now examine the techniques used by the Victorian campaigners which gradually took children out of the workplace and deposited them in the classroom, and we can identify key elements in the process which altogether provide a model for contemporary campaigns. The Victorian campaign was built firstly upon detailed *investigation,* which was of two kinds: leading figures in the campaign, like Shaftesbury, had to brief themselves and raise their own awareness; then, there were the institutional investigations of the Select Committees and the Royal Commissions. Any investigation necessarily leads to *abalysis:* in the case of child labour new social investigators like Henry Mayhew were helping to provide a classification of child workers for the first time. After analysis comes the need for *public exposure,* as the first step in raising public awareness: the 1830s and 1840s in Britain became the era of the great extra-parliamentary pressure groups; the factory movement drew much inspiration from the Anti-Slavery Movement, the most powerful and effective of these in publicising its cause. It was vital that the new knowledge of the factory conditions be *disseminated* widely. Robert Owen, the enlightened factory owner and model paternalist (it was Owen who established the first pre-school in Britain at his new Lanark factory in 1816), clearly recognised this, believing as he did in 'the multiplication of reason by means of its diffusion.'

To move a mass audience needs a transformation of abstract notions into a medium more concrete and emotional in its appeal. Significantly, Hanway, the first campaigner, called his book on child chimney sweeps, *A Sentimental History* (1785) in a deliberate attempt to engage the emotions of the public. Climbing boys were tailor-made for the early campaigners because of their high visibility (unlike factory children and child miners they entered the homes of the wealthy) and because their appearance and recruitment facilitated the slave/savage analogy; when the slave analogy was extended to factory children it became a powerful emotional tool (Cunningham, 1985, p. 2). Popular writers like Charles Dickens and Charles Kingsley transformed the new knowledge into a fictional from with which a mass audience could identify. Dickens could equally lay claim to the title of the 'children's champion' of Victorian Britain. His child heroes, from Little Nell (1840) to Jo in *Bleak House* (1853), presented for the first time the child's world from within. *Bleak House* in particular became proverbial and even the 'street arabs' treasured such tattered copies of the instalments as they could lay their hands on. Dickens's vast international appeal was instrumental in assisting both the factory reformers and more particularly the campaigners for universal free schooling.

The factory movement was able to utilise the remarkable pockets of literacy within the working class. It was workers' groups who established 'reading societies' to buy the new radical newspapers, such as the *Poor Man's Advocate* and the *Voice of the People*. The movement also produced its first pamphlets in 1836, and even the illiterate were not excluded from political discourse. Ballad singers and 'patteres' presented current political issues through song and theatre, and workers would walk miles to hear a radical speaker. The growing power of newspapers is graphically revealed by the case of W.T. Stead's account in the *Pall Mall Gazette* of buying a 13-year-old prostitute. This produced such a public clamour that it brought swift parliamentary action in 1885 to raise the age of consent and curb child prostitution. Contrast this with the painstaking efforts of Josephine Butler and others throughout the 1860s and 1870s to expose the 'white slave trade' which had consistently been ignored.

Such new opportunities for the *dissemination* of information fed into the consequent activities of *mobilisation* and *pressure for action*. These campaigns for political action did not always succeed (parliamentary inquiries were often as not a means of diffusing discontent), but from the *evaluation* of the points of resistance a new dissemination campaign could be mounted with a fresh attempt at mobilisation.

Out of the historically important experience of Victorian Britain, we can now construct a Child Labour Campaign Model.

Though all the elements of the models were present in the Victorian child labour campaign, they were not applied continuously either by individuals or pressure groups. Trade unions, which potentially could have activated the model, fully, had not yet developed a mass membership, and therefore the capacity for action, until after the education Acts sealed the fate of child labour. Dickens, though a genius at popular dissemination, never significantly involved himself in political mobilisation; while Shaftesbury, an expert in parliamentary pressure, kept himself aloof from popular movements.

To begin with, we only need to look at the means of mass communication available in developing countries. Perhaps for the first time large areas of the developing world have the organisation and communication structure to inform and support the majority to bring about change. Twenty years ago radios were a rarity. Today there are 8,000 radio stations in the developing world broadcasting to over one billion transistors. Twenty years ago the print media was relatively underdeveloped. Today there are 8,000 daily newspapers in the developing world. Television is also a growing force, reaching as it does some 50-60 per cent of the urban population. India has had a decade of experimentation with satellite TV to promote village education, and by 1990 almost three-quarters of its 670 million population will have access to TV. Such developments provide enormous scope for non-formal education, training and information dissemination. A number of campaigns already bear witness to this, from the spread of the Green Revolution to attempts to promote family planning, child health and adult literacy.

Equally, one can point to the educational opportunities provided by the remarkable expansion in schooling in the developing world during the 1960s and 1970s. By 1981, countries such as Sri Lanka, Tanzania, Kenya and Vietnam were achieving 100 per enrolled in formal education, making the school system one of the most important channels of communication for the vast majority of today's and tomorrow's parents. Nevertheless, this expansion makes fundamental defects. There are still major inequalities of access between urban and rural areas, and boys and girls. Drop-out rates continue to be universally high—up to 70 per cent in some cases. The absolute numbers not in school continue to rise with high birth-rates (110 million in 1960, rising to 121 million in 1975). What is also disturbing is the decline in educational expenditure (16.4 per cent of total government expenditure in 1982, reduced to 5.9 per cent in 1981) with the global recession. Despite this, primary schools, in particular, remain an important tool in any public awareness campaign against child labour as, for example, in the possibility of building child-to-child alliances.

The Green Revolution and child immunisation campaigns have shown that there is no substitute for the political will to mobilise all the possible channels of communication. Political leadership was vital in the promotion of the Green Revolution and Family Planning in Indonesia, and for the remarkable success of the Child Immunisation Campaign in Colombia in 1984. Equally significant is the growth of non-governmental organisations. India alone has 12,0000 voluntary organisations and Bangladesh, 6,000. Specifically, one can point to the growth of organised religion as a major development resource. Trade unionism, too, is on the increase in much of the developing world, albeit from a low base, and in the last decade there has been the growth of the Women's Movement. Additionally, one can mention the growth of the major youth movements of the Boy Scouts (16 million members world-wide) and Girl Guides (8 million members world-wide). To these indigenous NGOs should be added the over 3,000 NGOs in industrial countries, such as Radda Barnen and OXFAM, who are significant partners in grassroots development.

If the potential change agents and the tools for social mobilisation are in place, how can they be used in the campaign against child labour? This is the most difficult task of all because in a world where information technology has become the new wonder of the age, shamefully little is known about how to communicate information whose principal value is to the poor. Nevertheless, there are a number of initiatives which are indicative of how the Child Labour Campaign Model might operate in practice. In Kenya there is the recent WHO-sponsored Child Labour and Health Project run by Dr. Philista Onyango of the University of Nairobi. The project team engaged during 1984-5 in a number of activities which mirror the model. beginning with an investigation in eight districts in Nairobi they analysed the data and disseminated it through workshops and seminars. The project's dissemination strategy was initially aimed at parents and employers and, given the problem of illiteracy, they significantly used the medium of community drama. The team considered drama as perhaps the most powerful tool for not only presenting issues like child labour, but as a tool for collective problem analysis (Dr. Philista Onyango). The rationale behind the use of drama was its capacity both to hold the interest of large groups of parents and employers through entertainment, and to create awareness of the dangerous aspects of child labour. It was seen as vital that the people participated in this exercise through role play as part of the process of identifying the problem. This was followed by discussion out of which emerged suggested solutions. This is a good example of active learning which appears to have led to attitude shifts regarding the value of rural to urban migration (Onyango, 1986, p. 169).

In Peru, an NGO coalition co-ordinated by TIPACOM (Talleres Infantiles Procyectados a la (Comunidad) has, since the early 1980s mounted a Children's Rights Campaign mainly in the shanty-towns of Lima. Community participation was central to the strategy of creating awareness and mobilising people for action. In the shanty-town district of 3 de Mayo a Committee for the Defence of the Rights of the Child (CODEM) has been constituted by the parents and there is a similar children's committee. The aim of the committees is to investigate children's problems and to formulate possible solutions. The Committee of NGOs working in this all-year-round campaign has found direct communication through audio-visual presentations and drama the most effective channels of communication. Now, CODEM is producing its own newsletter. Though TV and radio were thought too costly by the Children's Rights Campaign, it is worth a small digression to point to the value of popular radio for the rural areas of Peru, and by extension to Latin America and the developing world. Radio is the medium best suited to the rural areas of Peru since it is both cheap and well adapted to the oral tradition of the peasantry. Recent experiments in educational radio are particularly noteworthy, such as *Tierra Fecunda* (Fertile Land) first broadcast in 1983. It has proved popular in disseminating a wide range of information not simply confined to agricultural practice. The impact achieved by *Tierra Fecunda* is evidenced by a network of over 700 correspondents throughout the country who receive 300 letters a month and about 3,000 correspondents bringing information and materials. This and similar radio programmes throughout the developing world represent an importants bringing information and materials. This and similar radio programmes throughout the developing world represent an important delivery system which could be out at the disposal of the Child Labour Campaign.

The Centre of Concern of Child Labour in Bangkok, Thailand, is a good example of an integrated approach to the raising to public awareness. Established in 1981 by an ecumenical association of Buddhists, Catholics and Protestants, the Centre operates across the activities of research, dissemination, pressure and welfare services provision. In 1982, the Centre published pamphlets containing warnings and advice for those rural families, especially in the impoverished north-east of the country, who are forced each year to send their children to work in Bangkok. The pamphlets were disseminated on a large scale to governors and governmental agencies for eventual distribution among villagers, labour officials and the media. In 1983 the Centre conducted research in Vierirem Province collecting information on children who had disappeared after obtaining work in Bangkok factories.

These grassroots organisations originating small-scale projects in the public education filed often work in isolation. There is a clear need not only to learn and, where possible, generalise from their experiences, but also to network them so that they can learn from each other. What these innovative projects generally have in common is a commitment to community participation which owes a great deal to the seminal work of the Brazilian educationalist Paulo Freire. In the early 1960s, Freire pioneered a new method of working with adult illiterates in his native north-east of Brazil. At the heart of this methodology is the concept of 'conscientisation'—the awakening of a critical consciousness in poor people. For Freire the way to break the 'culture of silence' characteristic of poor communities is through non-formal education. Indeed, Dickens's severe school-master, Mr. Gradgrind's obsession with facts, epitomizes what Friere terms the 'banking concept of education,' the aim of which is to fill people's minds with the facts and ideas of others. But to promote real awareness one needs to encourage people to think for themselves—to involve them in 'problem-posing education.' The coordinators of such programmes of education motivate through the use of the problem of poor people. These topics are typically raised in discussion groups or 'culture circles' using visual media like slides or pictures. Freire's ideas were highly influential in the 1970s but are essentially only a restatement of a precept and old as education itself; that people learn best by finding out for themselves. It was Pascal who observed that: '....we are usually convinced more easily by reasons we have found ourselves than by those which have occurred to others." Freire's methodology is important because of the principles of community involvement, and starting from where people are and are not from where you wish to take them. One could envisage 'learning circles' in which a discussion starter was: 'Is it better for our children to work rather than to go to school?'

These innovative projects are highly indicative of the types of techniques and strategies which might be further elaborated. What is needed now is a move beyond these fragmentary initiatives to a more systematic and integrated global strategy. In such a strategy one can identify at least three major action programmes. They are *workshops, training manuals,* and *mass communication campaigns.* Regional and national workshops are an important activity to enable people on the ground to share experiences and ideas. If participants are carefully selected, they offer an opportunity for identifying priorities and setting an agenda of feasible actions. They also provide the elements of a future network which is vital if the learning process is to be developed. Regional workshops to encompass the Americas, Africa, and Asia would need to have representatives of governments and workers' and employers' associations. The involvement of teacher unions should be particularly encouraged, given that they straddle both the world of child welfare and organised labour. In nineteenth and early twentieth-century Britain, teacher unions were an important factor in ensuring that poor children remained in school and had access to health and welfare services. Out of these well-prepared regional meetings it is important that a future agenda of regular reporting back on national experience is built in. Any programme of national workshops ought again to retain this basic tripartite core, added to which could be relevant NGOs, health professionals, the mass media and lawyers. The latter would seem to be another neglected professional group. Lawyers have a vested interest in child labour law, but they themselves may need educating first. As Jeremy Bentham pointed out: 'Lawyers are the only persons in whom the ignorance of the law is not punished.' Again, the basic aim would be to generate a deeper awareness of the problem with the objective of working towards the constitution of a national coalition for action. Perhaps these might be designated 'Child Protection Alliances' with a prominent patron. The CLC (Child Labour Campaign) Model outlined in this book would offer a practical tool for conceptualising the design of public awareness campaigns, either at the macro level of a nationally co-ordinated movement, or at the micro level of NGOs, workers' or employers, action. The field testing of the model at both levels would be vital and the experiences of its use, with suggestions for modifications, could be shared at regular regional meetings.

Training manuals for the literate trade union activist would make a significant contribution to the methodology of organising workers' education on a more informal and flexible basis at the community level. Such manuals would essentially be resources for tutors working with small groups of activists in workshop settings. They would function both as a resource and as a guide for people who would later run their own education programmes at the community level. As an exemplar the manual could offer a guide to co-operative learning. Active learning exercises built into manuals could increase participants' understanding of the issue of child labour, and their campaigning skills would be developed through the use and application of the CLC model.

The Trade Union Congress has already developed such a manual on child labour for its own membership. The Commonwealth Trade Union Council has, through its technical cooperation programme, particularly in Africa, experience of using training manuals and preparing 'study circle' books. One can envisage the adoption of a similar methodology with other appropriate groups. The use of manuals in teacher training is a clear possibility to develop teachers' child welfare capacity, and to enable them to improve curricula so that school children themselves can be mobilised in the campaign. Schools not only need a more relevant curriculum in order to retain children, they also need more flexible working arrangements to fit in with the needs of working children. In Peru, a national organisation of working children called MANTHOC, established since 1977, has attempted to create such awareness within the teaching profession. Employers, too, could be reached through an appeal to enlightened self-interest, as it would help erode chap labour competition. Many employers in the small-scale and marginal sector might be wiling to comply with the law if they were aware of the regulations and the penalties of non-compliance. Besides, employers could be appealed to in terms of the delivery of health services to child workers. Robert Owen used the argument with other employers that it was just as important to maintain human capital as physical capital if productivity was to be maximised. Both the and ILO recognised that it is possible to influence employers. There is little doubt too that a training manual resource would be an important tool for a range of NGOs to develop their advocacy function. After all training manuals provide the stimulus by which people educate themselves and develop their organisational skill.

Resource development to facilitate the mass dissemination

of information and to promote awareness is the third and final element in the integrated action programme. What can be done here to reach the mass of ordinary people, in particular parents? We must look to the mass communications media, particularly TV and radio, as powerful tools of social marketing. Again there are models to act as guides in the use of the mass media for public education. The ILO in 1985 began a mass media campaign in Latin American using a series of TV sports (of 15-30 seconds duration) to promote the message of equal rights for women. The ILO has been able to obtain the agreement of governments, workers and employers to this programme, and the national TV agreed to open up prime-time slots for these 'commercials.' The TV slots use a variety of media, including cartoons, to convey messages concerning equal fights for women. The series includes 12 TV sports which are repeated for 2-3 weeks before changing to the next. Argentina was the first to adopt the package in November 1985, followed by Bolivia, and similar agreements have been signed with the majority of the countries in the Americas Region. There is little doubt that such an approach would work equally well in urban area to deliver messages on the dangerous effects of child work, and particularly as a means of reaching those 'invisible' child workers who are employed as domestics in middle-class homes. It may well be that child domestic work (a priority concern in the field) is the most susceptible to this kind of public education campaign as so much of it rests on the attitudes and lifestyles of a group of affluent people who, unlike employers, have no collective strength.

In rural areas radio takes over, and we have already seen examples of attempts to use popular radio for development purposes. There is no reason to believe that programmes could not be devised, which, rather than castigating poor people for making their children work (for of course there are exploitative parents), communicated messages concerning the health and learning needs of children and how they could organise to press for improved services. Slide-tape presentations might also be used in village meetings. Already a group of Asian NGOs, collectively called Child Workers in Asia Support Group have used sets of slides based on a comic telling the story of a child worker from India. In addition, there is a cassette, a script, a copy of the comic, a set of eight pictures and a guide on how to organise group meetings, Any audio-visual package ought to be supported by such a group leader's guide. This proposed programme of integrated activities should not simply be a top-down' process. A 'bottom-up' feedback mechanism, in which lessons at the grassroots level are fed in at the national, regional and global levels, is vital if we are to improve the art of public awareness raising in relation to the child labour problem. It is the international agencies like ILO, UNICEF and WHO who are best placed to sponsor the piloting of such an integrated programme in public education, but it will be left to governments to engage in full-scale implementation. To conclude, it is worthwhile to say—'Where there is a wish there is way."

Chapter 13

Child Labour Laws: An Introduction

"No one ever would have crossed the ocean if the could have gotten of the ship in the storm."

—*C.F. Kettering*

Everywhere in every society, old traditions, values and norms create difficulty in adopting new changes for development and growth of its members. Therefore, reformation is needed to change its old system to meet the needs for their welfare and development. Long ago, child labour was not a social problem, but with the change in social understanding, child labour needed legislative protection against their exploitation and for their proper growth and development.

There are many laws and regulations in India to protect children from the adverse effects of employment especially on their physical and mental development. These laws are either derived from the Indian constitution or from the International Labour Organisation (ILO) recommendations, or from the declaration of the Rights of the Child unanimously adopted by the General Assembly of the United Nations on Nov. 20th, 1959.

Constitutional Commitment

The Constitution of India reflects its commitment to the welfare of children in the chapter on Directive Principles of State Policy. The Constitution makes were conscious of the requirements of children in need of extra care. Article 15 (3) lays down that "nothing it this article shall prevent the state from making any special provision for women and children." Article 24 proclaims that "no child below the age of 14 years shall be employed to work in any factory or mine or engaged in any other hazardous employment." Article 39 (c) provides that "the health, strength of the workers, man, women and the tender age of children are not abused and that the citizens are not forced by economic necessity to enter avocation unsuited to their age or strength." Article 39(f) enjoins "Childhood and youth are protected against exploitation and against moral and material abandonment"' Similarly, Article (45) provides that "the state shall endeavour to provide within a period of ten years from the commencement of the constitution for free and compulsory education for all children until they complete the age of 14 years."

International Labour Organisation (ILO) Efforts

Improvement of labour standards throughout the world is the basic aim of the ILO. It has paid particular attention to the protection of the employed children. It has sought to achieve its objective of protecting children by adopting international standards in the form of "conventions and recommendations." A convention seeks to create obligations of binding nature and its ratification requires complete compliance with all its provision. A recommendation, on the other hands, contains provision which are generally in the nature of guiding principles for action and may be implemented progressively and in parts. The ILO has so far adopted 18 conventions and 16 recommendation mainly in respect of children and young person in connection with their minimum age for entry to employment, medical examination before employment and work during nights. India has been able to ratify 6 of the ILO conventions concerning the employment of children and young persons in industrial and non-industrial occupations.

The United Nations declaration says that "the child by reason of his physical and mental immaturity needs special safeguards and care, including appropriate protection. The child shall enjoy the benefits of social security. He shall enjoy special protection and shall be given opportunities and facilities by law and by other means to enable him to develop in a healthy and normal manner and in conditions of freedom and dignity. In the enactments of laws for this purpose, the best interest of the child shall be the paramount considerations. The general assembly calls upon local authorities and national governments to recognise these rights, without discrimination on account of national or social origin, property, birth or other status whether or himself of his family.

Indian Statutory Provisions

1. *Statutory provisions regarding age for employment:* Almost all states regulate employment of children. The minimum age for employment differs from state to state. The relevant statutory provisions are briefly produced below:

A. *Factory Act, 1948:* The Act prohibits the employment of children below 14 years while ILO prescribes 15 years and above for employment in any factory using power and employing ten or more workers, and in a factory not using power and employing twenty or more workers on any date of the preceding 12 months. To safeguard the health of young persons between 14 to 18 years, the Act enjoins upon the employer to obtain a certificate of fitness from a surgeon and the certificate will be valid for a period of one year from the date of issue.

B. *Mines Act, 1952:* The minimum age of this Act for working in mines above ground is 15 years as recommended by ILO also. For underground employment, prescribed age limit is 16 years and above. In addition to this, a fitness certificate is also required from an authorised surgeon as in the factory Act, 1948.

C. *Plantation Labour Act, 1951:* Under this Act, a child of 12 years and below (according to ILO 14 years) shall not be employed in plantation of tea, coffee, rubber or cinchona within an area of 10,117 hectares of more and employing thirty or more persons. A child above 12 years willing to work in plantations is required to obtain a certificate of fitness which will be valid for the period of one year from the date of issue by certifying surgeon.

D. *Motor Transport Act, 1961:* Under this Act minimum age prescribed for employment in every transport undertaking employing five or more workers is 15 years and above. The ILO also recommends the same.

E. *Beedi and Cigarette Workers (Condition of Employment) Act, 1966:* Under this Act no child who has not completed his 14 years, shall be required or allowed to work in any industrial premises where any manufacturing process connected with making of beedi or cigar. Is carried on irrespective of the number of persons employed.

F. *Employment of Children Act, 1938:* To prevent employment of children inhazardous and unhealthy occupations the Act prohibits the employment of children below 15 years (as suggested by ILO) in any occupation connected with transport of passengers, goods or mails by railway, or a port-authority within the limits of a port. The Act prohibits the employment of children in railway particularly in construction work, catering services, track and line work as well as cleaning and picking of ash-pits and cinders. It also prohibits employment of children below 14 years in certain less hazardous occupations such as beedi-making, carpet weaving, cement manufacture, cloth printing, dyeing, and weaving, manufacture of matches, explosives and fire works, mica-cutting and splitting, shellac manufacture, soap manufacture and canning, etc. It may be mentioned that the Government of India has another bill to regulate employment of children.

G. *Merchant Shipping Act, 1958:* This Act prohibits the employment of children below 15 years of age in any capacity, on seagoing ships, except (a) in a school ship or training ship or (b) in a ship in which all persons employed are members of one family; or (c) in home made ship of less than two hundred tonnes gross; or (d) where such person is to be employed or nominal wages and will be in charge of his father or other adult male relative.

H. *Inland Steam Vessels Act, 1917* The Act applies to steam ships ordinarily playing in inland waters. The Act does not have any provision regulating employment of children. The reason for this omission seems to be that it is an old enactment when the community was not conscious of the need to have legislation for protection of children.

I. *Radiation Protection Rules, 1971:* Under this a child below 18 years of age is not to be employed at places where radiation takes place.

J. *State Shops and Commercial Establishment Act:* For the implementation of this act, different states have their own rules regulating employment and working hours in shops and establishment, restaurants and hotels, etc., to which the Factory Act does not apply. In Bihar, Gujarat, Jammu and Kashmir, Madhya Pradesh, Karnataka, Orissa, Rajasthan, Tripura, Uttar Pradesh, West Bengal, Goa Daman and Diu and Manipur, minimum age for employment in shops and commercial establishment is 12 years. In Andhra Pradesh, Assam, Haryana, Himachal Pradesh, Kerala, Tamil Nadu, Punjab, Delhi, Chandigarh, Pondicherry and Meghalaya, it is 14 years while 15 years in Maharashtra. According to the ILO it is 15 years.

K. *The Children (pledging of labour) Act, 1933:* The act prohibits any agreement written or oral to pledge the labour of child, whereby parents or guardians of such child undertakes to cause or allow the services of the child to be utilised for any employment in return for a payment received or to be received. A child under this Act is defined as a person who is under 15 years of age.

L. *The Apprentices Act, 1961:* Under this Act, a person shall not be qualified for being engaged as an apprentice to undergo apprenticeship training in any designated trade unless he has completed 14 years of age and fulfills the prescribed standard of education and physical fitness. The minimum educational qualification is 7th standard but for some jobs it is only 4th standard.

M. *The Contract Labour (regulations and abolition) Act, 1970:* Under this act, the permissible age for the working as contract labour is 18 and above. The second important aspect of the statutory provisions for the employment of children is the number of working hours. Different Acts have mentioned different working hours. The nature of these restrictions have been mentioned below:

1. *Hours of work:* Four and half hours per day have been prescribed for children under the Factory Act. Similarly, in Mines Act, for the adolescent who does not possess a fitness certificate from a surgeon working hour are 4 and a half per day. No limitation on daily working hours is prescribed under the Plantation Labour Act, 1951. Seven hours including rest period is prescribed in the Employment of Children Act, 1938. Different working hours have been prescribed in different provinces for the shops

and commercial establishments under the state acts.

2. *Limitations on weekly hours of work:* No clear-cut limitations have been prescribed for children under the Factory Act, 1948, the Mine Act, 1952 and the Railway (Hours of employment) Rules while Forty Hours a week for an adolescent and a child is prescribed in the Plantation Labour Act, 1951.
3. *Regulation of Rest Intervals:* The provision for the rest intervals has been prescribed under the Factory Act, 1948, and the plantation Labour Act, 1951. This provision is also made under the employment of children Act, 1938, and state Shops and commercial establishments Act.
4. *Night Work:* The provision for restriction of night work by children and in some cases even by young persons is available under the Factory Act, 1948. The Mines Act, 1952, the Plantation Act, 1951, Beedi and Cigar workers (conditions of employment) Act, 1966 and the State Shops and Commercial Establishments Acts. However, these provisions very in respect of age and prohibits work during nights.
5. *Provision on Shift relays and spread over:* Under the Factory Act, 1948, it is prescribed that the period of work of children shall be confined to two shifts which shall not spread over for more than 5 hours a day. Further, children shall be permitted to work only in one shift which can be changed for not more than once in a period of 30 days provided previous permission is obtained from the chief inspector of Factories.
6. *Double Employment:* Children are prohibited from working in more than one factory on any days under the Factory Act, 1948.
7. *Holidays:* Every working child under the Factory Act, 1948, Mines, Act, 1952, Motor Transport

Workers Act, 1961, and Beedi Workers, (condition of employment) Act is entitled to a weekly holiday.

8. *Safety:* Under the Factory Act, children are not allowed to work on pressing cotton where cotton opener is at work. Further the Act disallows the young person to clean lubricate or adjust any part of a prime-mover or of any transmission machinery while the prime-mover or transmission machinery is in motion or to clean, lubricate or adjust any part of any machine if it is likely to expose her or him to risk or injury from the part.
9. *Leave:* The annual leave with wages in available to the working children who have worked for more than 240 days or more during a calender year at the rate of one day for every 15 days of work performed by them under the Factory Act, 1948, the Plantation labour Act, 1951, The Motor Transport Workers Act, 1961 and the Beedi and Cigar Workers (condition of employment) Act, 1966. Provisions are different in different states for children working in the Shops and Commercial establishments.
10. *Wages:* Wages of the child workers are governed by the minimum Wages Act, 1948, and payment of Wages Act, 1936.
11. *Penalties:* Under the Factory Act, the occupier or manager of the factory is liable to be punished if found guilty of contravention of the provisions with a sentence of imparisonment upto 3 months of a fine upto Rs. 500 or with both. The adolescents using false certificates and parents or guardians permitting double employment of a child are also liable to be punished. The Employment of Children Act provides for punishment for contravention of the provisions of the Act with simple imprisonment extending to one month or fine upto Rs. 500 or with both. Children (pledging of Labour) Act, 1933

provides punishment to parents or guardians making an agreement to pledge labour of a child with a fine upto Rs. 50 and in the case of an employer with Rs. 200. Similarly, Beedi and Cigar Workers (conditions of employment) Act, 1966 provides for penalty of imprisonment upto 3 months and a fine upto Rs. 500 or both.

These Acts give an impression that the Government is doing its best to check the exploitation of children by employers and others, but the real picture in the field is otherwise. Various studies and reports by official and non-official organisations have pointed out a poor enforcement and gross violation of the provisions of these Acts by the employers in general and by shops and commercial establishments in particular. There have been a lot of debates on various aspects of this problem at various forums. The Law Association of Asia and Western Pacific have not been able to come out with a clear-cut opinion on the implementation of these acts. In fact, they are in a dilemma. If laws are enforced, on important supplementary family income is necessary for the survival of the family and as such laws become on absolute measures in the present Indian context. When the child labour is allowed, the unscrupulous persons and others motivated by a desire for higher profits fail to resist temptations to abuse child labour. This subject has generated a lot of heat in the minds of various segments of the population directly and indirectly concerned with this problem. The Concern expression in various forums led the Government to think about this problem more seriously.

Chapter 14

ILO Convention Concerning Minimum Age for Employment*

The General Conference of the International Labour Organistion,

Having been convened at Geneva by the Governing Body of the International Labour Office, and having met in its Fifty-eighth Session on 6 June 1973, and

Having a decided upon the adoption of certain proposals with regard to minimum age for admission to employment, which is the fourth item on the agenda of the session, and

Noting the terms of the Minimum Age (Industry) Convention, 1919, the Minimum Age (Sea) Convention, 1920, the Minimum Age (Agriculture) Convention, 1921, the Minimum Age (Trimmers and Stockers) Convention, 1921, the Minimum Age (Non-Industrial Employment) Convention, 1932, the Minimum Age (Sea) Convention (Revised), 1936, the Minimum Age (Industry) Convention (Revised), 1937, the Minimum Age (Non-Industrial Employment) Convention (Revised, 1937, the Minimum age (Fishermen) Convention, 1959, and the Minimum Age (Underground Work) Convention, 1965, and

Considering that the time has come to establish a general instrument on the subject, which would gradually replace the existing ones applicable to limited economic sectors, with a view to achieving the total abolition of child labour, and

Having determined that this instrument shall take the form of an international Convention,

* Convention No. 138.

adopts this twenty-sixth day of June of the year one thousand nine hundred and seventy-three the following Convention, which may be cited as the *Minimum Age Convention, 1973*:

Article 1

Each Member for which this Convention is in force undertakes to pursue a national policy designed to ensure the effective abolition of child labour and to raise progressively the minimum age for admission to employment or work to a level consistent with the fullest physical and mental development of young persons.

Article 2

1. Each Member which ratifies this Convention shall specify, in a declaration appended to its ratification, a minimum age for admission to employment or work within its territory and on means of transport registered in its territory; subject to Articles 4 to 8 of this Convention, no one under that age shall be admitted to employment or work in any occupation.

2. Each Member which has ratified this Convention may subsequently notify the Director-General of the International Labour Office, by further declarations, that it specifies a minimum age higher than that previously specified.

3. The minimum age specified in pursuance of paragraph 1 of this Article shall not be less than the age of completion of compulsory schooling and, in any case, shall not be less than 15 years.

4. Notwithstanding the provisions of paragraph 3 of this Article, a Member whose economy and educational facilities are insufficiently developed may, after consultation with the organisations of employers and workers concerned, where such exist, initially specify a minimum age of 14 years.

5. Each Member which has specified a minimum age of 14 years in pursuance of the provisions of the preceding paragraph shall include in its reports on the application of

this Convention submitted under article 22 of the Constitution of the International Labour Organisation a statement—

(a) that its reason for doing so subsists; or

(b) that it renounces its right to avail of the provisions in question as from a stated date.

Article 3

1. The minimum age for admission to any type of employment or work which by its nature or the circumstances in which it is carried out is likely to jeopardise the health, safety or morals of young persons shall not be less than 18 years.

2. The types of employment or work to which paragraph 1 of this Article applies shall be determined by national laws or regulations or by the competent authority, after consultation with the organisations of employers and workers concerned, where such exist.

3. Notwithstanding the provisions of paragraph 1 of this Article, national laws or regulations or the competent authority may, after consultation with the organisations of employers and workers concerned, where such exist, authorities employment or work as from the age of 16 years on condition that the health safety and morals of the young persons concerned are fully protected and that the young persons have received adequate specific instruction or vocational training in the relevant branch of activity.

Article 4

1. In so far as necessary, the competent authority, after consultation with the organisations of employers and workers concerned, where such exist, may exclude from the application of this Convention limited categories of employment or work in respect of which special and substantial problems of application arise.

2. Each Member which ratifies this Convention shall list in its first report on the application of the Convention submitted under article 22 of the Constitution of the International Labour Organisation any categories which may have been excluded in pursuance of paragraph 1 of this Article, giving the reasons for such exclusion, and shall state in subsequent reports the position of its law and practice in respect of the categories excluded and the extent to which effect has been given or is proposed to be given to the Convention in respect of such categories.

3. Employment or work covered by Article 3 of this Convention shall not be excluded from the application of the Convention in pursuance of this Article.

Article 5

1. A Member whose economy and administrative facilities are insufficiently developed may, after consultation with the organisations of employers and workers concerned, where such exist, initially limit the scope of application of this Convention.

2. Each Member which, avails, itself of the provisions of paragraph 1 of this Article shall specify, in a declaration appended to its ratification, the branches of economic activity or types of undertakings to which it will apply the provisions of the Convention.

3. The provisions of the Convention shall be applicable as a minimum to the following mining and quarrying; manufacturing; construction; electricity, gas and water; sanitary services; transport, storage and communication; and plantations and other agricultural undertakings mainly producing for commercial purposes, but excluding family and small-small holdings producing for local consumption and not regularly employing hired workers.

4. Any Member which has limited the scope of application of this Convention in pursuance of this Article—

(a) shall indicate in its reports under article 22 of the Constitution of the International Labour Organisation the general position as regards the employment or work of young persons and children in the branches of activity which are excluded from the scope of application of this Convention and any progress which may have been made towards wider application of the provisions of the Convention;

(b) may at any time formally extend the scope of application by a declaration addressed to the Director-General of the International Labour Office.

Article 6

This Convention does not apply to work done by children and young persons in schools for general, vocational or technical education or in other training institutions, or to work done by persons at least 14 years of age in undertakings, where such work is carried out in accordance with conditions prescribed by the competent authority, after consultation with the organisations of employers and workers concerned, where such exist, and is an integral part of—

(a) a course of education or training for which a school or training institution is primarily responsible;

(b) a programme of training mainly or entirely in an undertaking, which programme has been approved by the competent authority; or

(c) a programme of guidance or orientation designed to facilitate the choice of an occupation or of a line of training.

Article 7

1. National laws or regulations may permit the employment or work of persons 13 to 15 years of age on light work which is—

(a) not likely to be harmful to their health or development; and

(b) not such as to prejudice their attendance at school, their participation in vocational orientation or training programmes approved by the competent authority or their capacity to benefit from the instruction received.

2. National laws or regulations may also permit the employment or work of persons who are at least 15 years of age but have not yet completed their compulsory schooling on work which meets the requirements set forth in subparagraphs (a) and (b) of paragraph 1 of this Article.

3. The competent authority shall determine the activities in which employment or work may be permitted under paragraphs 1 and 2 of this Article and shall prescribe the number of hours during which and the conditions in which such employment or work may be undertaken.

4. Notwithstanding the provisions of paragraphs 1 and 2 of this Article, a Member which has availed itself of the provisions of paragraph 4 of Article 2 may, for as long as it continues to do so, substitute the ages 12 and 14 for the ages 13 and 15 in paragraph 1 and the age 14 for the age 15 in paragraph 2 of this Article.

Article 8

1. After consultation with the organisations, of employers and workers concerned, where such exist, the competent authority may, be permits granted in individual cases, allow exceptions to the prohibition of employment or work provided for in Article 2 of this Convention, for such purposes as participation in artistic performances.

2. Permits so granted shall limit the number of hours during which and prescribe the conditions in which employment or work is allowed.

Article 9

1. All necessary measures, including the provision of

appropriate penalties, shall be taken by the competent authority to ensure the effectively enforcement of the provisions of this Convention.

2. National laws or regulations or the competent authority shall define the persons responsible for compliance with the provisions giving effect to the Convention.

3. National laws or regulations or the competent authority shall prescribe the registers or other documents which shall be kept and made available by the employer; such registers or documents shall contain the names and ages or dates or birth, duly certified wherever possible, or persons whom he employes or who work for him and who less than 18 years of age.

Article 10

1. This Convention revises, on the terms set forth in this Article, the Minimum Age (Industry) Convention, 1919, the Minimum Age (Sea) Convention, 1920, the Minimum Age (Agriculture) Convention, 1921, the Minimum Age (Trimmers and Stokers) Convention, 1921, the Minimum Age (Non-Industrial Employment) Convention, 1932, the Minimum Age (Sea) Convention (Revised), 1936, the Minimum Age (Industry) Convention (Revised) 1937, the Minimum Age (Non-Industrial Employment) Convention (Revised), 1937, the Minimum Age (Fishermen) Convention, 1959, and the Minimum Age (Underground Work) Convention, 1965.

2. The coming into force of this convention shall not close the minimum Age (Sea) Convention (Revised), 1936, the Minimum Age (Industry) Convention, (Revised), 1937, the Minimum Age (Non-Industrial Employment) Convention (Revised), 1937, the Minimum Age (Fishermen) Convention, 1959, or the Minimum Age (Underground Work) Convention, 1965, to further ratification.

3. The Minimum Age (Industry) Convention, 1919, the

Minimum Age (Sea) Convention, 1920, the Minimum Age (Agriculture) Convention, 1921, and the Minimum Age (Trimmers and Stokers) Convention, 1921, shall be closed to further ratification when all the parties thereto have consented to such closing by ratification of this Convention or by a declaration communicated to the Director-General of the International Labour Office.

4. When the obligations of this Convention are accepted—

(a) by a Member which is a party to the Minimum Age (Industry) Convention (Revised), 1937, and a minimum age of not less than 15 years is specified in pursuance of Article 2 of this Convention, this shall *ipso jure* involve the immediate denunciation of that Convention,

(b) in respect of non-industrial employment as defined in the Minimum Age (Non-Industrial Employment) Convention, 1932, by a Member which is a party to that Convention, this shall *ipso jure* involve the immediate denunciation of that Convention.

(c) in respect of non-industrial employment as defined in the Minimum Age (Non-Industrial Employment) Convention (Revised), 1937, by a Member which is a party to that Convention, and a minimum age of not less than 15 years is specified in pursuance of Article 2 of this Convention, this shall *ipso jure* involve the immediate denunciation of that Convention,

(d) in respect of maritime employment, by a Member which is a party to the Minimum Age (Sea) Convention (Revised), 1936, and a minimum age of not less than 15 years is specified in pursuance of Article 2 of this Convention or the Member specifies that Article 3 of this Convention applies to maritime employment, this shall *ipso jure* involve the immediate denunciation of that Convention,

(e) in respect of employment in maritime fishing, by a Member which is a party to the Minimum Age (Fishermen) Convention, 1959, and a minimum age of not less than 15 years is specified in pursuance of Article 2 of this Convention or the Member specifies that Article 3 of this Convention applies to employment in maritime fishing, this shall *ipso jure* involve the immediate denunciation of that Convention,

(f) by a Member which is a party to the Minimum Age (Underground Work) Convention, 1965, and a minimum age of not less than the age specified in pursuance of that Convention is specified in pursuance of Article 2 of this Convention or the Member specifies that such an age applies to employment underground in mines in virtue of Article 3 of this Convention, this shall *ipso jure* involve the immediate denunciation of that Convention,

if and when this Convention shall have come into force.

5. Acceptance of the obligation of the Convention—

(a) shall involve the denunciation of the Minimum Age (Industry) Convention, 1919, in accordance with Article 12 thereof,

(b) in respect of agriculture shall involve the denunciation of the Minimum Age (Agriculture) Convention, 1921, in accordance with Article 9 thereof,

(c) in respect of maritime employment shall involve the denunciation of the Minimum Age (Sea) Convention, 1920, in accordance with Article 10 thereof, and of the Minimum Age (Trimmers and Stokers) Convention, 1921, in accordance with Article 12 thereof,

if and when this Convention shall have come into force.

Article 11

The formal ratifications of this Convention shall be

communicated to the Director-General of the International Labour Office for registration.

Article 12

1. This Convention shall be binding only upon those Members of the International Labour Organisation whose ratifications have been registered with the Director-General.

2. It shall come into force twelve months after the date on which the ratifications of two Members have been registered with the Director-General.

3. Thereafter, this Convention shall come into force for any Member twelve months after the date on which its ratification has been registered.

Article 13

1. A Member which has ratified this Convention may denounce it after the expiration of ten years from the date on which the Convention first comes into force, by an act communicated to the Director-General of the International Labour Office for registration. Such denunciation shall not take effect until one year after the date on which it is registered.

2. Each Member which has ratified this Convention and which does not, within the year following the expiration of the period of ten years mentioned in the preceding paragraph, exercise the right of denunciation provided for in this Article, will be bound for another period of ten years and, thereafter, may denounce this Convention at the expiration of each period of ten years under the terms provided for in this Article.

Article 14

1. The Director-General of the International Labour Office shall notify all Members of the International Labour Organisation of the registration of all ratifications and denunciations communicated to him by the Members of the Organisation.

2. When notifying the Members of the Organisation of the registration of the second ratification communicated to him, the Director-General shall draw the attention of the Members of the Organisation to the date upon which the Convention will come into force.

Article 15

The Director-General of the International Labour Office shall communicate to the Secretary-General of the United Nations for registration in accordance with Article 102 of the Charter of the United Nations full particulars of all ratifications and acts of denunciation registered by him in accordance with the provisions of the preceding Articles.

Article 16

At such times as it may consider necessary the Governing Body of the International Labour Office shall present to the General Conference a report on the working of this Convention and shall examine the desirability of placing on the agenda of the Conference the question of its revision in whole or in part.

Article 17

1. Should the Conference adopt a new Convention revising this Convention in while or in part, when unless the new Convention otherwise provides—

(a) the ratification by a Member of the new revising Convention shall *ipso jure* involve the immediate denunciation of this Convention, notwithstanding the provisions of Article 13 above, if and when the new revising Convention shall have come into force;

(b) as from the date when the new revising Convention comes into force this Convention shall cease to be open to ratification by the Members.

2. This Convention shall in case remain in force in its actual form and content for those Members which have ratified it but have not ratified the revising Convention.

Article 18

The English and French versions of the text of this Convention are equally authoritative.

RECOMMENDATION CONCERNING MINIMUM AGE FOR ADMISSION TO EMPLOYMENT*

The General Conference of the International Labour Organisation,

Having been convened at Geneva by the Governing Body of the International labour Office, and having met in its Fifty-eighty Session on 6 June 1973, and

Recognising that the effective abolition of child labour and the progressive raising of the minimum age for admission to employment constitute only one aspect of the protection and advancement of children and young persons, and

Noting the concern of the whole United Nations system with such protection and advancement, and

Having adopted the Minimum Age Convention, 1973, and

Desirous to define further certain elements of policy which are the concern of the International Labour Organisation, and

Having decided upon the adoption of certain proposals regarding minimum age for admission to employment, which is the fourth item on the agenda of the session, and

Having determined that these proposals shall take the form of a Recommendation supplementing the Minimum Age Convention, 1973.

adopts this twenty-sixth day of June of the year one thousand

---

* Recommendation No. 146.

nine hundred and seventy-three the following Recommendation, which may be cited as the Minimum Age Recommendation, 1973:

I. National Policy

1. To ensure the success of the national policy provided for in Article 1 of the Minimum Age Convention, 1973, high priority should be given to planning for and meeting the needs of children and youth in national development policies and programmes and to the progressive extension of the inter-related measures necessary to provide the best possible conditions of physical and mental growth for children and young persons.

2. In the connection special attention should be given to such areas of planning and policy as the following:

(a) firm national commitment to full employment, in accordance with the Employment Policy Convention and Recommendation, 1964, and the taking of measures designed to promote employment-oriented development in rural and urban areas;

(b) the progressive extension of other economic and social measures to alleviate poverty wherever it exists and to ensure family living standards and income which are such as to make it unnecessary to have recourse to the economic activity of children;

(c) the development and progressive extension, without any discrimination, of social security and family welfare measures aimed at ensuring child maintenance, including children's allowances;

(d) the development and progressive extension of adequate facilities for education and vocational orientation and training appropriate in form and content to the needs of the children and young persons concerned;

(e) the development and progressive extension of appropriate facilities for the protection and welfare of children and young persons, including employed young persons, and for the promotion of their development.

3. Particular account should as necessary be taken of the needs of children and young persons who do not have families or do not live with their own families and of migrant children and young persons who live and travel with their families. Measures taken to that end should include the provision of fellowships and vocational training.

4. Full-time attendance at school or participation in approved vocational orientation or training programmes should be required and effectively ensured up to an age at least equal to that specified for admission to employment in accordance with Article 2 of the Minimum Age Convention, 1973.

5. (1) Consideration should be given to measures such as preparatory training, not involving hazards, for types of employment or work in respect of which the minimum age prescribed in accordance with Article 3 of the Minimum Age Convention, 1973, is higher than the age of completion of compulsory full-time schooling.

(2) Analogous measures should be envisaged where the professional exigencies of a particular occupation include a minimum age for admission which is higher than the age of completion of compulsory full-time schooling.

II. Minimum Age

6. The minimum age should be fixed at the same level for all sectors of economic activity.

7. (1) Members should take as their objective the progressive raising to 16 years of the minimum age for admission to employment or work specified in pursuance of Article 2 of the Minimum Age Convention, 1973.

(2) Where the minimum age for employment or work covered by Article 2 of the Minimum Age Convention, 1973, is still below 15 years, urgent steps should be taken to raise it to that level.

8. Where it is not immediately feasible to fix a minimum age for all employment in agriculture and in related activities in rural areas, a minimum age should be fixed at least for employment on plantations and in the other agricultural undertakings referred to in Article 5, paragraph 3, of the Minimum Age Convention, 1973.

III. Hazardous Employment or Work

9. Where the minimum age for admission to types of employment or work which are likely to jeopardise the health, safety or morals of young persons is still below 18 years, immediate steps should be taken to raise it to that level.

10 (1) In determining the types of employment or work to which Article 3 of the Minimum Age Convention, 1973, applies, full account should be taken of relevant international labour standards, such as those concerning dangerous substances, agents or processes (including ionising radiations), the lifting of heavy weights and underground work.

(2) The list of the types of employment or work in question should be re-examined periodically and revised as necessary, particularly in the light of advancing scientific and technological knowledge.

11. Where, by reference to Article 5 of the Minimum Age Convention, 1973, a minimum age is not immediately fixed for certain branches of economic activity or types of undertakings, appropriate minimum age provisions should be made applicable therein to types of employment or work presenting hazards for young persons.

IV. Conditions of Employment

12 (1) Measures should be taken to ensure that the

conditions in which children and young persons under the age of 18 years are employed or work reach and are maintained at a satisfactory standard. These conditions should be supervised closely.

(2) Measures should likewise be taken to safeguard and supervise the conditions in which child and young persons undergo vocational orientation and training within undertakings, training institutions and schools for vocational or technical education and to formulate standards for their protection and development.

13. (1) In connection with the application of the preceding Paragraph, as well as in giving effect to Article 7, paragraph 3, of the Minimum Age Convention, 1973, special attention should be given to—

(a) the provision of fair remuneration and its protection, bearing in mind the principle of equal pay for equal work;

(b) the strict limitation of the hours spent at work in a day and in a week, and the prohibition of overtime, so as to allow enough time for education and training (including the time needed for homework related thereto), for rest during the day and for leisure activities;

(c) the granting, without possibility of exception save in genuine emergency, of a minimum consecutive period of 12 hours' night rest, and of customary weekly rest days;

(d) the granting of an annual holiday with pay of at least four weeks and, in any case, not shorter than that granted to adults;

(e) coverage by social security schemes, including employment injury, medical care and sickness benefit schemes, whatever the conditions of employment or work may be;

(f) the maintenance of satisfactory standards of safety and health and appropriate instruction and supervision.

(2) Subparagraph (1) of this Paragraph applies to young seafarers in so far as they are not covered in respect of the matters dealt with therein by international labour Conventions or Recommendations specifically concerned with maritime employment.

V. Enforcement

14. (1) Measures to ensure the effective application of the Minimum Age Convention, 1973, and of the Recommendation should include—

(a) the strengthening as necessary of labour inspection and related services, for instance by the special training of inspectors to detect abuses in the employment of work of children and young persons and to correct such abuses; and

(b) the strengthening of services for the improvement and inspection of training in undertakings.

(2) Emphasis should be placed on the role which can be played by inspectors in supplying information and advice on effective means of complying with relevant provisions as well as in securing their enforcement.

(3) Labour inspection and inspection of training in undertakings should be closely co-ordinated to provide the greatest economic efficiency and, generally, the labour administration services should work in close co-operation with the services responsible for the education, training, welfare and guidance of children and young persons.

15. Special attention should be paid—

(a) to the enforcement of provisions concerning employment in hazardous types of employment or work; and

(b) in so far as education or training is compulsory, to the prevention of the employment or work of children and young persons during the hours when instruction is available.

16. The following measures should be taken to facilitate the verification of ages:

(a) the public authorities should maintain an effective system of birth registration, which should include the issue of birth certificates;

(b) employers should be required to keep and to make available to the competent authority registers or other documents indicating the names and ages or dates of birth, duly certified wherever possible, not only of children and young persons employed by them but also of the those receiving vocational orientation or training in their undertakings;

(c) children and young persons working in the streets, in outside stalls, in public places, in itinerant occupations or in other circumstances which make the checking of employers' records impracticable should be issued licences or other documents indicating their eligibility for such work.

INTERNATIONAL YEAR OF THE CHILD (1979): INFORMATION RECEIVED FROM GOVERNMENTS OF MEMBER STATES ON ACTION IN RESPECT OF THE MINIMUM AGE CONVENTION (NO. 138) AND RECOMMENDATION (NO. 146), 1973

1. At its 204th Session (November 1977) the Governing Body of the International Labour Office considered that the ILO's contribution to the International Year of the Child should include a special effort to promote the implementation of the ILO's most recent comprehensive standards on the minimum age for admission to employment. It accordingly decided to invite the governments of member States:

(a) to consider taking such further action as might be necessary to give effect to the provisions of the Minimum Age Convention (No. 138) and Recommendation (No. 146), 1973, and to consider the ratification of the Convention, if not yet ratified; and

(b) to inform the Director-General, by 31 July 1978, of any such action taken or contemplated and of any difficulties which in their view stand in the way of the implementation of the instruments in question and the ratification of the Convention.

The Governing Body requested the Director-General to submit to the Committee on Standing Orders and the Application of Conventions and Recommendations, in November 1978, a report summarising the information received, as a basis for consideration of any further action which might be called for at that stage.

2. The Governments of the following 58 States have supplied information: Argentina, Austria, Bahrain, Belgium, Bolivia, Brazil, Bulgaria, Burundi, Byelorussian SSR, Canada, Cuba, Cyprus, Czechoslovakia, Ethiopia, Finland, France, Gabon, German Democratic Republic, Federal Republic of Germany, Ghana, Guatemala, Hungary, India, Indonesia, Iran, Iraq, Ireland, Japan, Kenya , Libyan Arab Jamahiriya, Mali, Mauritius, Mexico, Morocco, New Zealand, Niger, Norway, Pakistan, Panama, Papua New Guinea, Paraguay, Philippines, Poland, Romania, Rwanda, Senegal, Spain, Sri Lanka, Suriname, Sweden, Switzerland, Tunisia, Ukrainian SSR, United Kingdom, Uruguay, Venezuela, Zaire, Zambia.

Ratification Position and Prospects with Respect to Convention No. 138

3. Convention No. 138 has so far been ratified by the following 13 countries: Cost Rica, Cuba, Finland, Federal Republic of Germany, Ireland, Libyan Arab Jamahiriya,

Luxembourg, Netherlands, Poland, Romania, Spain Uruguay, Zambia.

4. In two countries—Bolivia and Iraq—the ratification of the Convention has been approved but not yet formally communicated to the ILO. The Government of Kenya proposes to ratify the Convention. In Burundi, Gabon, Italy and Zaire, a proposal for its ratification has been submitted to the legislature or the President. The Government of Tunisia, on the basis of a comparative study, has concluded that national legislation is in full conformity with the Convention; its ratification is being examined. The Government of Czechoslovakia considers that national legislation is in conformity with Convention No. 138 and Recommendation No. 146 and when certain minor points have been clarified, will examine the possibility of ratifying the Convention. Ratification is being considered in Rwanda. In Ghana, a recommendation in favour of ratification made by the tripartite Labour Advisory Committee is under consideration by the Government. The Governments of Mauritius and Norway have indicated that the implementation and rectification of the Convention are to be further considered by tripartite advisory bodies. The Government of the German Democratic Republic states that, on the occasion of the International Year of the Child, all ILO Conventions relating to the employment and training of children and young persons are being examined to decide whether they should be ratified or any other measures taken. In Cyprus a committee consisting of representatives of all the services concerned has been set up to consider the possibility of taking such action as may be necessary to give effect to Convention No. 138 and Recommendation No. 146.

5. The Government of the Byelorussian SSR states that its legislation and practice fully meet, and in many respects go beyond, the standards laid down in Convention No. 138. The Government of the Ukrainian SSR has provided particulars

of legislation and practice corresponding to those given by the Byelorussian SSR.

6. The Government of the Federal Republic of Germany, which has ratified Convention No. 138, indicates that its legislation was amended to make the ratification possible. A number of governments which consider that their country is not at present in a position to ratify the Convention also refer to measures which have been taken or are contemplated to improve the protection in employment of children and young persons. The Government of India has adopted a National Policy for Children and established a National Children's Board for planning, review and co-ordination (of which the Prime Minister of India is president); the Government is committed to the gradual elimination of child labour, and measures to raise the minimum age in certain sectors are contemplated or in course of adoption. In the Philippines a "Decade of the Filipino Child 1977-87" has been declared and a National Plan of Action adopted. In Canada it is proposed to include consideration of the application of Convention No. 138 and Recommendation No. 146 in the agenda of the next federal-provincial meeting of Deputy Ministers of Labour. The Austria Government has referred to the influence of Convention No. 138 on the raising of the minimum age for employment in agriculture and forestry. The Government of Suriname intends to raise the minimum age for employment of young persons as fishermen to 15 years, in conformity with Convention No. 112, and the Government of the United Kingdom is considering the adoption of regulations concerning minimum age for employment at sea which would make possible the ratification of Convention No. 58. Further particulars of measures contemplated are given below in the review of difficulties in the implementation of Convention No. 138 and Recommendation No. 146.

7. A number of governments, while providing some

indications concerning their legislation on minimum age for employment, state that they are not in a position to ratify Convention No. 138. Many of them consider it difficult, at their country's present stage of development, to extend minimum age protection to all sectors of activity, to raise the minimum age to the required level, or to ensure general observance of minimum age standards. Problems of this kind are mentioned by the Governments of Argentina, Brazil, Ethiopia, India, Indonesia, Iran, Mali, Mexico, Morocco, Pakistan, Papua New Guinea, Paraguay, Sri Lanka, Suriname and Venezuela. It is not apparent from the replies whether, in all these cases, full account has been taken of the range of flexibility permitted by the Convention as regards the sectors to be covered by minimum age provisions, the possibility of excluding limited categories of employment, the fixing of the general minimum age at 14 years (instead of 15 years) in the case of developing countries, and the authorisation of employment in light work as from the age of 13 years (or 12 years, for countries fixing the general minimum age at 14 years). More specific difficulties mentioned by government are analysed below.

Difficulties in the Implementation of Convention No. 138

Scope

8. The Convention, in contrast to earlier minimum age Conventions applicable to limited economic sectors (which it is designed gradually to replace), applies to all forms of employment or work. However, a State whose economic and administrative facilities are insufficiently developed may initially limit the scope of application of the Convention, but must apply it at least to mining and quarrying; manufacturing; construction; electricity, gas and water; sanitary services; transport, storage and communication; and plantations and other agricultural undertakings mainly producing for commercial purposes, but excluding family and small-scale holdings producing for local consumption and not regularly

employing hired workers. In addition, limited categories of employment or work in respect of which special and substantial problems of application arise may be excluded, provided that they do not involve danger to health, safety or morals.

9. The Government of Canada indicates that, although school attendance is compulsory everywhere at least up to 15 years, it remains necessary to establish a minimum age for employment in agriculture; in addition, in two jurisdictions no minimum age exists for work in factories, hotels and restaurants. In Norway and Switzerland minimum age provisions do not at present apply to agriculture; in the former country it is proposed to extend them to that sector. In India minimum age legislation dos not cover all activities to which the Convention must be applied even under the special relaxation for developing countries. In Pakistan minimum age provisions do not apply in agriculture and the rural industrial sector. The reply from the Government of Bahrain mentions only legislation applicable to the private sector.

10. The Governments of Sweden and Switzerland indicate that the existing minimum are legislation applies only to persons working under an employment relationship, whereas the Convention is not confined to such persons.

Minimum Age

11. The Convention requires ratifying States to specify a minimum age which should not be less than the age of completion schooling, and in any case not less than 15 years. A country whole economy and educational facilities are insufficiently developed may, however, initially specify a minimum age of 14 years. Of the 13 countries which have so far ratified the Convention, all but two have specified a minimum age of 15 years; the Libyan Arab Jamahiriya and Romania specified 18 and 16 years respectively. Most of the non-ratifying States which have supplied information on

their legislation appear to have set their general minimum age at a level consistent with the minimum standard of 15 years (or 14 years permitted initially for developing countries) laid down in the Convention.

12. The Belgian Government states that the only obstacle to ratification of the Convention is the fact that compulsory schooling ends at 14 years, whereas the Convention fixes a minimum age for employment of 15 years; the extension of compulsory schooling is contemplated. In Hungary compulsory schooling covers eight classes, which must children complete by the age of 14; however, more than 90 per cent continue their studies. The Government considers that it would be inappropriate to deprive the small number who do not continue their studies after the age of 14 of the possibility of entering employment, and refers to special conditions applicable to workers under 16 years (reduced hours, additional paid leave, prohibition of night work and of employment in arduous or unhealthy work). In Switzerland, in cantons where the school-leaving age is 14 years children who have completed their schooling may be employed, without limitation of such employment to light work. The Austrian Government mentions that, while in general children complete their compulsory education and can take up work only after they have reached the age of 15 years, exceptionally compulsory education may be completed and employment taken for a brief period before that age. The Canadian Government states that in one province with a school-leaving age of 16 years the minimum age for employment is 15.

13. A number of developing countries indicate that their legislation does not yet meet the 14-year minimum age standard which Convention No. 138 would permit them to apply initially. In Indonesia, Iran and Morocco the general minimum age for entry into employment is 12 years. The Government of Iran states that draft amending legislation now under consideration would raise this age to 14 years. The Government

of Indonesia is examining the possibility of similar action. In Morocco a draft Labour Code would provide for a minimum age of 13 years. In India, while a minimum age of 14 or 15 years is laid down for employment in a wide range of industrial activities, rail and motor transport, merchant shipping, etc., the minimum age for work on plantations is 12 years and for employment in shops and commercial establishments it varies from 12 to 14 years (but was recently raised to 15 in one state). The raising of the minimum age under the Plantations Act to 14 years is to be examined when that Act is next amended, and state governments have been requested to raise the minimum age for shops and commercial establishments to 14 years, where this is not already the case; some state governments have already agreed to take such action. The Government of Pakistan reports that the minimum age under the Factories Act and the legislation on shops and commercial establishments was recently raised from 12 to 14 years. In Argentina children under 14 years may be permitted to work when this is necessary for their own or their family's subsistence. The Government of Venezuela states that, although the minimum age for employment is 14 years; economic factors frequently lead children to take up work before that age, and it considers that it would be justified to lower the minimum age to 13 years in such cases provided that it is limited to light work as permitted by the Convention.

14. In general, where the minimum age standard provided for in the Convention cannot yet be fully attained, it would seem appropriate to re-examine the legislation with due regard to the provisions of the Convention relating to light work. In some cases the possibility of excluding limited categories of employment or work from the application of the Convention may also make it possible to overcome marginal problems.

Dangerous Work

15. The Convention provides that the minimum age for admission to employment or work dangerous to health, safety

or morals shall be not less than 18 years or, under certain conditions, 16 years. It leaves the employments in question to be determined by each State after consultation with employers' and workers' organisations.

16. From the information supplied it would appear that the principle of setting the level for admission to dangerous work at 18 years is widely accepted, although the range of jobs to which that standard applies varies considerably. The Government of Canada, however, indicates that in general Canadian legislation does not contain a definition of "dangerous employment" and that, while the minimum age for underground work in mines is generally 18 years, it is 17 years in one province and the federal jurisdiction. In Mexico and Morocco the minimum age for dangerous work is in general 16 years. In Austria, for agriculture and forestry, there exists no list of employments prohibited for persons under 18 years. In France the application to employment in agriculture of the general provisions on dangerous work prohibited for young persons is dependent on the issue of a decree now under consideration. In Norway, where a number of specific prohibitions of employment in dangerous work of persons under 18 years are contained in the basic legislation, detailed regulations to supplement these provisions are being prepared. In Sweden measures to meet the requirements of Convention No. 138 as regards dangerous work on board ship are under consideration.

Light Work

17. The Convention leaves it open to ratifying States to permit the employment on light work which is not harmful to their health or development, and not prejudicial to attendance at school or participation in vocational orientation or training programmes, of children between 13 and 15 years (or between 12 and 14 years for States having specified a general minimum age of 14 years) and of children above that age who are still subject to compulsory schooling. From the

information supplied it appears that most countries permit the employment on light work of children below the general minimum age. However, in several countries where the general minimum age is 15 (Austria, Japan) or 16 (France) light work is permitted as from the age of 12, instead of 13 as specified in the Convention. The Government of Sweden indicates that, while light work is permitted only in limited circumstances, there is no lower age limit for such work. The Government of New zealand indicates that children may be employed part-time on certain forms of light work, the prohibition of which would not have public support or appear necessary. The Government of Mauritius mentions the possibility for children under 15 to be employed in light work in agriculture and the construction industry, without indicating whether this is subject to any minimum age condition.

18. The Convention also permits exceptions from minimum age standards to be made, by permits granted in individual cases, for such purposes as participation in artistic performances. The United Kingdom Government states that its legislation allows children to take part without permit in such performances subject to defined conditions, observance of which is subject to inspection and enforced by penal sanctions. The Government considers that the welfare of the children is safeguard and does not propose to alter the legislation.

Consultation

19. The Convention provides for the consultation of the employers' and workers' organisations concerned on various matters such as the determination of dangerous occupations and certain exclusions or exceptions. The Government of Brazil states that, while national legislation already contains provisions on child labour corresponding to those of the Convention, with due regard to conditions obtaining in developing countries, the system does not permit the

consultation of employers' and workers' organisations in the form required by the Convention.

Enforcement

20. The Convention contains various provisions relating to the enforcement of its provisions, including the provision of appropriate penalties and the keeping of registers or other documents by employers. The United Kingdom Government indicates that its legislation requires the keeping of registers only in industrial employment and that the standard of record-keeping is poor especially among small employers. However, legislation on non-industrial employment of school children is being reviewed, and the making of regulations to require employers to keep records of children employed is contemplated. The Governments of several other countries (Indonesia, Mali, Pakistan, Venezuela) refer more generally to the difficulties encountered in enforcing existing minimum age legislation in view of prevailing economic conditions.

Comments Regarding the Implementation of Recommendation No. 146

21. Only relatively few replies refer specifically to the situation with regard to Recommendation No. 146. The Government of Ireland and Norway state that they have accepted this Recommendation. The Government of Sweden states that the aspirations expressed in the Recommendation are in general agreement with Swedish attitudes (although national legislation prescribes a night rest of 11 hours for young persons, as compared with the 12-hour rest provided for in the Recommendation). The Government of India, while giving particulars of its national policy to promote the welfare of children and of its efforts to raise the minimum age for employment, states that the objective of the progressive raising of the minimum age to 16 years stated in the Recommendation is not easy of attainment in developing countries like India. The Government of Kenya also states that it cannot at present ensure full-time education or training of all children under

16 years. The Governments of the Byelorussian SSR, Czechoslovakia, France, Norway Romania, the Ukrainian SSR and the United Kingdom indicate that the general minimum age for employment in their countries is 16 years; in Spain the minimum age is being raised to this level in conjunction with the introduction of new educational and training measures. The Government of Japan considers that the raising of the minimum age from 15 to 16 years requires careful study, including its relation to the completion of compulsory education. It also mentions that national legislation does not ensure a night rest of 12 hours for young persons nor entitle them to a special annual holiday with pay. The Government of Austria and the United Kingdom refer to the difficulties mentioned in connection with the Convention. The latter Government also states that it cannot accept responsibility for application of certain provisions of the Recommendation relating to matters (hours of work, night rest, holidays with pay) which are normally dealt with by collective bargaining.

Conclusions

22. The information available indicates that the general principles underlying Convention No. 138 and recommendation No. 146 find a very wide measure of support and that the problem of child labour is receiving close attention from national policy makers, both within the framework of the International Year of the Child and as an important aspect of economic and social development planning. In many countries measures to improve the protection of children and young persons in regard to work have recently been taken or are under consideration. It would appear that Convention No. 138 and Recommendation No. 146, as a comprehensive and up-to-date statement of internationally agreed principles, are providing a direct source of inspiration and reference in this process. Their use in this connection is facilitated by the dynamic but flexible approach adopted in these instruments: they aim at a progressive raising of

standards; they permit the gradual integration of young persons into active life on the basis of distinctions between light work, employment in general and dangerous occupations; and they make allowance for the varying possibilities of countries at different stages of development.

23. Nevertheless, the information so far available does not permit of a full or precise analysis of the situation with regard to the implementation of Convention No. 138 and Recommendation No. 146. Less than half the member States have provided information. The replies received vary considerably in volume and detail, and frequently they do not clearly identify the problems which may impede acceptance of these standards. In particular, while a number of developing counties express doubt as to their ability to ratify Convention No. 138, many of them do not provide any detailed analysis of the difficulties encountered or seek to accommodate these difficulties within the different flexibility devices embodied in the Convention. A more detailed examination of these questions would be useful, bearing in mind the relationship between the raising of minimum age standards and other aspects of social policy to which reference is made in Recommendation No. 146 (such as measures to combat youth unemployment and to develop and adapt facilities for education and training). Furthermore, it has not been possible within the present context to analyse ways in which the various difficulties mentioned by governments might be resolved. This aspect also would merit further review.

24. To permit fuller study of national law and practice regarding the minimum age for admission to employment and to facilitate the application of the Convention and Recommendation of 1973, it would appear useful to obtain reports from member States under the provisions of article 19 of the Constitution (reports on unratified Conventions and Recommendations). This would provide a basis for a general survey of the situation by the Committee of Experts

on the Application of Conventions and Recommendations. A proposal that Convention No. 138 and Recommendation No. 146 should be chosen for reports under this procedure in 1980 is made in another paper presented to the Committee. The Committee, in considering that proposal, will no doubt wish to take into account the information and comments, contained in the represent paper.

Geneva, 1 Nov. 1978.

DECLARATION BY THE DIRECTOR-GENERAL OF THE ILO CONCERNING THE INTERNATIONAL YEAR OF THE CHILD*

Resolution 31/169 adopted by the General Assembly on 21 December 1976 proclaimed 1979 the International Year of the Child, with the general objectives of promoting the well-being of children, drawing attention to their special needs and encouraging national action on behalf of children, particularly for the least privileged and those who are at work.

This International Year is of special importance to the ILO, which, even since its foundation in 1919, has sought to restrict child labour and provide protection for children. In doing so, the ILO has acted in accordance with the principle set forth in the United Nations Declaration of the Rights of the Child—that a child has a right to protection against exploitation. Despite the efforts made by the ILO and by many countries which have laid down regulations on the minimum age for admission of children to employment and on the conditions of employment of children, child labour is still widespread and a disturbing problem in many parts of the world where poverty and tradition have precluded its elimination.

---

* Declaration endorsed by the ILO Governing Body at its 209th Session, February-March 1979.

In the light of ILO standards, the International Year should enable governments and employers' and workers' organisations the world over to assess the situation of children at work and also give the competent national bodies and the ILO an opportunity and the means to strengthen their action programmes for children. For that purpose the ILO urgently appeals to them to apply its standards on the minimum age for admission to employment and the conditions of employment of children. Action should be based on the following principles: (a) a child is not a "small adult" but a person entitled to self-fulfilment through work at an early age; (b) governments should, in co-operation with all the national organisations concerned, take all necessary social and legislative action for the progressive elimination of child labour; (c) pending the elimination of child labour, it must be regulated the humanised.

I therefore declare the ILO's endorsement of the aims of the International Year of the Child and its pledge to make every effort and lend all support to member States for their earliest possible fulfilment.

RESOLUTION CONCERNING THE INTERNATIONAL YEAR OF THE CHILD AND THE PROGRESSIVE ELIMINATION OF CHILD LABOUR AND TRANSITIONAL MEASURES*

The General Conference of the International Labour Organisation,

Recalling resolution 31/169 adopted by the United Nations General Assembly proclaiming 1979 as the International Year of the Child, with the general objectives of promoting the well-being of children, drawing attention to their special needs and encouraging national action on behalf of children, particularly for the least privileged and those who are at work,

* Adopted by the International Labour Conference, at its 65th Session in June 1979.

Noting the activities that were undertaken at the national, regional and international levels in preparation for the International Year of the Child and the progress made since,

Convinced that the International Year of the Child provides for all member States an opportunity to review their economic and social policies concerning child welfare and to formulate guidelines in this sphere,

Considering that a new and fair international economic order would greatly contribute towards genuine economic and social development, primarily of benefit to children,

Recalling the endorsement by the ILO of the aims of the International Year of the Child and its pledge to make every effort and lend all support to member States for their earliest possible fulfilment,

Recalling the United Nations Declaration of the Rights of the Child, 1959, and particularly Principle 9, which stipulates that the child should be protected against all forms of neglect, cruelty and exploitation; that he should not be admitted to employment before an appropriate minimum age; and that he should in no case be caused or permitted to engage in any occupation or employment which would prejudice his health or education, or interfere with his physical, mental or moral development,

Considering that since its foundation the International Labour Organisation has sought to eliminate child labour and to provide protection of children,

Noting with approval the Director-General's Declaration on the International Year of the Child,

Deeply concerned that child labour still remains widespread in many parts of the world and that working children frequently work under conditions including those of exploitation detrimental to their health and welfare,

Recognising the need to ensure that the health and strength and the tender age of children are not abused and that children are not permitted to enter avocations unsuited to their age or strength,

Considering that the International Year of the Child should be an occasion to reaffirm with practical measures and deeds that the well-being of today's children to the concern of all people everywhere.

Recalling the decision of the Governing Body of the International Labour office, taken at its 208th Session (November 1978), to request the member states to supply a report in 1980 under article 19 of the Constitution on the extent to which effect has been given or is proposed to be given to the Minimum age Convention (No. 138) and Recommendation (No. 146) of 1973:

1. Calls upon member States to strengthen their efforts for the elimination of child labour and for the protection of children, and in this context—

(a) to implement the provisions of the Minimum Age Convention, 1973 (No. 138), and, where they have not already done so, to ratify this Convention as early as practicable;

(b) to ensure in particular full recognition of the principle that any work undertaken by children who have not completed their compulsory education shall not be such as would prejudice their education or development;

(c) to apply the Minimum Age Recommendation, 1973 (No. 146), and the Minimum Age (Underground Work) Recommendation, 1965 (No. 124);

(d) to report in detail in 1980 under the procedure of article 19 of the Constitution on the progress reached in the implementation of the Minimum Age Convention (No. 138) and Recommendation (No. 146), 1973;

(e) pending the elimination of child labour, to take all necessary social and legislative action for the progressive elimination of child labour and, during the transitional period until the elimination of child labour, to regulate and humanise it and to give particular attention to the implementation of special standards for children relating to medical examination, night work, underground work, working hours, weekly rest, paid annual leave and certain types of hazardous and dangerous work embodied in a number of ILO instruments;

(f) to make every effort to extend the provisions of appropriate educational facilities, in order fully to apply compulsory education and to introduce it where it does not exist and, where education is compulsory, to make it effective;

(g) to ensure that appropriate protective labour legislation applies to all children at work in the sectors of activity in which they are employed;

(h) to ensure that special attention is given to the provision of fair remuneration and to its protection for the benefit of the child;

(i) to strengthen, where appropriate, labour inspection and to undertake all other measures conducive to the elimination of child labour;

(j) (i) to identify the special needs of children, to strengthen efforts to improve the general economic and social well-being of the family, and to launch a national campaign aimed at creating awareness among the general public of the adverse effects of child labour on his/her development;

(ii) to develop international solidarity and co-operation with the developing countries and to activate efforts to establish a new and fair international economic order so as to respond more effective to the basic measures undertaken by each State for better child protection.

2. Calls upon governments and employers' and workers' organisations to assess the situation of child work and to assist the competent bodies and the ILO to strengthen their action programme for children.

3. Invited the Governing Body of the International Labour Office to instruct the Director-General to continue and reinforce the ILO's action through such means as factual surveys of national situations and practices for the elimination of child labour and for the protection of children at work, and to make the necessary preparations for a global revision of the relevant ILO instruments.

Chapter 15

Laws for Child Labour Welfare

"The victory of success is half won when one gains the habit of work."

—*Sarah A. Boltom*

The constitution-makers in India were conscious of the need for special care for children and, therefore, provisions to the welfare of children dealing specially with the protection of child labour have been envisaged in our National Charter. Accordingly, our National Policy Resolution for Children, 1974, lays special stress on the responsibility of the national for physical, mental, moral and special development of children. All this calls for great deal of legislative activity. The subject of "child" does not fall exclusively either in the Union (Central) or the State field. Different matters related to child care and development are distributed among the Union; state and concurrent list of the constitution. It is not only in India but in other industrialised countries including those developed ones that the present labour legislation is aimed to provide legal protection to child labour who constitute an important section of wage-earning population. The underlying conviction of all labour legislations is that it is one of the principal duties of the state to protect and safeguard the interest and well-being of workers irrespective of their age, caste, creed and colours.

It may be submitted that the labour legislation in India including protective legislation for children has been greatly influenced and is the result of various conventions and recommendations adopted by International Labour Organisation (ILO). Besides constitutional provisions, there are at present 13 major legislative enactments which provides legal protection to children in various occupations. These are:

(i) The Children (Pleading of Labour) Act, 1933;
(ii) The Employment of Children Act, 1938;
(iii) The minimum Wages Act, 1948; and rules made thereunder by the government;
(iv) The Factories Act, 1948;
(v) The Plantations Labour Act, 1951;
(vi) The Mines Act, 1952;
(vii) The Merchant Shipping Act, 1958;
(viii) The Motor Transport Workers Act, 1961;
(ix) The Apprentices Act, 1961;
(x) The Atomic Energy Act, 1962;
(xi) The Beedi and Cigar Workers (Conditions of Employment) Act, 1966;
(xii) The Shops and Establishments Act in various states.
(xiii) Child Labour (Prohibition and Regulation) Act, 1986.

From time to time, amendments have been made in most of the above statutes, because of the progressive outlook of the governments for improving the conditions of the important legislations which regulate the working conditions of child workers and mitigate the adverse effect of employment on their health, education and training, etc.

TEXT OF LEGISLATION

(i) The Children) (Pledging of Labour) Act, 1933

The main object of this Act is to eradicate the evils arising from the pledging of labour of young children by their parents employers in lieu of loans or advances.

Previously, the Act extended to whole of India except Jammu and Kashmir, but after September 1, 1971, it has been extended to the Jammu and Kashmir also.

The Act declares an agreement, oral or written, to pledge the labour of children, whereby the parents or the guardian of child, in return of any payment or benefit to be received, undertakes to cause or allow the services of a child to be utilised in any employment, to be void. "However, an agreement made without detriment in a child and not made in consideration of any benefit other than reasonable wages to be paid for the child's service and terminable at more than a weak's notice is not to be deemed to be an illegal agreement. A person who knowingly enters into an agreement with a parent or guardian of a child whereby such parent or guardian pledges the labour of child, or an employer who knowingly employs such a child is liable to a fine upto Rs. 200. A parent or a guardian who knowingly pledges the labour of his child is liable to be wished with a find which may extend upto Rs. 50.

Child means, under this Act, a person who has not complete the age of 15 years.

(ii) The Employment of Children Act, 1938

This Act is also applied to the whole of India. To prevent employment of children in hazardous employment and certain categories of unhealthy occupations, the Act prohibits the employment of children below 15 years of age in any occupation connected with the transport of passengers, goods or mail by railway, or a port authority within the limits of a port.

With the exception of children employed as apprentices or trainees, no child between the age of 15-17 can be employed or permitted to work in these occupations unless he is allowed a rest interval of at least 12 consecutive hours in a day. The period of rest is to include at least 7 such consecutive hours between 10 P.M. and 7 A.M. as may be prescribed by the appropriate government.

The Act also prohibits the employment of children below

the age of 14 in workshops connected with bidi-making; carpet-weaving; cement manufacture including bagging of cement, cloth printing; dyeing and weaving; manufacture of matches; explosives and fire works; mica cutting and splitting; shellac manufacture; soap manufacture tanning and wool cleaning. These provisions, however, do not apply to workshops where the work is done by the occupier with the aid of his family only or to any school established, aided or recognised by any state government. The State governments are empowered to extend the scope of this provision of the Act to any other employment also. In exercise of this power the government of Madras has extended the Act to children working as cleaners in workshops attached to motor transport companies. The Government of Uttar Pradesh has also extended this provision of the Act to brassware and glass bangle industries. The penalty for the breach of the Act is imprisonment upto one month or fine upto Rs. 500 or both. The Act also require the Railway and port authorities to maintain registers showing names, date of birth, rest intervals, etc. of children under 17. It is however imperative to mention here that this Act has been repeated to the extent it is in consistent with the child labour (Prohibition and Regulation) Act, 1986.

(iii) The Factory Act, 1948

The Act extends to the whole of India except the state of Jammu and Kashmir. It applies to establishments employing 10 or more workers with power or 20 or more workers without power. A child under the Act., is defined as a person who has not completed the fifteen years of age. A 'young person' is defined as either a child or an adolescent, who has completed his fifteen years but not eighteen years. Thus, "young person" may be divided into three categories:

(i) Those who are under fourteen years. They are totally prohibited by this Act from entering into employment in factory.

In *Walker T. Ltd. v. Martindale,* it was held that the prohibition is absolute and not restricted to employment in one of manufacturing processes; thus a child employed as a sweeper to clean the floor of a factory is in contravention of the 'provisions of the section, even though he is not employed in any of the manufacturing processes.

The following employments are also prohibited by the court:

(a) Shorting of groundnuts in a courtyard near the machinery rook for decorticating *Ramanathan* v. *K.E.*

(b) To employ children under 7 years in plating straw in a workroom, the benefit of which goes to the mother, was held liable to penalty—*Beedon* v. *Parrot.*

(c) Oiling of parts of machinery of the spinning mill by a young person during meal time, though done without orders and for workers own amusement was held in *Prior* v. *Slaith-Waite Spinning Co.*

Violation of law making the occupier liable to fine.

(ii) Persons who are between 14 and 15 years, they can be employed under the following restrictions provided under Sections 68, 69 and 71 to 75 of the Act:

(i) Such persons should have a certificate of fitness issued by a surgeon and should carry a token of such certificate.

(ii) The certifying surgeon should follow the procedure laid down in Section 69.

(iii) They should not work at night, i.e., twelve consecutive hours including the period from 10 P.M. To 6 A.M.

(iv) They should work not more than four and half hours a day.

(v) The period of work is to be limited to two shifts.

(vi) The shift should not overlap.

(vii) Each child has to be employed in one relay.

(viii) The spread over is not to exceed five hours and should also not change except once in 30 days.

(ix) They should not be employed in two separate factories on the same day.

(x) The employer should display a notice regarding the periods of work for such children.

(xi) The manager of the factory should maintain a register in respect of such child-workers.

(xii) No such child be employed except in accordance with the notice of periods of work displayed at the entries against his name in register of child workers.

Section 75 empowers the inspectors to require any such person for re-examination by surgeon and he may prohibit the employment till the examination is made.

Person between 15 and 18: They are employed as adults if they possess a certificate of physical fitness issued by the certifying surgeon and they also carry a token of such certificate. The adolescents under 17 are not allowed to work at night.

The object of those statutory restriction over the employment of young person is to prevent exploitation of young labourers and to provide for their safety. This was the view expressed by Chief Justice Narasimha. Orissa High Court in *Jhunjhunwalla* v. *B.K. Patnaik,* where the occupier of a glass factory was severely punished for employing 14 adolescent in blowing section of the factory, which is a hazardous occupation, without a certificate of fitness required under sections 68 and 69 of the Factories Act.

In *Mechnitosh* v. *First Brook Book Co.,* it was observed that it was the duty of the employer to ascertain by reasonable means that the applicant was a requisite age and merely the statement of child about his age should not be treated as correct.

The Act also prohibits the employment of children to any part of the factory for pressing cotton in which a cotton opener is at work, except where the feed end of a cotton opener is in a room separated from the delivery end.

The state government is empowered by this Act to make rules prescribing the maximum weights which may be lifted by adolescents and children. Besides a weekly day of rest, every child worker who has worked for a period of 240 days or more in a factory during a calendar year is entitled during the subsequent year of leave with wages at the rate of one day for every 15 days of work as against every 20 days in the case of an adult worker. Rest-shelters, canteens, etc. are also to be provided to all workers including children.

(iv) The Plantation Labour Act, 1951

The Act covers in the first instance all tea, coffee, rubber, cinchona, cordamom plantation and areas 10.117 hectares or more, in which 30 or more persons are employed, or were employed on any day of the preceding 12 months. Further the state government is, however, empowered to extend, all or any of the provisions of this Act to any land used or intended to be used for growing and plantation even if it measures less than 10.117 hectares and the number of persons employed therein is less than thirty. provided that land which measured less than 10.117 hectares or in which measured less than 30 persons are employed immediately before the commencement of the Act would not be covered.

The Act prohibits the employment of children under 12 years. An adolescent between 15-18 years cannot be employed for work unless he is certified fit for work by a surgeon. Such certificate is valid only for one year. Use of a false certificate of fitness is punishable by imprisonment which may extend to one month, or with fine or both.

This Act is, however, more comprehensive in the sense that this Act alone makes the provisions for education as a responsibility of the employer and so is for the housing and medical and recreational facilities. Perhaps the legislators were moved to make all these provisions in this Act because of the fact that plantation labour is commonly known as "family labour" as against `individual' child labour.

(v) The Mines Act, 1952

This Act also extends to the whole of India and includes all excavations where any operation for the purpose of searching for or obtaining minerals is carried out. This Act also defines child as a person who has not completed his fifteen years. This Act not only prohibits the employment of children in mines, but also prohibits the presence of children in any part of a mine which is below ground or in any open cast working in which any mining operation is being carried on. Even an adolescent is not allowed to work in part of a mine which is below ground, unless he has completed his 16th year and has a medical certificate of fitness for work. A certificate is valid only for 12 months. The act also says that adolescent is allowed to be employed in any mine except between 6 A.M. and 6. P.M. This act also includes:

(i) All bearing, bore holes and oil well;

(ii) all shafts, in or adjacent to and belonging to mine, whether in the course of being sunk or not;

(iii) all levels and inclined planes in the course of being driven;

(iv) all converse or alrial railways provided for the bringing into or removal from mine of minerals or other articles or for the removal of refuse thereform;

(v) all adits, level, planes, machinery, works, railways, tramways, and riding;

(vi) in or adjacent to and belonging to a mine;

(vii) all workshops situated within the precinct of a mine and under the same management and used solely for purposes connected with that mine or a number of mines under the same management;

(viii) all power stations for supplying solely for the purpose of working the mines or a number of mines under the same management;

(ix) any premise exclusively occupied by the owner of the mines and for the time being used for depositing refused from a mine or in which any operation in connection with such refuse is being carried on; and

(x) unless exempted by the central government by notification in the official gazette, any premises for part thereof in or adjacent to and belonging to a mine, on which any process ancillary to getting, dressing or preparation for sale of minerals or of coke is carried on.

(vi) The Merchant Act, 1958

The Act prohibits the employment of children in any capacity, who are below 15 years of age, on sea-going ships. This Act applied to ships registered in India. It also prohibits the employment of young persons under 15 as trimmers and stakers except under certain specific conditions. Such persons, if employed, are required to produce a certificate of fitness. Further the Act empowers the government to make necessary rules regarding employment of young persons as and when the occasion demands.

(vii) The Apprentices Act, 1961

The main object of the Act is to provide for the regulation and control of training of apprentices in trades and for matters connected therewith. The Act extends to the whole of India and provides for the regulations and control of training of apprentices in trade and for matters connected therewith. Under the Act. an apprentice has been defined "as person who is undergoing apprenticeship training in a designated trade in pursuance of control of apprenticeship." The Act provides that no person shall be qualified for engaged as an apprentice or to undergo apprenticeship training in any designated trade unless he is atleast 14 years of age and satisfies such standards of education and physical fitness as may be prescribed. If he is a minor. His guardian is required to enter into a contract of apprenticeship with the employer and it shall be registered with the Apprenticeship Advisor.

Initially the Act was enforced in 12 industries but in order to met the growing and changing demands of all skilled workers in other industries, the coverage of the Act has been extended to 1995 industries. The central government has also specified 56 designated trades for the purpose of the Act.

(viii) The Motor Transport Workers Act, 1961

This act applies to the whole of India, it covers every motor transport undertaking employing 5 or more transport workers. The state governments are authorised to apply all or any of the provisions of this Act to any motor transport undertakings employing less than 5 workes. This Act also prohibits the employment of children under 15 in any capacity in the motor transport undertakings. The adolescents are prohibited to work unless a certificate of fitness is granted, which is valid only for 12 months. An adolescent can work only for 6 hours including a rest interval of half an hour and between 10 A.M. and 6 P.M. only.

(ix) Bidi and Cigar Works (Conditions of Employment) Act, 1966

The Act also extends to whole of India. The Act provides that no child should be required or allowed to work in any industrial premises; the Act defines the child as a person who has not completed his fourteen years of age. The employment of young persons between 14 to 18 years is prohibited between 7 P.M. to 6 A.M. The Administration of Act rests with the state who appoint Chief Inspectors or Inspectors for the purpose. The Act provides the penalties for breach which may be imprisonment upto three months or a fine upto Rs. 500 or both.

(x) Contract Labour (Regulations and Abolition) Act, 1970

The Act also extends to the whole of India. The Act applies to establishments and contractors employing 20 or more workers. It is not applied to establishment in which work only of an intermittent or casual nature is performed. There are no specific provisions under the Act pertaining to employment of children.

(xi) Shops and Commercial Establishment Act, 1969

Provisions relating to minimum age also exists in different state shops and commercial establishments Act. These acts applied to shops, commercial establishments, restaurants and hotels and place of amusement and notified urban areas, to which the Factories Act does not apply. Further the state governments are empowered to extend the coverage of the Act in any establishment.

The minimum age of employment in shops and commercial establishment is 12 years in Bihar, Gujarat, J and K, Madhya Pradesh, Karnataka, Orissa, Rajasthan, Tripura, Uttar Pradesh, West Bengal, Goa, Daman and Diu and Manipur, and 14 years in Andhra Pradesh, Assam, Haryana, Himachal Pradesh, Kerala, Tamil Nadu, Punjab, Delhi, Chandigarh, Pondicherry and Meghalaya. The minimum age of employment is 15 years in Maharashtra. There is no separate Shops and Commercial Establishment Act in Andaman and Nicobar, Arunachal Pradesh, Dadra and Nagar Haveli Lakshdweep, Nagaland and Sikkim.

(xii) The Child Labour (Prohibition and Regulation) Act, 1986

The Act states right in the beginning that its aim is to prohibit the engagement of children in certain employments and to regulate the conditions of work of children in certain other employments.

According to this Act, the Employment of Children Act, 1938 is repealed. All rules made in this Act will be in addition to the provisions of the Factories Act, 1948, the Plantations Labour Act, 1951 and Mines Act, 1952:

(i) According to this Act "Child" means a person who has not completed his fourteen years of age.

(ii) Again, family units and training centres are not included in the purview of the Act.

(iii) The Act provides for the setting up of "Child Labour Technical Advisory Committee" for the purpose of addition of occupations and processes to the schedule. A notice of at least three months will be given by the Central Government before adding any occupation or process to the schedule.

(iv) The Act clearly lays down that no child will be allowed to work for more than six hours per day with a rest period of one hour after three hours of work. Once a week he will be given a holiday.

(v) No child will be allowed to work between 7 P.M. and 8 A.M. No over time will be permitted.

(vi) The Act clearly states that the government can make rules for the health and safety of children who are permitted to work in any establishment. These rules can provide for matters such as cleanliness, ventilation. dust and fumes, lighting, drinking water, and sanitary facilities, etc. But there is no mention of nutrition or medical facilities.

(vii) The penalty of violation of the Act will range from three months to one year of imprisonment with a fine of Rs. 10,000 to Rs. 20,000.

(viii) If a person is found guilty he will be liable for punishment under the clauses given in Section 14 (1 and 2) and not under any of the previous Acts.

(ix) Any person, policy officer or an inspector can file a complaint of an offence under this Act in any Court of Competent jurisdiction.

(x) Part 'B" of the schedule has added one more process into existing list and that is "building and construction industry." All other provisions are similar to the ones already existing in the Act of 1938.

The government proposes to bring in amendment to The Child Labour (Prohibition Regulation) Act, 1986, to make it more effective.

REFERENCES

B.D. Rawat (1988), *Labour Welfarism in India*, p. 185.

Bidi and Cigar Works (Conditions and Employment) Act, 1966, Section 1(2).

Child Labour in India, Document 4, (1979), *The Indian Journal of Public Administration*, Vol. XXV (No. 3). p. 933.

Encyclopaedia of Social Work in India (1987), Vol. I, 69.

Factory Act, 1948, Section 68.

M.C. J. Kazi (1984), *Constitution of India*, Vol. II. p. 858.

Mahajan, Krishan (1993), "US Bill Seek to Strike at Child Labour." *Indian Express*, March 29, p. 15.

Mines Act, 1952, Section 1(2).

Narayan, Ashok (1988), "Child Labour Policy and Programme: The Indian Experience," Assefe Bequele and Jo Bovden (ed.) *Combating Child Labour*, p. 147.

Suresh C. Srivastava, "Labour Laws Relating to Children in Employment: Their Impact and implementation," *Punjab University Law Review*, (1980), p. 335.

The Apprentices Act, 1961, Section (2).

The Child Labour (Prohibition and Legislation) Act, 1986, Section 2(ii).

The children (Pledging of Labour) Act, 1933, Section 1(2).

The Contract Labour (Regulation and Abolition) Act, 1970, Section 1(2).

The Employment of Children Act, 1938, Section 3(3).

The Factory Act, 1948, Section 1(2).

The Indian Labour Year Book (1974), p. 175.

The Motor Transport Workers Act, 1961, Section 14.

The *Plantation Labour Act*, 1951, Section 4(a).

Appendix

IMPORTANT RELEVANT PORTIONS OF THE INDIAN CONSTITUTION AND LEGISLATIONS PERTAINING TO CHILD LABOUR

Indian Constitution: Article 24 of the Indian Constitution lays down: No child below the age of 14 years shall be employed to work in any factory or mine or engaged in any other hazardous employment."

Article 39 (c) lays down that: "The health, strength of workers, man and woman and the tender age of children are not abused and that citizens are not forced by economic necessity to enter a vocation unsuited to their age or strength."

Article 39(f) proclaims: "That childhood and youth are protected against exploitation and against moral and material abandonment."

Legislations: With a view to eradicate the problems of child labour, the following two legislations have been enacted regulating the employment of children:

A. The children (Pledging of Labour) Act, 1933: The Act defines 'child' as a person who is under the age of 15 years. The act prohibits the making of agreements to pledge the labour of children and the employments of children whose labour has been pledged. The act also lays down that any agreements or contracts to pledge the labour of a child is void and imposes penalties on any such agreement or employment of a pledged child.

The Child Labour (Prohibition and Regulation) Act, 1986 which is reproduced as Annexure.

Several other legislations and acts have laid down special provisions and clauses pertaining to the employment of children.

I. The 'Child" is defined a follows in the different Acts:

1) *Beedi and Cigar Workers (Conditions of Employment)* Act, 1966:

   Section 2 (b): 'Child' means a person who has not completed 14 years of age.

2) *Factories Act, 1948,* and *Minimum Wages Act, 1948:*

   Section 2 (c) : 'Child' means a person who has not completed his 15 years.

3) *Mines Act, 1952:*

   Section 2(c) : 'Child' means a person who has not completed his 15 years.

4) Motor Transport Workers Act, 1961:

   Section 2 (c): 'Child' means a person who has not completed his 15 years,

5) *Plantations Labour Act, 1951:*

   Section 2(c): 'Child' means a persons who has not completed his 15 years.

II. The minimum age of employment is given in various acts as follows:

1) *Factories Act, 1948:*

   Section 67: No child who has not completed his fourteenth year shall be required or allowed to work in any factory.

2) *Mines Act, 1952:*

   Section 45: No person below 18 years of age shall be allowed to be present in any part of a mine above ground where any operation connected with or incidental to any mining operation is being carried on.

3) *Indian Merchant Shipping Act, 1958:*

Section 109: No person under 15 years of age shall be engaged or carried to sea to work in any capacity in any ship, except —

- in a schoolship or trainingship, in accordance with the prescribed conditions; or,
- in a ship in which all persons employed are members of one family; or,
- in a home-made ship of less than 200 tons gross; or,
- where such person is to be employed on nominal wages and will be in the charge of his father or other near male adult relative.

4) *Motor Transport Workers Act, 1961:*

Section 21: No child who has not completed his 15 years shall be required or allowed to work in any capacity.

5) *Beedi and Cigar Workers (Conditions of Employment)* Act, 1966:

Section 24: No child who has not completed his 14 years shall be required or allowed to work in any industrial premises.

6) State Shops and Commercial Establishments Act:

The minimum age of employment in shops and commercial establishments is 12 years in Bihar, Gujarat, Jammu and Kashmir, Madhya Pradesh, West Bengal, Goa, Daman and Diu and Manipur, and 14 years in Andhra Pradesh, Assam, Haryana, Himachal Pradesh, Kerala, Tamil Nadu, Punjab, Delhi, Chandigarh, Pondicherry and Meghalaya. The minimum age of employment is 15 years in Maharashtra. There are no separate shops and Commercial Establishments Acts in Andaman and Nicobar Islands, Arunachal Pradesh, Dadra and Nagar Haveli, Lakshadweep, Nagaland and Sikkin.

7) *Radiation Protection Rules, 1971:*

Persons below 18 years of age cannot be employed under the Radiation Protection Rules, 1971.

8) *Apprentices Act, 1961:*

Section 3 (a): A person shall not be qualified for being engaged as an apprentice to undergo apprenticeship training in any designated trade, unless he is not, less than 14 years of age.

9) *The Children (Pledging of Labour) Act, 1933:*

Section 3: An agreement to pledge the labour of child (below 15 years of age) shall be void.

III. Prohibition of allowing children (below the age of 14 years to 18 years) to work in hazardous occupations under the Factories Act, 1948, is given below:

1) *Factories Act, 1948*

Section 22 (2) : No young person shall be allowed to clean, lubricate or adjust any part of the prime mover or transmission machinery when in motion, or to clean, lubricate or adjust any part of machine, if the cleaning, lubrication or adjustment thereof would expose the young person to risk of injury from any moving part either of that machine or of any adjacent machinery.

Section 23 (1): No young person shall work at any machine to which this section applies unless he has been fully instructed as to the dangers arising in connection with the machine and the precautions to be observed and : (a) has received sufficient training at work on machines, or, (b) is under adequate supervision by a person who has a thorough knowledge and experience of the machine.

Section 23 (2): Sub-section (1) shall apply to such machines as may be prescribed by the (state) government, being machines which in its opinion are of such a dangerous character that young persons ought not to work at them unless the foregoing requirements are complied with.

Section 27: No child (that is, above the age of 14 years, but below the age of 15 years) shall be employed in any part of a factory for pressing cotton in which a cotton opener is at work. Provided that if the feed-end of a cotton opener is in a room separated from the delivery and by a partition extending to the roof or to such a height as the inspector may in any particular case specify in writing; children may be employed on the side of the partition where the feed-end is situated.

Section 34(2): The (state) government may make rules prescribing the maximum weights which may be lifted, carried or moved by children employed in factories or in any class or description of factories or in carrying on any specified process.

IV. The hours of work for children are regulated as follows:

1) *Factories Act, 1948:*

   Section 21 (a): No child shall be employed or permitted to work in any factory for more than four and a half hours a day.

2) *Minimum Wages (Central) Rules, 1950:*

   Section 24: The number of hours which shall constitute a normal working day shall be four and a half hours in case of children.

3) *Plantations Labour Act, 1951:*

   Section 19: No child shall be required or allowed to work on any plantation for more than 40 hours a week.

4) *State Shops and Commercial Establishments Acts:*

   The hours of work for young persons in shops and Commercial Establishments are seven per day in

Andhra Pradesh, Bihar, Tamil Nadu, Tripura, Pondicherry and West Bengal; six per day in Gujarat, Maharashtra, Jammu and Kashmir, Uttar Pradesh and Delhi; five per day in Himachal Pradesh, Madhya Pradesh, Karnataka, Orissa and Punjab and three per day in Rajasthan.

5) *Apprentices Rules, 1962:*

Section 8: The weekly hours of work of an apprentice while undergoing practical training shall be as follows:

- The total number of hours per week shall be 42 to 48 hours (including the time spent on related instructions).
- Apprentices undergoing basic training shall ordinarily work for 42 hours per week including the time spent on related instructions.
- Apprentices during the second year of apprenticeship training shall work for 42 to 45 hours per week including the time spent on related instructions.
- Apprentices during the third and subsequent years of apprenticeship shall work for the same number of hours per week as the workers in trade in the establishments in which the apprentices are undergoing apprenticeship training, provided however, that short- term apprentices may be engaged to work up to a limit of 48 hours per week.

V. Children are prohibited from working at night according to the following acts:

1) *Factories Act, 1948: -*

Section 71 (b): No child shall be employed or permitted to work in any factory during the night.

2) *Plantations Labour Act, 1951:*

Section 25: Except with the permission of the state government, no child, worker shall be employed in any plantation otherwise than between the hours of 6 a.m. and 7 p.m.

3) *Beedi and Cigar Workers (Conditions of Employment)* Act, 1966:

Section 25: No young person shall be required or allowed to work in any industrial premises except between 6 a.m. and 7 p.m. (Young persons means a person who has completed 14 years of age but has not attained 18 years of age.)

4) *State Shops' and Commercial Establishment Acts*

Night work for children and young person is also prohibited under state laws relating to shops and commercial establishments. The children and young persons are allowed to work between 6 a.m. and 7 p.m. in Andhra Pradesh, Gujarat, Maharashtra, Tamil Nadu, Pondicherry ; 7 a.m. and 7 p.m. in Bihar, and Kerala; 7 a.m. and 9 p.m. in Jammu and Kashmir and Madhya Pradesh 6 a.m. and 8 p.m. in Karnataka; 6 a.m. and 10 p.m. in Orissa and Rajasthan, and 6. a.m. and 8 p.m. during winter and 7 a.m. and 9 p.m. during summer in Delhi. They cannot be employed after 8 p.m. in West Bengal and Tripura.

5. *Apprentices Rules, 1962*

Section 8(2): No apprentice, other than a short term apprentice, shall be engaged in such training between the hours of 10 p.m. and 6 a.m. except with the prior approval of the apprenticeship adviser who also shall give his approval if he is satisfied that it is in the interest of the training of the apprenctice or of the public interest.

Bibliography

Addam, Jane (1983), *Child Labour and Pauperism.*

B.D. Rawat (1988), *Labour Welfarism in India.*

Baig, Tara Ali (1988), 'The Child: The Trauma of a Change' *Social Welfare,* pp. 7 and 39.

Bhagoliwala, T.N. (1982), *Economics of Labour and Industrial Relations,* Sahitya Bhavan, Agra.

Bidi and Cigar Works (Conditions and Employment) Act, 1966, Section 1(2).

Burra, Neera (1988), "Where Children are Cast in Misery's Mould," *The Hindustan Times,* Feb. 14.

Burra, Neera (1988), "Where Children are Caste in Misery's Mould," *The Hindustan Times.*

Chandra, Ramesh (1961), "Effect of Law Income on the Size of Labour Force and Unemployment in India," *Indian Labour Journal,* p. 1164.

Child Labour in India, Document 4, (1979), *The Indian Journal of Public Administration,* Vol. XXV (No. 3). p. 933.

Dahrendorf, Ralph (1967), *Gesellschaft und Demokratie in Deutschland* (Society and Democracy in Germany), Muenche.

Ebeling, Hans/Birkenfeld, Wolfgang (1972), Die Reise in die Vergangenheir. Ein geschichtliches Arbeitsbuch. Band 3, Das Werden der modernen Welt. Lehrerausgabe, Braunschweig.

Engels, Friedrich (1973), The Condition of the Working Class in England, *From personal observation and authentic sources,* Moscow.

Enid, Schildkrout (1981), "The employment of Children in

Kano (Nigeria)" in *Child Work, Poverty and Underdevelopment*, International Labor Office, Geneva.

Gangrade, K.D. & Gathia, J.A. (ed.) (1983), Women and Child Workers in Unorganised Sector. Concept Publishing Company, New Delhi, p. 60.

Gangrade, K.D. (1978-79), *Child Labour in India*, Department of Social Work, Delhi University, Delhi, (Unpublished).

Gathia, J.A. (1983), 'Child Workers in the Informal Sector' in *Women and Child Workers in Unorganised Sector*. Concept Publishing Company, New Delhi.

Gebhardt, Bruno (1965), Handbuch der deutschen Geschichte. Band 3: Von der Franzoesischen Revolution bis zum Ersten Weltkrieg. (Handbook of German history. Vol. 3: From the French revolution to world war I). Stuttgart.

George, K.N. (1977), "Child Labour in the City of Madras," in National Seminar on Employment of Children in India, organised by National Institute of Public Cooperation and Child Development, New Delhi.

George, K.N. (1977), Child Labour in the City of Madras," in National Seminar on Employment of Children in India, organised by the National Institute of Public Cooperation and Child Development, New Delhi, August, (Unpublished).

Giri, V.V. (1958), *Labour Problems in Indian Industries*, Asia Publishing House, Bombay.

Herzfeld, Hans (1961), Die Moderne Welt, 1989-1945. Teil I: Die Epoche der buergerlichen Nationalstaaten. (The modern world, 1789-1945. Part I: The era of the bourgeois nation states). Braunschwei.

Herzig, Arno (1983), Kinderarbeit in Deutschland in Manufacture und Proto-Fabrik (1950-1850), S. 311-375, in: "Archiv fuer Sozialgeschichte," herausgegeben von der Friedrich-Ebert-Stiftung in Verbindung mit dem Institut fuer Sozialgeschichte. Braunschweig—Bonn. XXIII, Band 1, Bonn.

Hull, Terence (1981) "Perspectives and Data Requirements for the Study of Children's Work," *Child Work, Poverty and Underdevelopment,* ed. Rodgers and Standing, 49.

Institute of Public Opinion (1973), *Monthly Commentary on Indian Economic Condition.*

International Labour Organisation's Report (1990) published in *The Hindustan Times,* May 2.

Jain, S.N. (1982), "Preventive Legal Measures in the Area of Child Labour," read at the National Seminar on Child and the Law, Organised by National Institute of Public Co-operation and Child Development, New Delhi.

Justice Bhagwati in L.K. Pandey v Union of India 1982 (2) SCC 249.

Juyal, B.N. (Dr), Kumari Sudarshan Chandola, L.M (1985), 'Child Labour: The twice exploited', Gandhian Institute of Studies, Varanas.

Karl Marx, *Das Kapital,* Ch. XV sec. 3-a.

Ketkar, Kumar (1977) 'Bombay Workers up in Arms', *Economic Times,* 26 May, 1977.

Khan, A.M. (1988), 'Child Labour, Causes and Remedy', *Yojana,* December 16-31, p. 18.

Khandekar, M. (1970), *A Report on the situation of Children and Youth in Greater Bombay,* Tata Institute of Social Sciences, Bombay.

Kulshreshtha, J.C. (1978), *Child Labour in India,* Ashish Publishing House, New Delhi.

Lorenzo, A.M., *Agricultural Conditions in Northern India,* New Book Company Ltd., Bombay.

Lumpkin, K.D. and Douglas D.W. (1938), *Child Workers in America.*

M.C. J. Kazi (1984), *Constitution of India,* Vol. II.

Madan, G. (1975), *Review of Legal Provisions Relating to Facilities for, and Working Conditions of Employed Children—The Impact on Their Health, Education and Development,"* (Unpublished).

Mahajan, Krishan (1993), "US Bill Seek to Strike at Child Labour." *Indian Express,* March 29, p. 15.

Mathur, Deep (1984), While They Should Have Been Playing. *The Hindustan Times,* August 19.

Mead, Cain & A.B.M. Khorshed (1981), "Labour Market Structure and Reproductive Behaviour in Rural South "Asia" in *Child Work, Poverty and Underdevelopment,* International Labour Office, Geneva.

Meena Gupta (1992), 'Special problems of enforcement of child labour and Regulations' Workshop on child labour in U.P.

Mines Act, 1952, Section 1(2).

Mohinder Singh, Child Labour and Law Constraints and Policy—Workshop, on Child Labour in U.P. organised by Deptt. of Labour and UNICEF.

Mukhopadhyaya, Ashim (1989), 'Children Without Childhood', *Frontier,* June 24, p. 23.

N. Vaidyanathan (1975), 'I.L.O. convention and India', p. 39.

Narayan, Ashok (1988), "Child Labour Policy and Programme: The Indian Experience," Assefe Bequele and Jo Bovden (ed.) *Combating Child Labour,* p. 147.

Nigam, Sevanti (1982), 'Child Labour and Education', *Voluntary Action,* Vol. 24, No. 7, pp. 286-287.

Panwar, Brijendra Singh (1988), 'Pledged for Rs. 100,' *Free Press Journal,* September, p. 11.

Patel, B.B. (1980), *Slums in Ahmedabad: A study of Migration, Employment and Housing* (Mimeo), Sardar Patel Institute of Economic and Social Research, Ahmedabad, India.

Patel, B.B. (1986), *Work, Working Conditions and Earnings: Agarbathi Workers in Ahmedabad,* Gandhi Labour Institute, Ahmedabad, India.

Plan for Action for Implementing the World Summit for children held at the United Nation (1990), New York.

Punekar, S.D. (1975), 'Child Labour in Unorganised Industries'. Rural Vocation paper presented at the National Seminar on the Exployment of Children in India, New Delhi, November 25-28.

Quandt, Siegfried (1978), Kinderarbeit und Kinderschutz in Deutschland, 1783-1976. Quellen und Anmerkungen. (Child labour and legislation in Germany, 1783-1976. Sources and Notes). Paderborn.

Rawat, B.D., *Labour Welfare in India.*

Report IV-1 of the 57th Session of the International Labour Conference (1972), Geneva.

Report of National Commission on Labour (1969), p. 386.

Report of the Committee on Child Labour (1979), Ministry of Labour, Government of India.

Report of the Committee on Child Labour (1979), p. 7.

Report of the Committee on Child Labour (Gurupadaswamy Committee) (1979), Ministry of Labour, Government of India, December.

Report of the Director General (1960), International Labour Organisation; Youth and Work (Part I).

Report of the Indian Factory Labour Commission (1908), Vol. I.

Report of the International Labour Organisation quoted in the book *"Needs of Children"* pub. by UNICEF.

Report of the Labour Investigation Committee (1958), Government of India, Delhi.

Report of the Labour Investigation Committee (1969), Government of India, Ministry of Labour and Employment and Rehabilitation.

Report of the Royal Commission on Labour in India (1931), Government of India, Central Publication Branch.

Report on Child Labour in Indian Industries (1981).

Richard II Young (1993), 'Labour Exploitation and the Rights of the Child', UNICEF publication.

Rodger, Gerry and Guy Standing (1981), *Child Work, Poverty and Underdevelopment*, International Labour Office, Geneva.

Roy Choudhary, S.C. (1978), *'Social Cultural and Economic History of India'* (Modern Times), Surjeet Publications, Delhi, p. 50.

S. Marla (1977), "Bonded Labour in Medak District (Andhra Pradesh)" In *National Labour Institute Bulletin* (New Delhi), Vol. 3 No. 10.

Sanat Mehta Committee Report on Child Labour (1984), Ministry of Labour, Government of India.

Schindkrout, Enid (1981), The Employment of Children in Kano (Nigeria), *Child Work, Poverty and Underdevelopment*, ed. Rogers and Standing.

Seal, K.C. (1980), *Profile of the Child in India*, Ministry of Social Welfare, Government of India, New Delhi, p. 181.

Sen, Sukomal (1977), *Working Class of India, History of Emergence and Movement* (1830-1970), K.P. Bagchi and Company.

Sengupta, Padmini, *Child Labour as a Social Problem* (Unpublished).

Singh R.C. (1990), 'Economic Rights of the Child'.

Sinha, Swapan Kumar (1985), 'A Profile of Child Labour in Calcutta' *Social Welfare*, Vol. XXXII, November-December, p. 24.

Study of Child Labour in Bombay (1978), National Institute of Public Cooperation and Child Development, New Delhi, (Unpublished).

Suresh C. Srivastava, "Labour Laws Relating to Children in Employment: Their Impact and implementation," *Punjab University Law Review*, (1980), p. 335.

The Child Labour (Prohibition and Legislation) Act, 1986, Section 2(ii).

The Children (Pledging of Labour) Act, 1933, Section 1(2).

The Contract Labour (Regulation and Abolition) Act, 1970, Section 1(2).

The Employment of Children Act, 1938, Section 3(3).

The Factory Act, 1948, Section 1(2).

The Hindustan Times (1989), April 27.

The Indian Labour Year Book (1974).

The Motor Transport Workers Act, 1961, Section 14.

The *Plantation Labour Act*, 1951, Section 4(a).

Tripathy, S.N., *Bonded Labour in India*, Discovery Publishing House, New Delhi.

Upendra Baxi (1993), 'Unconstitutional Polities and Child Labour', *Mainstream*.

Woodward, S.W., "A Businessman's Views on Child Labour," *Charties and the Commons*, XV (1905-6) pp. 800-1.

Index

●●●●